OVER THERE

OVER THERE
HOLLYWOOD IN BRITAIN

BY ALAN FRANK

BearManor Media
2019

Over There – Hollywood in Britain

© 2019 Alan Frank

All rights reserved.

No portion of this publication may be reproduced, stored, and/or copied electronically (except for academic use as a source), nor transmitted in any form or by any means without the prior written permission of the publisher and/or author.

Published in the United States of America by:

BearManor Media
P. O. Box 71426
Albany, GA 31708

BearManorMedia.com

Printed in the United States.

Typesetting and layout by John Teehan

ISBN—978-1-62933-245-1

For Gilly,
who drove me to completion

Table of Contents

Acknowledgements ix

Introduction 1

Chapter 1: The 1940s 7

Chapter 2: The 1950s 17

Chapter 3: The 1960s 117

Chapter 4: The 1970s 189

Milestones and Millstones 207

Epilogue 283

About the Author 285

Acknowledgements

Heartfelt thanks to Warren Sherman, good friend and terrific literary agent, Carol Reyes, Kate, Liza, Nigel, the British Film Institute without whom… and, of course, alphabetically, to Izzy, Jake and Lara whose frequent welcome interruptions gave me a chance to take it easy, quit staring at the screen for a while and stop cursing the spell-check (which seems unable to cope with names without seeking to change them, notably offering me "Al gallstone" for "Al Jolson").

And, finally, enormous thanks are due to Sir Timothy Berners-Lee who invented the World Wide Web in 1989 and so made it possible for me to watch and enjoy again myriads of long-forgotten B feature films happily brought back to life for viewing on the Internet.

Introduction

"Life is like a B-picture script. It is that corny. If I had my life story offered to me to film, I'd turn it down."
— Kirk Douglas

By the age of 17 when I began studying Natural Sciences as an undergraduate at Cambridge University I was already a committed movie addict since I had grown up in a British Colony where there was no television but where frequent cinema-going cost very little.

I learned a considerable amount at Cambridge, much of it from lectures and tutorials. However, my most memorable discovery was the mind-blowing for me "two-movies-for the-price-of-one" programs on offer at every one of the several cinemas in the city.

Cambridge was celluloid heaven.

I couldn't believe my good fortune and naturally made the most of it, soothing my conscience with the realization that cinemas were considerably warmer than my freezing college rooms.

(Ironically, at that time, Leslie Halliwell of *Halliwell's Filmgoer's Companion* and *Halliwells Film Guide* fame ran two invaluable specialist cinemas in Cambridge that enabled me to catch up with all the movies that had yet to make it to East Africa by the time I left.

Years later, when I was working with Halliwell in television, we decided to check the record of all the movies he had screened during the time I was an undergraduate. I then discovered that while I had missed more than a few lectures, I had never missed any of the films he had screened).

I still genuinely believe that there is always something worthwhile—the good, the bad and the execrable—to learn from every movie: and, moreover, films often deliver unusual insights that even the internet is unable to provide.

B features opened my eyes to a brave new cinema world where movies ran for only seventy minutes or thereabouts and, when they were filmed in Britain, frequently headlined Hollywood stars I had assumed were either dead or had retired. These actors were most often cast as an American private eye helping Scotland Yard solve crimes in Darkest London or a Yank having to turn detective to prove themselves innocent of the accusation of law-breaking in Great Britain.

Years later, when I became a film extra, it seemed even weirder when I found myself standing around in British studios talking to Hollywood stars whose Westerns and thrillers I had shown when I was my school's projectionist.

In those days double features were proven cinema staples in the United States and rather more so in Britain where television was limited to one channel that too often seemed to be more dedicated to patronizing and/or educating the masses than providing entertainment.

Inevitably, when commercial television invaded Great Britain in September 1955, second features began to fade away before finally petering out and vanishing in the mid 1960s and early 1970s.

After the demise of the double feature in Britain, short-lived attempts were made to tempt moviegoers with two slightly more positively cast and produced "co-features": but inevitably as television prospered, the profitability and popularity of double-bills petered out.

Two less-than-wonderful films for the price of one no longer seemed much of a bargain.

In the United States too, the arrival of multiple television broadcasters badly eroded cinema audiences and had also predictably led to the inevitable demise of the double feature. It did not help, either, that new movies were also becoming longer as well which almost unavoidably meant a double-bill program would simply run too long and would not be able to be shown sufficient times in a day to make a profit for the exhibitors.

As a result, many British stars who had made it to Hollywood now needed to return home to find work.

(The disastrous failure to revive the double feature in 2007 with the dismal *Grind House* which unsurprisingly ended up more dead than

Dracula and, unlike the Count, highly unlikely ever to be raised from the grave again, wretchedly confirmed the demise of the genre).

During the heyday of the double feature in post WW2 Britain, a large number (and usually the most popular) second features were imported from the United States.

Which was understandable since then (as now) Hollywood and its stars were preeminent in the world of movies.

Obviously while there was a busy indigenous British film industry dedicated to producing sufficient first and second features to satisfy post-war moviegoers, large sectors of the British audience still preferred their B films flavoured with American actors.

Then, as now, Hollywood input was not simply an ingredient of choice but a valuable commercial requirement for profit-seeking British exhibitors in the heyday of the second feature.

Of course many Hollywood stars as well as, importantly, American directors, producers and screenwriters had been contributing to British movies for many years prior to the post-war heyday of the B feature.

In 1935, for example, after having escaped the giant paws of *King Kong* in 1933, Fay Wray fell into the arms of English comic Jack Hulbert in the comedy-thriller *Calling Bulldog Drummond* (1951). William Henry Pratt had returned to his native Great Britain, this time as Boris Karloff to spread fear in 1933's *The Ghoul* while in 1937 Hollywood's Harold Schuster, editor of Murnau's 1927 classic *Sunrise,* turned director to make Britain's first Technicolor feature film *Wings of the Morning* (1937) which starred Henry Fonda.

Then, significantly accelerating this Hollywood influence after World War Two, there was the notorious public blacklisting by the House Un-American Activities Committee (HUAC) of the "Hollywood Ten" (Alvah Bessie, Herbert Biberman, Lester Cole, Edward Dmytryk, Ring Lardner, Jr., John Howard Lawson, Albert Maltz, Sam Ornitz, Robert Adrian Scott, Dalton Trumbo) who had variously written and directed hundreds of movies) triggered an exodus to Britain of more talented Hollywood exiles seeking to continue to work in films—which they did but frequently to begin with by being forced to use pseudonyms.

And consequently, as moviemaking started to become more internationally based after the 1950s, it became notable that more and more frequently Hollywood directors, writers and producers went east to contribute to made-in-Britain movies.

But while Hollywood then still ruled the world of film, indigenous moviemaking was still alive and well and busy in Great Britain.

Next, and fortuitously for the British B movie industry in particular, in 1950 the British Government injected a potent commercial stimulant into film production with the creation of the Eady Levy.

Eady established the voluntary levy on a proportion of the cost of cinema tickets. The exhibitors would retain half the proceeds, while the remaining 50 percent was allocated for the future funding of new British movies.

The levy became compulsory in 1957 and remained in action until 1985 when it was terminated because the British Government had discovered that it was no longer fit for purpose since most of the levy money was being taken by distributors rather than by film producers.

While it lasted, however, the Eady Levy helped create the surprisingly large number of B films that provided roles for Americans in Britain before the growth of popular and profitable European-filmed Spaghetti Westerns lured them further east in search of celluloid shootouts.

Although B feature double bills and co-features may have petered out in the late 1960s and early 1970s, the genre movies still serve to provide vital film fodder to fill the voracious needs of thousands of television channels world wide that are consistently desperate to leave no gaps in their demanding 24/7 schedules.

And so B films from the heyday of the genre once more see the light and strut on the small screen to entertain legions of vintage movie lovers and, hopefully, to make new converts to an old genre.

These films still make fascinating viewing since, by preserving the past, they restore to life (albeit "life" as seen through the camera/projector) long-ago performers, interesting locations that vanished years previously along with reviving still fascinating old-fashioned themes and moral attitudes.

Watching these movies again has eerily confirmed for me the (admittedly not in this context) accuracy of Haley Joel Osment's classic admission "I see dead people" in *The Sixth Sense* (1999).

Over There is intended to provide a wide-ranging and informative record of the sizeable and fascinating genre of Hollywood-led British-made second features produced from the end of World War Two until the mid-1970s when co-features (fewer and fewer made in Britain) briefly replaced second-features prior to stand-alone movies becoming endemic.

I have covered the 30 years since the end of World War Two although by 1975, co-features had finally replaced second features: that said, their makers carried on the traditions of the B feature—but longer, louder, more expensively—and in color as well.

(Incidentally Hammer Films who revived gothic horror from the grave in gory color, makes frequent appearances here having played a major role in creating the sub-genre. Hammer were among the first and most frequent British filmmakers to import Hollywood actors to enhance their programmers since they realized early on that American names could endow their B films with greater appeal for export to the US as well as satisfying British filmgoers).

Major Milestones and Millstones in the careers of these Hollywood imports from both sides of the camera are indexed.

The 1940s

"One of the worst things you can do is have a limited budget and try to do some big looking film. That's when you end up with very bad work."

– Roger Corman

"There are no rules in filmmaking. Only sins. And the cardinal sin is dullness."

– Frank Capra

Give Me The Stars (1945) 90 mins (black&white (b&w))

British National Films; director (d): Maclean Rogers; producer (p): Frederick Zelnik, William Howard Borer; screenplay: Maclean Rogers, Austin Melford; story by: A Hilarius, Rudolph Bernauer; cinematographer (ph): James Wilson, Arthur Grant; editor (ed): Donald Ginsberg; music (m): Kennedy Russell
    Synopsis: When a music hall artist who has fallen on hard times is injured his orphaned American niece Leni Lynn takes his place singing to the theatre queue and is propelled to stardom.
    Cast: Leni Lynn (Toni Martin), Will Fyffe (Hector MacTavish), Jackie Hunter (Lyle Mitchell), Olga Lindo (Lady Hester), Emrys Jones (Jack Ross), Margaret Vyner (Patricia Worth), Anthony Holles (Achille Lebrun), Grace Arnold (Mrs Gossage), Patric Curwen (Sir John Worth), Robert Griffith (Dick Winter)
    Milestones and Millstones: Leni Lynn

Comment: Mild second feature musical starring a former child star whose short film career was nearing its end.

Reviews: "Obvious story ... Fairy-tale narrative nothing more than framework for array of naïve clichés, supplemented by powerful coloratura singing of star... Liberally padded development offers ingenious sentiment. Average direction." *Cinema*

Woman to Woman (1946) 100 mins (b&w)

British National Films; d: Maclean Rogers; p: Louis H Jackson, Fred A Swann; screenplay: James Seymour; adaptation: Marjorie Deans, from the play by Michael Morton; ph: James Wilson, Gerald Moss; ed: Daniel Birt; art director (ad): R Holmes Paul; m: George Melachrino; choreographer (choreo): Andrée Howard

Synopsis: Working with the British Secret Service married Canadian Officer Douglass Montgomery falls for a cabaret dancer in Paris. Years later he learns that she fell pregnant and searches for her and her son.

Cast: Douglass Montgomery (David Anson), Joyce Howard (Nicolette Bonnet), Adele Dixon (Sylvia Anson), Yvonne Arnaud (Henriette), Paul Collins (David Junior), Eugene Deckers (De Rillac), John Warwick (Dr Gavron), Kay Young (Pauline), Gehard Kempinski (Cafe Proprietor), Martin Miller (Postman)

Milestones and Millstones: Douglass Montgomery

Comment: Michael Morton's play had been filmed twice before, directed by Graham Cutts in 1923 and in 1929 by Victor Saville. Sentiment-sodden and rendered more over-melodramatic by Montgomery's stagey performance.

Reviews: "Although there are no important marquee names, it is definitely a woman's picture and should benefit from mouth-to-mouth. Should find a good place on dual bills in the U.S. Montgomery's overplaying occasionally throws the whole thing out of balance." *Variety*

The Shop at Sly Corner/US: Code of Scotland Yard (1947)
91 mins (b&w)

Pennant Pictures; director/producer (d/p): George King; screenplay: Katherine Streuby; additional dialogue (add dial); Reginald Long; from the play by Edward Percy; ph: Hone Glendinning; ed: Manuel del Campo; ad: Bernard Robinson; m: George Melachrino
   Synopsis: Apparently benign antique dealer Oscar Homolka doubles as a fence who turns to murder when a blackmailer threatens his daughter.
   Cast: Oskar Homolka (Descius Heiss), Derek Farr (Robert Graham), Muriel Pavlow (Margaret Heiss), Manning Whiley (Corder Morris), Kathleen Harrison (Mrs Catt), Gary Marsh (Major Elliot), Kenneth Griffith (Archie Fellowes) Jan Van Loewen (Professor Vanetti), Johnnie Schofield (Inspector Robson)
   Milestones and Millstones: Oskar Homolka
   Comment: Film noir, British-style, driven by Homolka whose enjoyable, slightly larger-than-life performance complements a melodramatic storyline.
   Reviews: "…the yarn can be sold on its blackmail and murder angles…Homolka is well-cast." *Variety*

The Gay Duellist/Meet Me at Dawn (1947) 81 mins (b&w)

20th Century-Fox; d: **Thornton Freeland,** Peter Creswell; p: Marcel Hellman: screenplay: Lesley Storm, James Seymour, Peter Creswell, Maurice Cowan; from the story *Le Tueur* by Marcel Archard and Anatole Litvak; ph: Gunther Krampf; ed: Edward B Jarvis; ad: Norman G Arnold; m: Mischa Spoliansky: lyrics (l): Robert Musel
   Synopsis: In turn-of-the-century Paris young swordsman Charles Morton who makes his living anonymously fighting duels for others falls for the woman he exploits to bring down a senator for the politicians who hire him.
   Cast: William Eythe (Charles Morton), Stanley Holloway (Emile), Beatrice Campbell (Margot), George Thorpe (Senator Renault), Irene Browne (Mme. Renault), Hazel Court (Gabrielle Vermorel), Basil Sydney (Georges Vermorel), Margaret Rutherford (Mme. Vermorel), Ada Reeve (Concierge), Wilfred Hyde White (News Editor), Graeme Muir (Count de Brissac)

Milestones and Millstones: William Eythe, Thornton Freeland

Comment: Eythe, enjoyed brief leading man status at 20th Century Fox during WW2 because his 4F status prevented him from being conscripted, he fell out with studio head Darryl F Zanuck who sentenced him to make this B feature in England. Little to recommend it: ironically, given its initial title, Eythe (briefly married to actress Buff Cobb) was gay and had a long-time relationship with fellow actor Lon McCallister.

Reviews: "…extremely artificial and there is an air of unreality about the whole show… the leading character being typically American and the rest obviously British…might get by as a second feature." *CEA Film Report*

"…producer Marcel Hellman has provided a good entertainment… director Thornton Freeland, conscientious as he is, lacks the Lubitsch touch, and Eythe, competent actor, lacks the Gallic effervescence the part cries out for." *Variety*

White Cradle Inn/US: High Fury (1947) 83 mins/US: 71 mins (b&w)

"Between their love…the shadows of a man, a boy, and a mountain!"

Peak Films; d: Harold French; p: A E Hardman, Ivor McLaren, Mary Pickford; screenplay: Basil Mason, Lesley Storm; ph: Derick Williams; ed: A S Bates, Walter Klee; ad: Carmen Dillon; m: Bernard Grun

Synopsis: A Swiss innkeeper and her profligate husband battle because she intends to adopt a young French orphan displaced by the war who does not want to return home.

Cast: Madeleine Carroll (Magda), Ian Hunter (Anton), Michael Rennie (Anton), Anne-Marie Blanc (Louise), Michael McKeag (Roger), Arnold Marle (Joseph), Willy Feuer (Benno) Max Haufler (Frederick), Margarete Hoff (Maria), Gerhardt Kempinski (President)

Milestones and Millstones: Madeleine Carroll

Comment: Carroll, who achieved international stardom in Hitchcock's *The 39 Steps* (1935), was the first female British star to win a major Hollywood film contract, with Paramount, starring in the hit *The Prisoner of Zenda* (1937), before returning to Britain to make this minor movie. Only for die-hard Carroll admirers and cinema completists.

Reviews: "...looks like a fairly mild entry in the U.S....Carroll may prove something of a draw, but the picture will need plenty of selling both here (UK) and in America." *Variety*

"It is not an outstanding production, but is good average entertainment for the masses. Madeleine Carroll gives a pleasing performance." *CEA Film Report*

"The story is simple and straightforward and even unromantic. In fact it is of little consequence. It is the mountains and the photography which provide the high spots." *Monthly Film Bulletin*

Bond Street (1948) 109 mins (b&w)

World Screenplays (aka De Grunwald Productions)/ABPC; d: Gordon Parry; p: Anatole de Grunwald, associate producer (ap): Teddy Baird; screenplay: Terence Rattigan, Rodney Ackland, Anatole de Grunwald; ph: Otto Heller, Brian Langley; ed: Gerald Turney-Smith; ad: Peter Glazier; m: Benjamin Frankel

Synopsis: Four separate stories linked by the bride's dress purchased in London's Bond Street, along with a veil, pearls and flowers.

Cast: Jean Kent (Ricki Merritt), **Roland Young** (George Chester-Barratt), Kathleen Harrison (Mrs. Brawn) Derek Farr (Joe Marsh), Hazel Court (Julia Chester-Barratt) Ronald Howard Steve Winter), Patricia Plunkett (Mary), Paula Valenska (Ella), Adrianne Allen (Mrs. Traverner), Robert Flemyng (Frank), Kenneth Griffith (Len Phipps), James McKechnie (Inspector Yarrow), Joan Dowling, (Norma) Wilfred Hyde White (Jeweller).

Milestones and Millstones: Roland Young

Comment: Enjoyable mélange of comedy, suspense, romance, character-driven drama, a murder and future horror film star Hazel Court.

Reviews: "Competent direction in main, competent all-round portrayals. Holding entertainment." *Cinema*

"Dialogue is witty, the situations well contrived, and Roland Young and Paula Valenska make the most of their acting opportunities. The same can hardly be said for the rest of the film." *Monthly Film Bulletin*

Night Comes too Soon/The Ghost of Rashmon Hall (1948) 52 mins (b&w)

"A story of razor-edge suspense. They stood stark still, she trembled in his arms...and it came closer and closer...!"

Federated Film Corporation; d: Dennis Kavanagh; p: Harold Baim; ap: A Jarrett; screenplay: Pat Dixon; from the story *The Haunters and the Haunted* by Edward George Bulwer-Lytton; ph, special effects (sfx): Ray Densham; ed: Dorothy Elliot; ad: George Ward

Synopsis: An expert in the occult is called in to a strange old house to exorcise it of malign spirits.

Cast: Valentine Dyall (Dr George Clinton), **Ann Howard** (Phyllis), Alec Faversham (John), Beatrice Marsden (Mrs Paxton), Anthony Bird (Lionel Waddell), David Keir (Realtor), Monty DeLyle (Ghost of Rinaldo Sabata), Nina Erber (Ghost of Marianna Sabata), John Desmond (Ghost of the Sailor).

Milestones and Millstones: Ann Howard

Comment: The patently low budget and the equally muted aspirations of its makers deliver a feeble ghost story that tends to drag even with its relatively short running time.

Reviews: "Popular offering for the masses... apparitions appear, and mysterious noises, whispering voices, screams, and mad laughter are heard...Howard and Alec Faversham are good as the married couple." *CEA Film Report*

"The story, as filmed, is unlikely to chill any spines...the film's chief interest lies in the effective use of lighting in the "ghostly" sequences." *Monthly Film Bulletin*

No Orchids for Miss Blandish (1948) 92 mins (b&w)

"Shocking as a book! Sensational as a motion picture!"

Tudor-Alliance; director/producer/ screenplay (d/p/s): St. John L. Clowes; from the novel by James Hadley Chase; ph: Gerald Gibbs; ed: Manuel del Campo; ad: Harry Moore; m: George Melachrino

Synopsis: Sadistic gangster Jack LaRue kidnaps pampered heiress

Miss Blandish on her wedding night and kills her fiancé: then she becomes attracted to her abductor.

Cast: Jack La Rue (Slim Grisson), Linden Travers (Miss Blandish), Hugh McDermott (Dave Fenner), Walter Crisham (Eddie Schultz), MacDonald Parke (Doc), Danny Green (Flyn), Lilli Molnar (Ma Grisson), Charles Goldner (Louis, Head Waiter), Zoe Gail (Margo), Leslie Bradley (Ted Bailey)

Milestones and Millstones: Jack La Rue

Comment: James Hadley Chase's famed 1939 novel was set in the United States. This infamous film version also takes place in the USA but was filmed in Britain, thus accounting for the poor-to-dreadful American accents perpetrated by British players. Character actor LaRue, making his worst film in a 53-year-long career embracing over 140 screen credits, was American.

The film was rightly castigated for its violence and wide-ranging (for the period) nastiness, with the British C this is censor cutting 114 feet from the movie: after a first sold-out five-week run in New York it was extensively edited and re-cut for subsequent US screenings. By any standards, it is a truly dreadful movie, cut or uncut, and deserving of much of the opprobrium spewed on it by appalled contemporary reviewers.

(Ironically, the movie's current DVD reissue rating is 'U'—not entirely surprising in an era when four-letter words are frequent in low-rated kids' films). In 1971, Robert Aldrich remade *No Orchids for Miss Blandish* as *The Grissom Gang*.

Reviews: "A lurid bestseller has been converted into a deplorable picture… on the talky side but has been well paced…as a supposed America thriller, this film touches bottom in sadism, morbidity and bad taste…" *Variety*

"… the film sets out to appeal to the prurient-minded, the twisted, the unbalanced." *Daily Express*

"… this is an exceedingly sordid and unsavory film, dealing with American racketeers…the film is, in fact, an orgy of sadistic brutality." *CEA Film Report*

"…the morals of an alley cat" (and) "the sweetness of a sewer." *Observer*

Noose/US: The Silk Noose (1948) 76 mins (b&w)

Edward Dryhurst Productions/Associated British Picture Corporation (ABPC); d/p: Edmond T Greville; ap: Eric L'Epine-Smith; screenplay: Richard Llewellyn, from his play; ph: Hone Glendinning/Otto Heller; ed: David Newhouse; ad: Bernard Robinson; m: Charles Williams.

Synopsis: Chicago fashion journalist Carole Landis turns crime reporter in post WW2 London and, helped by her former commando fiancé, goes after black marketeering gangster Joseph Calleia.

Cast: Carole Landis (Linda Medbury), **Joseph Calleia** (Sugiani), Derek Farr (Captain Jumbo Jyde), Stanley Holloway (Inspector Kendall), Nigel Patrick (Bar Gorman), Ruth Nixon (Annie Foss), Carol van Derman (Mercia Lane), John Slater (Pudd'n Bason), Leslie Bradley (Basher), Reginald Tate (Editor), Edward Rigby (Slush), John Salew (Greasy Anderson), Hay Petrie (Barber)

Milestones and Millstones: Carole Landis, Joseph Calleia

Comment: Patently a second feature but with some effective film noir overtones and Calleia's crooked character well contrived to meet the needs of then chauvinistic British moviegoers.

Reviews: "Lively story... ingenious direction sets swift pace in development of material which alternates thrills and comedy... Excellent entertainment assured of whole-hearted approval of the masses." *Cinema*

"The film moves at a smart pace from start to finish, there is much humour...alert direction...Landis is both clever and attractive." *Monthly Film Bulletin*

"*Noose* is a nice subject to fit the quota bill at home, but isn't likely to go big in the export market, despite American names in leads...the late Carole Lombard is attractive." *Variety*

The Small Voice/US: The Hideout (1948) 67 mins (b&w)

"Packed with high voltage Tension!"

Constellation Films; d: Fergus McDonnell; p: Anthony Havelock-Allan; screenplay: Derek Neame, Julian Orde, George Barraud; based on the novel *The Small Voice* by Robert Westerby; ph: Stanley Pavey; ed: Manuel del Campo; ad: Andrew Mazzei; m: Stanley Black

Synopsis: A writer and his wife stop to help two men in a car crash, only to be taken hostage by Howard Keel and a fellow criminal on the run.

Cast: Harold Keel (Boke), Valerie Hobson (Eleanor Byrne), James Donald (Murray Byrne), David Greene (Jim), Michael Balfour (Frankie), Joan Young (Housekeeper), Angela Fouldes (Jenny Moss), John Dearman (Ken Moss), Norman Claridge (Superintendent), Edward Evans (Police Inspector)

Milestones and Millstones: Harold Keel

Comment: Crisp suspense thriller that does not overstay its relatively short running time and made Keel (billed as 'Harold' and then appearing on the London stage in *Oklahoma*) a person of interest for MGM and later earned him Hollywood stardom.

Reviews: "… slow in places… Good suspense values and competent acting, however, make the film a fairly good entertainment of its type for the masses. Howard Keel makes an interesting gangster…" *CEA Film Report*

"…a neatly contrived thriller, strong in suspense values. … should make a worthwhile dualer… Harold Keel, as the big shot, and David Greene and Michael Balfour as his two confederates, turn in meaty, convincing performances." *Variety*

Forbidden/Scarlet Heaven (1949) 87 mins (b&w)

Pennant Pictures (George King Productions); d/p: George King; screenplay: Katherine Strueby; story by: Val Valentine; ph: Hone Glendinning, Robert Day; ed: Douglas Myers; ad: Bernard Robinson; m: George Melachrino

Synopsis: Unhappily married scientist Douglass Montgomery, reduced to selling patent medicines on the front at Blackpool, plans to murder his wife—but his scheme misfires.

Cast: Douglass Montgomery (Jim Harding), Hazel Court (Jane Thompson) Patricia Burke (Diana Harding) Garry Marsh (Jerry Burn) Ronald Shiner (Dan Collins), Kenneth Griffith (Johnny), Eliot Makeham (Mr Thompson), Frederick Leister (Dr Franklin) Richard Bird (Jennings), Michael Medwin (Cabby)

Milestones and Millstones: Douglass Montgomery

Comment: Average second feature in danger of being posthumously overrated: *Forbidden* was their final film for Montgomery and director King.

Reviews: "There are moments of romance, plus touches of humour and the film is well made and convincingly acted... and, although not delectable fare, is good entertainment for tolerant audiences." *CEA Film Report*

Miss Pilgrim's Progress (1949) 82 mins (b&w)

Angel Productions; director/screenplay (d/s): Val Guest; p: Daniel M Angel, Nat Cohen; ph: Bert Mason; ed: Douglas Myers; ad: George Paterson; m: Philip Martell, Ronald Hanmer

Synopsis: American factory girl Yolande Donlan comes to England as an exchange worker and ends up saving her village and new friends from the local land developer exploiting them.

Cast: Yolande Donlan (Laramie Pilgrim), Michael Rennie (Bob Thane), Garry Marsh (Mayor), Emrys Jones (Vicar), Reginald Beckwith (Mr. Jenkins), Jon Pertwee (Postman Perkins), Avril Angers (Factory Girl), Marianne Stone (2nd factory girl), Helena Pickard (Mrs Jenkins), Peter Butterworth (Jonathan)

Milestones and Millstones: Yolande Donlan

Comment: Donlan is good fun in this light-hearted British comedy. The following year saw Donlan's co-star Michael Rennie being signed up in Hollywood by 20th Century Fox's Darryl F Zanuck.

Reviews: "The Anglo-American theme... raised hopes that it might appeal on both sides of the Atlantic. Unfortunately the finished product lacks the polish and sophistication to justify US success... Donlan has an easy stint." *Variety*

"8 ¼ marks for the masses...It is well acted and makes good entertainment...the role of the American visitor is charmingly played by Yolande Donlan." *CEA Film Report*

"After a slow and sticky start full of conventional good neighbourly jokes about drug stores and English coffee, the comedy improves owning to a performance of engaging idiocy by Yolande Donlan." *Monthly Film Bulletin*

The 1950s 2

"Self-plagiarism is style."

– Alfred Hitchcock

Cairo Road (1950) 83 mins (b&w)

> *"A ceaseless war against the drug traffic... and the men who build a mountain of dirty money in every city of the world!"*

Mayflower Productions; d: **David MacDonald**; second unit director: Don Weeks; p: Aubrey Baring, Maxwell Setton; screenplay and story: Robert Westerby; ph: Oswald Morris, Arthur Ibbetson; ed: Peter Taylor; ad: Duncan Sutherland; m: Naim al Basri, Louis Levy, Robert Gill

Synopsis: Cairo police chief Eric Portman and dedicated junior officer Laurence Harvey battle to bring drug traffickers to justice.

Cast: Eric Portman (Youssef Bey), Laurence Harvey (Lieutenant Mourad), Harold Lang (Humble), Karel Stepanek, (Edouardo Pavlis), Coco Aslan (Lombardi), Maria Mauban (Marie), Oscar Quitak (Bedouin Boy), Anna Mickelis (Camilla}, John Bailey (Mental Hospital Doctor)

Milestones and Millstones: David MacDonald

Comment: Location filming in Cairo, Port Said and the Suez add impact to a slick, quick thriller.

Reviews: "There are plenty of thrills and the film moves at a lively pace... interesting and entertaining." *CEA Film Report*

"A thriller with oriental flavouring, stock characterisations and clumsy handling. Adequate location work." *Monthly Film Bulletin*

Double Confession (1950) 80 mins (b&w)

A Harry Reynolds Production; d: Ken Annakin; p Harry Reynolds; ap: George Brass; screenplay: William Templeton, Ralph Keene; from the novel *All On a Summer's Day* by John Garden; ph: Geoffrey Unsworth; ed: Carmen Beliaeff; ad: Bernard Robinson; m: Benjamin Frankel

Synopsis: Derek Farr finds his ex-wife murdered and, attempting to avoid becoming a suspect, frames her lover and comes up against criminals, including Peter Lorre, who try to dispose of him.

Cast: Derek Farr (Jim Medway), Joan Hopkins (Ann Corday), **Peter Lorre** (Paynter), William Hartnell (Charlie Dunham), Naunton Wayne (Inspector Tendby), Ronald Howard (Hilary Boscombe), Leslie Dwyer (Leonard), George Woodbridge (Sergeant Sawnton), Kathleen Harrison (Kate)

Milestones and Millstones: Peter Lorre

Comment: Now (after being lost for years) somewhat overrated as a period *film noir,* Annakin tells his tall story well, makes good use of British seaside locations and ensures that Lorre, while overdoing it at times, makes a potent impact.

Reviews: "This intricate plot is told in an interesting but baffling way and the surprise ending does not convince... Lorre does his best with a rather overdrawn character." *CEA Film Report*

"The longer the film goes on the less we know about its plot, but the more we learn about the inhabitants of Bexhill and Hastings." *Picturegoer*

"Melodrama with an extremely confused plot... breaks off into touches of stereotyped humour." *Monthly Film Bulletin*

Highly Dangerous (1950) 90 min (b&w)

"Caught in a blaze of intrigue!"

Two Cities Films; d: Roy Ward Baker; p: Anthony Darnborough; executive producer (ep): Earl St John; screenplay: Eric Ambler; ph: Reginald Wyer; ed: Alfred Roome; ad: (Alex) Vetchinsky; m: Richard Addinsell

Synopsis: Entomologist Margaret Lockwood is saved time and again by American reporter Dane Clark when she goes on a secret mission behind the Iron Curtain to investigate insects being developed as disease-spreading weapons.

Cast: Margaret Lockwood (Frances Gay), **Dane Clark** (Bill Casey), Marius Goring (Police Chief Anton Razinski), Naunton Wayne (Hedgerley), Wilfrid Hyde White (Mr Luke, British Charge D'affaires), Eugene Deckers (Alf), Olaf Pooley (Razinski's assistant), Gladys Henson (Attendant)

Milestones and Millstones: Dane Clark

Comment: The sometimes-ludicrous combination of dramatic spy thriller and seriously silly segues works well enough; the players keep commendably straight faces.

Reviews: "… starts as a serious espionage thriller, but develops into satire of this type of film and the Dick Barton type of yarn, and the absurd recklessness of the typical hero and heroine of such stories is subtly characterised… Clark makes an excellent partner (for Lockwood)." *CEA Film Report*

"Ambler's script is a curious mixture of genuine adventure and of comedy…the adventures, unfortunately, follow an all-too conventional pattern …undistinguished thriller. Of the players, only Dane Clark succeeds in overcoming the obstacles of the script." *Monthly Film Bulletin*

My Daughter Joy/US: Operation X (1950) 81 mins (b&w)

London Film Productions; d/p: Gregory Ratoff; ap: Philip Brando; screenplay: **Robert Thoeren**, William Rose; from the novel *David Golder* by Irène Némirowsky; ph: Georges Périnal; ed: Raymond Poulton; ad André Andrejew; m: R. Gallois-Montbrun

Synopsis: Ambitious businessman Edward G Robinson organizes the arranged marriage of his daughter and the son of a millionaire sultan but she loves the journalist investigating her father.

Cast: Edward G. Robinson, (George Constantin), Peggy Cummins (Georgette Constantin), **Richard Greene** (Larry), Nora Swinburne, (Ava Constantin), Walter Rilla (Andreas), Finlay Currie (Sir Thomas McTavish), James Robertson Justice (Professor Keval) **Gregory Ratoff** (Marcos), Ronald Adam (Colonel Fogarty)

Milestones and Millstones: Edward G Robinson, Gregory Ratoff, Richard Greene, Robert Theoren

Comment: Nothing special, apart from the sad sight of Robinson trapped in a cheap British picture.

Reviews: "Despite its powerful cast, it is not going to help the cause of British pictures, it's a vague and insincere piece of entertainment...and barely merits a place on the American screens... Robinson is virtually wasted." *Variety*

Cloudburst (1951) 92 mins (b&w)

"He had murdered once! NOW he was ready to strike again... and no one could catch him but HIMSELF!"

Hammer Film Productions; d/s: Francis Searle; p: Anthony Hinds, Alexander Paal; screenplay and story: Leo Marks; ph: Walter Harvey; ed: John Ferris; ad: Donald Russo; m: Frank Spencer

Synopsis: Canadian intelligence officer Robert Preston who is working at the Foreign Office sets out to track down the criminals who killed his pregnant wife while making their getaway.

Cast: Robert Preston (John Graham), Elizabeth Sellars (Carol Graham), Colin Tapley (Inspector Davis), Sheila Burrell (Lorna Dawson), Harold Lang (Mickie Fraser), Mary Germaine (Peggy), George Woodbridge (Sergeant Ritchie), Lyn Evans (Chuck Peters), Thomas Heathcote (Jackie) Edith Sharpe (Mrs Reece)

Milestones and Millstones: Robert Preston

Comment: Competent thriller establishing the type of Hammer Films pre-horror offering made with an American star for US box-office. Future Hammer Films director/producer Michael Carreras is credited with casting and writer/producer to-be Jimmy Sangster gets an assistant second unit director credit. Also first Hammer Film to be shot at their Bray Studios.

Reviews: "After a rather doubtful opening, the picture develops intriguing situations, building up suspense as it proceeds... the critical may not find it acceptable, although is holding and exciting. Robert Preston plays the leading character with great sincerity and conviction." *CEA Film Report*

"...palatable meller for filmgoers with a leaning towards mellers. Picture, however, calls for some intense selling for aside from Robert Preston the cast is composed of British players unknown to American audiences." *Variety*

"Violent and implausible thriller." *Monthly Film Bulletin*

I'll Get You for This/US: Lucky Nick Cain (1951) 87 mins (b&w)

"The stakes were slim blonde, beautiful ... the action was fast and dangerous..."

Kaydor/Romulus Films; d: **Joseph M Newman**; p: Joe Kauffman; screenplay: George Callahan, David Rose; from the novel *High Stakes* by James Hadley Chase; ph: Otto Heller; ed: Russell Lloyd; ad: Ralph Brinton; m: Walter Goehr

Synopsis: Aircraft engineer George Raft vanishes in London but it turns out he is an undercover FBI agent on the trail of an international abduction ring smuggling scientists behind the Iron Curtain.

Cast: George Raft (Nick Cain), **Coleen Gray** (Kay Wonderly), Enzo Staiola (Toni), Charles Goldner (Massine), Constance Smith (Nina) Walter Rilla (Mueller, Martin Benson (Sperazza), Peter Illing (Ceralde), Hugh French (Travers), Peter Bull (Hans), Greta Gynt (Claudette Ambling), Elwyn Brooke Jones (The Fence)

Milestones and Millstones: George Raft, Coleen Gray, Joseph M Newman

Comment: Location shooting in San Remo adds a touch of class to an otherwise fairly routine programmer with Raft scoring in a role requiring little new work from him.

Reviews: "... finishes fairly excitingly... the film as a whole makes good entertainment of its kind with a predominant appeal to men. George Raft, if not quite as youthful as before, still makes a virile hero. Coleen Gray is most attractive." *CEA Film Report*

The Late Edwina Black/US: Obsessed (1951) 78 mins (b&w)

"WAS THIS THE KISS... of a murderer?"

Romulus Films; d: Maurice Elvey; p: Ernest Gartside; screenplay: David Evans; from the play *The Late Edwina Black* by William Dinner and William Morum; ph: Stephen Dade; ed: Douglas Myers; ad: George Provis; m: Allan Gray

Synopsis: When a Scotland Yard Inspector investigates the murder by arsenic poisoning of a sickly Victorian woman suspicion falls on her unfaithful husband and his lover Geraldine Fitzgerald.

Cast: David Farrar (Gregory), **Geraldine Fitzgerald** (Elizabeth), Roland Culver (Inspector Martin), Jean Cadell (Ellen, Housekeeper), Mary Merrall (Lady Southdale), Harcourt Williams (Dr Septimus Prendergast), Ronald Adam (Headmaster), Charles Heslop (Vicar), Sidney Moncton (Horace)

Milestones and Millstones: Geraldine Fitzgerald

Comment: What might have worked as on stage signally fails to engage on the screen: the screenplay, direction and performances remain sedulously stage-bound and tedium rapidly sets in.

Reviews: "The stage play from which this picture was taken does not adapt well to the screen...the play's thrilling moments tend to fall flat ... slow moving, laboured and unexciting." *CEA Film Report*

"...an excruciating waste of talent...a plodding, pedantic duplicate, moving at a snail's pace and talking itself deader than the corpse in question." *The New York Times*

The Long Dark Hall (1951) 86 mins (b&w)

"TWO GREAT BROADWAY STARS AT THEIR GREATEST!"

Cusick International Films/Five Ocean Films; d: Anthony Bushell, Reginald Beck; p: Peter Cusick; ap: Rex Harrison; screenplay: **Nunnally Johnson**, W E Fairchild; from the novel *A Case to Answer* by Edgar Lustgarten; ph: Wilkie Cooper; Tom Simpson; ad: George Paterson; m: Benjamin Frankel

Synopsis: Circumstantial evidence puts unfaithful husband and father Rex Harrison on trial for the murder of his mistress.

Cast: Rex Harrison (Arthur Groome), Lilli Palmer (Mary Groome), Tania Held (Sheila Groome), Henrietta Barry (Rosemary Groome), Dora Sevening (Mary's Mother), Ronald Simpson (Mary's Father), Raymond Huntley (Chief Inspector Sullivan) William Squires (Sergeant Cochran), Anthony Dawson (The Man), Ballard Berkeley (Superintendent Maxey)

Milestones and Millstones: Rex Harrison, Nunnally Johnson

Comment: Harrison and Palmer, well served by Johnson's potent screenplay, compel attention.

Reviews: "A very tidy murder drama ... from England...an unusually literate and impressively acted film. Rex Harrison and Lilli Palmer easily walk off with the honors in a cast of uniformly competent perform-

ers...a happy example of Anglo-American motion-picture cooperation."
The New York Times

"...treads no fresh paths and is rather awkwardly presented in flashbacks...the ending is somewhat of a let-down... in spite of its weaknesses, the film holds the interest." *CEA Film Report*

Mr Drake's Duck (1951) 75 mins (b&w)

*"The Army's Got Her! The Navy Wants Her! The Air Force Claims Her!
... and there's an international RIOT in the barn!"*

Angel Productions/Douglas Fairbanks Productions; d/s: Val Guest; from the radio play by Ian Messiter; p: Daniel M Angel, Douglas Fairbanks Jr; ph: Jack Cox; ed: Adam Dawson, Sam Simmonds; ad: Maurice Carter; m: Bruce Campbell

Synopsis: The armed forces move in when honeymooners Douglas Fairbanks Jr and Yolande Donlan discover a duck that lays uranium eggs on their farm.

Cast: Douglas Fairbanks Jr (Donald Drake), **Yolande Donlan** (Penny Drake), Jon Pertwee (Reuben), Wilfrid Hyde-White (Mr May), Reginald Beckwith (Mr Boothby), Howard Marion-Crawford, (Major Travers), Peter Butterworth (Higgins), A.E. Matthews (Brigadier Matthews), Tom Gill (Captain White)

Milestones and Millstones: Douglas Fairbanks Jr, Yolande Donlan

Comment: Cool modernized comic riff on the fairy tale about the goose that lays the golden eggs featuring some sharp swipes at authority. Future Hollywood character star Arthur Hill has a minor role as the US Vice Consul.

Reviews: "*Mister Drake's Duck* is responsible for some chuckles, a few good-natured gibes at the British armed services and civil servants and the international race for atomic supremacy... they do come up with enough laughs to make *Mister Drake's Duck* a pleasant if slight lampoon." *New York Times*

"This uproarious comedy is a sheer delight and should prove highly amusing entertainment for almost any type of audience...the acting leaves nothing to be desired." *CEA Film Report*

Whispering Smith Hits London/US: Whispering Smith Versus Scotland Yard (1951) 77 mins (b&w)

"MAD KILLERS STALK YANK SLEUTH!"

Hammer-Lesser; d: Francis Searle; p: Anthony Hinds, Julian Lesser (uncredited); screenplay/ story by: John Gilling, Steve Fisher (uncredited), Francis Searle uncredited; story by: Frank H Spearman (uncredited); ph: Walter J Harvey; ed: James Needs

Synopsis: An Englishwoman hires American private eye Richard Carlson to investigate a suicide in London that turns out to be a murder and marks him for death.

Cast: Richard Carlson (Whispering Smith), Greta Gynt (Louise), Herbert Lom (Roger Ford), Rona Anderson (Anne), Alan Wheatley (Hector Reith), Dora Bryan (Miss La Fosse), Reginald Beckwith (*Manson*), Daniel Wherry (Dr Taren), Michael Ward (Photographer), Stanley Baker (Reporter)

Milestones and Millstones: Richard Carlson

Comment: Minor Hammer thriller that moves briskly enough and doesn't outstay its welcome.

Reviews: "A fast moving and quite exciting thriller, well acted by Richard Carlson, and made with modest competence." *Monthly Film Bulletin*

"All British cast, with the exception of Richard Carlson, picture will rate secondary bookings in most situations…a hole or two develops in the script, but overall it proves to be acceptable…Carlson does a likeable job." *Variety*

Babes in Baghdad (1952) 79 mins (color)

"The Shapes that Shook a Harem Empire!" All its Spectacle captured in EXOTIC COLOR

Danziger Productions Limited (English version)/Orphea Film (Spanish version); d: **Edgar G Ulmer**/Jerónimo Mihura; p: **Edward J Danziger, Harry Lee Danziger** (English version); Daniel Aragonés, Antonio Pujol; screenplay: Joe Ansen, Felix E. Feist, Reuben Levy, John Roeburt; ph: Jack

Cox (English version), José Luis Pérez de Rozas, Georges Périnal (Spanish version); ed: Edith Lenny (English version), Teresa Alcocer, Ángeles Pruña (Spanish version); m: J. Leoz

Synopsis: Paulette Goddard joins a Caliph's harem and demands equal rights for women, upsetting caliph John Boles: but his godson Richard Ney supports her.

Cast: Paulette Goddard (Kyra), **Gypsy Rose Lee** (Zohara), **John Boles** (Hassan), **Richard Ney** (Ezar), Thomas Gallagher (Sharkhan), Sebastian Cabot (Sinbad), MacDonald Parke (Caliph), Natalie Benesh (Zelika), Hugh Dempster (Omar), Christopher Lee (Slave Trader)

Milestones and Millstones: Paulette Goddard, Gypsy Rose Lee, John Boles, Richard Ney, Edgar J Ulmer, Edward J Danziger, Harry Lee Danziger

Comment: A cinematic low point for all concerned that makes a mockery of director Ulmer's largely undeserved auteur status. Drivel in either version.

Reviews: "Presumably intended as a take-off on Arabian Nights films, this heavy and witless romp only succeeds in being more dreary than the real (Walter Wanger) thing." *Monthly Film Bulletin*

"Even the youngest of the three leads, Gypsy Rose Lee, was far too mature for the childish proceedings at hand.... Even the staunchest auteurist defenders of director Edgar G Ulmer are hard-pressed to justify his participation in this relentlessly silly effort." *The New York Times*

The Gambler and the Lady (1952) 72 mins (b&w)

"THEIR WHEEL OF FORTUNE WAS SPUN by the COLD STEEL of an AUTOMATIC!"

Hammer Film Productions/Lippert Films; d: Patrick Jenkins; **Sam Newfield** (additional material for USA release); p: Anthony Hinds; screenplay: Sam Newfield; ph: Walter Harvey; ed: Maurice Rootes; ad: J Elder Wills; m: Ivor Slaney

Synopsis: Social-climbing American gambler Dane Clark lands in trouble with gangsters and an ex-girlfriend in London when he starts to romance a British blueblood.

Cast: Dane Clark (Jim Forster), Kathleen Byron (Pat), Naomi Chance (Lady Susan Willens), Meredith Edwards (Dave Davies), Anthony Forwood (Lord Peter Willens), Eric Pohlmann (Arturo Colonna), Anthony Ireland (Richard Farning), Max Bacon (Maxie), Mona Washbourne (Miss Minter)

Milestones and Millstones: Dane Clark, Sam Newfield

Comment: Routine and predominantly depressing B feature thriller.

Reviews: "A heavy and somber picture with scant light relief... Clark ... gives a good performance." *CEA Film Report*

Lady in the Fog/US: Scotland Yard Inspector (1952) 73 mins (b&w)

"SHE'LL KISS OR KILL... Depending upon the MAN!"

Hammer Film Productions/Lippert films; d: **Sam Neufield**; p: Anthony Hinds; screenplay: **Orville H Hampton**; from the BBC radio serial by Lester Powell; ph: Walter J Harvey; ed: James Needs; ad: Wilfred Arnold: md: Muir Matheson

Synopsis: A woman persuades American journalist Cesar Romero to help her investigate the murder of her brother who was murdered in the London fog.

Cast: Cesar Romero (Bill O'Dell), Lois Maxwell (Margaret/'Peggy' Maybrick), Bernadette O'Farrell (Heather McMara), Geoffrey Keen (Christopher Hampden), Campbell Singer (Inspector Rigby),Alastair Hunter (Detective Sergeant Reilly), Mary Mackenzie (Marilyn Durant)

Milestones and Millstones: Cesar Romero, Sam Newfield/Neufeld, Orville H Hampton

Comment: Typical minor pre-*The Curse of Frankenstein* (1957) Hammer B film: here Hammer regulars include producer Anthony Hinds, future director/producer Michael Carerras as casting director, Philip Leakey (who made up Christopher Lee as the Creature) and future cinematographer Moray Grant

Reviews: "Routine mystery with Cesar Romero somewhat miscast as the reporter and some unconvincingly "Americanised" English settings." *Monthly Film Bulletin*

"Undeveloped psychological thriller: weak grosses indicated...Mason walks through the role with little animation and gets virtually no support from Miss Havoc in her superficial playing of a difficult part." *Variety*

The Last Page/US: Man Bait (1952) 78 mins (b&w)

"LOOK IF YOU LIKE...BUT Look Out! SHE'S MAN BAIT"

Hammer Films/Exclusive Films, in association with Lippert Films; d:Terence Fisher; p: Anthony Hinds; screenplay: Frederick Knott; based on a story by James Hadley Chase; ph: Walter J Harvey; ed: Maurice Rootes; ad: Andrew Mazzei; m: Frank Spencer

Synopsis: After American West End book manager George Brent reprimands his clerk Diana Dors, her criminal boyfriend starts to blackmail him with Brent ending up being suspected of murdering Dors.

Cast: George Brent (John Harman), **Marguerite Chapman** (Stella), Raymond Huntley (Clive Oliver), Peter Reynolds (Jeff Hart), Eleanor Summerfield (Vi), Meredith Edwards (Dale), Harry Fowler (Joe), Diana Dors (Ruby), Conrad Phillips (Todd), Lawrence Ward (Lang), Nelly Arno (Miss Rossetti)

Milestones and Millstones: George Brent, Marguerite Chapman

Comment: Most notable now as Fisher's first film for Hammer, efficiently made and acted but rarely rises above its second-feature level.

Reviews: "A confused and not altogether likely melodrama, handicapped by two competent but uninteresting American stars... Some of the direction has conciseness and there is one exciting shot." *Monthly Film Bulletin*

"Okay program melodrama for secondary bookings... story handling has interest and names of George Brent and Marguerite Chapman are familiar enough to help its market chances... performances are universally good." *Variety*

The Lost Hours/US: The Big Frame (1952) 67 mins (b&w)

"SIX BLACKED OUT HOURS that branded him KILLER!"

Tempean Productions; d: **David MacDonald**; p: Monty Berman, Robert S Baker; screenplay: Steve Fisher, John Gilling; story by: Robert S Baker; Carl Nystrom; ph: Monty Berman; ed: Reginald Beck; ad: Andrew Mazzei; m: William Hill-Bowen

Synopsis: Former WW2 American pilot Mark Stevens passes out drunk at a reunion in London and wakes up next morning suspected of murdering a friend with whom he fought the previous evening.

Cast: Mark Stevens (Paul Smith), Jean Kent (Louise Parker), John Bentley (Clark Sutton), Gary Marsh (Insp. Foster), Cyril Smith (Det. Sgt. Roper), Dianne Foster (Dianne Wrigley), Bryan Coleman (Tom Wrigley), Leslie Perrins (Dr Morrison), Duncan Lamont (Bristow), John Horsely (Brown)

Milestones and Millstones: David MacDonald

Comment: Brisk "American-in-England" B film that emerges as well put together and justifies the majority of its relatively short running time.

Reviews: "Undistinguished British thriller made with more than one eye on the American B picture market, *The Lost Hours* has its full share of improbabilities of character and action. The actors can make little of their roles, which is certainly a waste of Mark Stevens." *Monthly Film Bulletin*

Monsoon (1952) 79 mins (color)

> *"ECSTASY ... flaming into passion sweet adventure...*
> *in the most daring picture ever filmed!"*

CFG Productions, Film Group Judd; d: Rod Amateau p: Gordon S Griffith, Forrest Judd; screenplay: Forrest Judd, David Robinson, Leonardo Bercovici; based on the play *Romeo et Jeanette* by Jean Anouilh; ph: Ernest Haller; second unit ph: Malcolm Gasper; ed: George Gale; ad: George Jenkins, Leslie Thomas; m: Vasant Desai

Synopsis: When Diana Douglas brings fiancé George Nader and his mother to a small village in India to meet her father and brother, the arrival of her younger sister causes problems.

Cast: Ursula Thiess (Jeannette), Diana Douglas (Julia), **George Nader** (Burton), Ellen Corby (Katie), Philip Stainton (Putsi), Myron Healey (Rault), Eric Pohlmann (Molac),

Milestones and Millstones: George Nader

Comment: The scenery is rather more convincing than the melodrama confected by a strange screenplay and seemingly over-emphatic direction.

Reviews: "Studiously strives for novelty and winds up being an odd number... erratic and self-conscious little conversation piece does likewise... the talk is endless and full of philosophical twaddle, at the expense of conviction and an impressive scenic background …a strange little film that chooses to sham instead of shine." *The New York Times*

"Unlikely to appeal to the average cinema audience…little plot and even less action, an ending which is too symbolic for words, while the characters are patterned and artificial, with dialogue to match… Nader is not distinguished." *CEA Film Report*

The Reluctant Bride/US: Two Grooms for a Bride (1952) 75 mins (b&w)

"THE GAY HILARIOUS STORY OF A PROPER MISS…who should have said "no" when she said "yes"!"

Tempean Films; d: Henry Cass; p: Monty Berman, Robert S Baker: screenplay: Frederick Stephani; ph; Monty Berman; ed: Maurice Rootes; ad: C Wilfred Arnold; m: Ivor Slaney

Synopsis: When their parents vanish on an African safari, two children try maneuvering their father's brother John Carroll and mother's sister Virginia Bruce into a romantic relationship.

Cast: John Carroll (Jeff Longstreet), **Virginia Bruce** (Laura Weeks), Brian Oulton (Professor Baker), Kay Callard (Lola Sinclair), Michael Caridia (Tony), Barbara Brown (Ra), Kit Terrington (Big), Alexander Gauge Humbold), Anita Sharpe-Bolster (Mrs Fogarty), Arthur Lowe (Mr Fogarty), Tom Gill (McCarthy)

Milestones and Millstones: John Carroll, Virginia Bruce

Comment: Eminently predicable: even with two past their peak Hollywood stars *The Reluctant Bride* was not shown in Britain until 3 years later and did not receive a release in the United States (as *Two Grooms for a Bride)* until 1957.

Reviews: "Although the material of this comedy is familiar enough, the treatment is moderately lively, with some bright dialogue capably put over by John Carroll and Virginia Bruce… quite good-humoured entertainment." *Monthly Film Bulletin*

"This kind of script is strictly from tritesville. One scene segues into the next with about as much surprise as Thursday following Wednesday… Carroll can't do much with the material he has to work with…Bruce is pleasant." *Variety*

Top Secret/Mr Potts Goes to Moscow (1952) 93 mins (b&w)

"It's the HOT COMEDY About the COLD WAR!"

Transocean/ABPC; d/p: Mario Zampi; screenplay/story by: Jack Davies, Michael Pertwee; ph: Stanley Pavey; ed: Giulio Zampi; ad: Ivan King; m: Stanley Black

Synopsis: Russian secret agent Oscar Homolka goes after British sanitary engineer George Cole when he goes on holiday after mistakenly getting hold of the plans for a new atomic device.

Cast: George Cole (George), **Oskar Homolka** (Zekov), Nadia Gray, (Tania) Frederick Valk (Rakov), Wilfrid Hyde-White (Sir Hubert Wells), Geoffrey Sumner (Pike), Ronald Adam (Barworth Controller), Ernest Jay (Professor Layton), Edwin Styles (Barworth Superintendent), Richard Wattis (Barnes)

Milestones and Millstones: Oscar Homolka

Comment: Routine second feature spy caper capped by Homolka's enjoyably bravura performance.

Reviews: "...characterisation and incident stem from the hoariest traditions of British farce, and the technique of the film is theatrical." *Monthly Film Bulletin*

"... a laugh-making espionage yarn...Homolka fits naturally into the role." *Variety*

Old Mother Riley Meets the Vampire/Mother Riley Meets the Vampire/ My Son the Vampire/ US: Vampire Over London (1952) 74 mins (b&w)

Fernwood Productions; d/p: John Gilling; ap: Stanley Couzins; screenplay: Val Valentine; ph: Stan Pavey; ed: Len Trumm; ad: Bernard Robinson; m: Lindo Southworth

Synopsis: Mysterious Bela Lugosi, known as the Vampire, comes to England to complete the experiments he needs to take over the world only to be brought to book by the old lady to whom the robot has been wrongly delivered.

Cast: Arthur Lucan (Mrs Riley), **Bela Lugosi** (Van Houten), Dora

Bryan (Tilly), Philip Leaver (Anton Dashcomb), Judith Furse (Freda), Ian Wilson (Hitchcock), Richard Wattis (PC Freddie), David Hurst (Mugsy), Graham Moffat (The Yokel), Maria Mercedes (Julia Loretti), Charles Lloyd-Pack (Sir Joshua Bing)
Milestones and Millstones: Bela Lugosi
Comment: Reduced to playing stooge to lowbrow British comedian Lucan's popular transvestite character Irish washerwoman Old Mother Riley in a witless comedy that flopped on both sides of the Atlantic, Lugosi keeps a commendably straight face in the face of dedicated nonsense. This was Lucan's last movie (and his only film to get a US release).
Reviews: "Stupid, humourless and repulsive." *Monthly Film Bulletin*

Saturday Island/Island of Desire (1952) 93 mins (color)

"A SOUTH SEA ISLAND SHANGRI-LA BEYOND YOUR WILDEST DREAMS!"

Coronado Productions; d: **Stuart Heisler**; p: David E Rose; screenplay: Stephanie Nordli; screen story: Stuart Heisler; from the *Saturday Evening Post* story *Saturday Island* by Hugh Brooke; ph: Arthur Ibbetson, Oswald Morris; ed: Russell Lloyd; ad: John Howell; m: William Alwyn; sfx: George Blackwell
Synopsis: Nurse Linda Darnell and Marine corporal Tab Hunter are sole survivors when their ship hits a mine off an island in the South Pacific during WW2: but their idyllic lives are disrupted by British pilot Donald Grey whose plane crashes on the island.
Cast: Linda Darnell (Elizabeth Smythe), **Tab Hunter** (Michael J. "Chicken" Dugan), Donald Gray (William Peck), John Laurie (Grimshaw), Russell Waters (Dr Snyder), Michael Newell (Eddie), Lloyd Lamble (Officer of the Watch), Peter Butterworth (Wounded Marine), Diana Decker (Mike)
Milestones and Millstones: Tab Hunter, Stuart Heisler
Comment: Routine romantic melodrama: Hunter's physique and attractively photographed Jamaican locations steal the show without any noticeable major acting involved.
Reviews: "...British offering has extra pictorial qualities and colourful backgrounds. These, however, are its main assets...it takes far

too long for the picture to get moving... Darnell plods through the role...Hunter...displays a healthy torso, but not a great deal of talent." *Variety*

"...this slick and glossy, Technicolor-drenched romantic melodrama stars two onetime screen heartthrobs, Linda Darnell and Tab Hunter... This saga was originally released under the title Saturday Island but was also issued in some quarters as the more-alluring Island of Desire." *The New York Times*

Stolen Face (1952) 72 mins (b&w)

"Wrong for any man... desired by all!
CROSS THIS DAME OFF YOUR LIST!"

Hammer Film Productions/Lippert Films; d: Terence Fisher; p: Anthony Hinds; screenplay: Martin Berkeley, **Richard H Landau**; story by: Alexander Paal, Steven Vas; ph: Walter J Harvey; ed: Maurice Rootes; ad: Wilfred Arnold; m: Malcolm Arnold

Synopsis: Plastic surgeon Paul Henreid remodels the face of a psychopathic woman criminal on the run to resemble concert pianist Lizabeth Scott whom he loves with ultimately unfortunate results.

Cast: Paul Henreid (Dr Philip Ritter), **Lizabeth Scott** (Alice Brent/Lily Conover) Mary Mackenzie (Lily Conover, before surgery) Andre Morell (David), John Wood (Dr Jack Wilson), Susan Stephen (Betty Arnold), Arnold Ridley (Dr Russell), Diana Beaumont (May), Russell Napier (Detective Cutler)

Milestones and Millstones: Paul Henreid, Lizabeth Scott, Richard H Landau

Comment: Tense, atmospheric low-budget thriller was Fisher's 11th film as director and his third for Hammer whose future he assured with his 1956 shocker *The Curse of Frankenstein*. Small scale but significant: improbably, for Hammer's usual low budgets, Hollywood legend Edith Head designed Scott's costumes.

Reviews: "Program drama, filmed in England, with only mild chances despite names of Paul Henreid and Lizabeth Scott..." *Variety*

"Personally, I would have thought that a drama based on plastic surgery, had scope. But what opportunities the subject may offer for getting off the beaten track certainly haven't been taken up ...Henreid does well and convinces as the surgeon... Scott makes what she can of the dual role." *Picturegoer*

36 Hours/US: Terror Street (1952) (b&w)

"ONE-WAY ROAD TO VIOLENCE HER FRAME WAS ONLY THE BUILD-UP TO A FRAME-UP!"

Hammer Film Productions/Lippert Films; d: Montgomery Tully; p: Anthony Hinds; screenplay: Steve Fisher; ph: Walter Harvey; ed: James Needs; ad: J Elder Wills; m: Malcolm Arnold

Synopsis: American pilot Dan Duryea who is training in the USA gets an unauthorised flight to England to pay a surprise visit to his Norwegian wife and ends up framed for her murder and has just 36 hours to prove his innocence.

Cast: Dan Duryea (Major Bill Rogers), Elsie Albiin (Katherine 'Katie' Rogers), Gudrun Ure (Sister Jenny Miller), Eric Pohlmann (Slossen, the smuggler), John Chandos (Orville Hart), Kenneth Griffith (Henry Slosson), Harold Lang (Desk Clerk), Jane Carras (Soup Kitchen Supervisor), Marianne Stone (Pam Palmer)

Milestones and Millstones: Dan Duryea

Comment: Duryea commands attention in an otherwise average *film noir* B.

Reviews: "Far-fetched and complicated plot ... some dramatic situations, a number of fierce fights, shooting and jewel smuggling... moderate entertainment for indulgent audiences... Duryea gives a virile performance." *CEA Film Report*

Dan Duryea in English-made melodrama offering only fair escapism for lowercase market...Duryea manages to bolster up the show with good histrionics but gets little help from the others." *Variety*

24 Hours of a Woman's Life/US: Affair in Monte Carlo
(1952) 75 mins (color)

*"THEY GAMBLED LIFE, LOVE, EVERYTHING...
IN A PARADISE OF TEMPTATION!"*

The J Arthur Rank Organisation/A Two Cities Film; d: Victor Saville; p: Ivan Foxwell; screenplay: Warren Chetham Strode; from the novella *24 Stunden aus dem Leben einer Frau* by Stefan Zweig; ph: Christopher Challis; ed: Richard Best; ad: Terence Verity; m: Philip Green, Robert Gill

Synopsis: Worldly writer Leo Genn tells people in a café about Merle Oberon who fell in love in less than 24 hours with compulsive gambler Richard Todd who had just lost the last of his money in Monte Carlo.

Cast: Merle Oberon (Linda Venning), Richard Todd (The Boy), **Leo Genn** (Robert Sterling), Joan Dowling (Mrs Barry), **June Clyde** (Mrs Roche), Joan Dowling (Mrs Barry), Peter Reynolds (Peter), Stephen Murray (Father Benoit), Mara Lane (Alice Brown), Isabel Dean (Mrs Johnson), Robert Ayres (Frank Brown)

Milestones and Millstones: Leo Genn, June Clyde

Comment: Morose melodrama with little to recommend it other than the Monte Carlo locations.

Reviews: "...a film of such artificiality and bathos the very typewriter keys cling together to avoid describing it." *The Spectator*

"A solemn tearjerker dressed up with Riviera photography in Technicolor... the three stars perform with unusual woodenness, the direction is lifeless, the pace almost unbearably retarded." *Monthly Film Bulletin*

"Merle Oberon, Richard Todd, Leo Genn wasted in unrealistic story...the plot is developed with unrealistic incident and unrealistic characters." *Variety*

Wings of Danger/US: Dead on Course (1952) 73 mins (b&w)

"Suspense Soars ON—WINGS of DANGER"

Hammer Film Productions/Lippert Films; d: Terence Fisher; p: Anthony Hinds; screenplay: John Gilling; based on *Dead on Course'* by Elleston

Trevor and Packham Webb; ph: Walter J Harvey; ed: James Needs; ad: Andrew Mazzei; m: Malcolm Arnold

Synopsis: Pilot Zachary Scott romances the girlfriend of a criminal when he takes on the crooks blackmailing his friend into helping them in a major smuggling racket.

Cast: Zachary Scott (Richard Van Ness), Robert Beatty (Nick Talbot), Naomi Chance (Avril Talbot), Kay Kendall (Alexia LaRoche), Colin Tapley (Inspector Maxwell), Arthur Lane (Boyd Spencer), Harold Lang (Snell), Diane Cilento (Jeannette). Jack Allen (Triscott), Douglas Muir (Dr Wilner)

Milestones and Millstones: Zachary Scott

Comment: Another efficient pre-*Curse of Frankenstein* (1957) B-film Hammer thriller by Terence Fisher: here Phil Leakey, who transformed Christopher Lee's into the Frankenstein Creature, simply does routine, unmemorable, work.

Reviews: "Thriller with a moral ending, in which the good people survive and the bad ones don't. In this, as in other ways, quite unremarkable." *Monthly Film Bulletin*

"The picture is solidly constructed and tells its story slickly." *Picturegoer*

"Uninspired, uninteresting plot ingredients hamper this weak British entry. Action is confusing throughout, and the U.S. going will even be tough in secondary markets." *Variety*

The Woman's Angle (1952) 86 mins (b&w)

*"3 SMART GIRLS WITH ONE SINGLE THOUGHT
(about the same man!)"*

Walter C Mycroft Productions/Bow Wells; d: Leslie Arliss; p: Walter C Mycroft; screenplay: Leslie Arliss, Mabbie Poole; based on the novel *Three Cups of Coffee* by Ruth Feiner; ph: Erwin Hillier; ed: Edward B Jarvis; ad: Terence Verity; m: Robert Gill

Synopsis: During a divorce hearing, flashbacks reveal the busy love life of composer Edward Underdown.

Cast: Edward Underdown (Robert Mansell), **Cathy O'Donnell** (Nina Van Rhyne), Lois Maxwell (Enid Mansell), Claude Farell (Delysia

Veronova), Peter Reynolds (Brian Mansell), Marjorie Fielding (Mrs Mansell) Joan Collins (Marina), Dana Wynter (Elaine), Isobel Dean (Isobel Mansell)

Milestones and Millstones: Cathy O'Donnell

Comment: Competently made but hardly interesting: not too surprisingly, Joan Collins has no lines.

Reviews: "*The Woman's Angle,* a baffling little exercise on the subject of masculine behavior. It is also a mildly vexing picture, a grim little sample of bad writing, bad acting and bad directing all around!" *The New York Times*

"...no more than the filming of a woman's magazine story, and has the traditional air of unreality. The ingredients—eccentric genius, misunderstandings, music and a variety of settings—are put together without inspiration." *Monthly Film Bulletin*

The Fake (1953) 80 mins (b&w)

"NOW HE KNEW...IN <u>ANY</u> COUNTRY A RACKET'S A RACKET ... and A MURDER IS A MURDER!"

Pax Films; d:Godfrey Grayson; p: Steven Pallos; ap: Ambrose Grayson; screenplay: Patrick Kirwan, Bridget Boland; original story: James Daplyn; ph: Cedric Williams; ed: Charles Hasse; ad: Denis Wreford; m: Matyas Seiber

Synopsis: American detective Dennis O'Keefe, who is investigating the thefts of great paintings, believes London's Tate Gallery may be the thieves' next target.

Cast: Dennis O'Keefe (Paul Mitchell), **Coleen Gray** (Mary Mason), Hugh Williams (Sir Richard Aldingham), Guy Middleton (Smith), John Laurie (Henry Mason), Eliot Makeham (Pavement Artist), Gerald Case (Peter Randall), Seymour Green (Weston), Stanley Van Beers (Cartwright), Dora Bryan (Barmaid) Ellen Pollock (Miss Fossett), Billie Whitelaw (Waitress)

Milestones and Millstones: Dennis O'Keefe, Coleen Gray

Comment: Most notable as the first movie to be allowed to film in the Tate Galley: the blandly directed narrative is just about sufficient to maintain interest.

Reviews: "O'Keefe is forthright and typically the he-man as the American detective." *Picturegoer*.

"A crime thriller that runs along the usual lines... the American stars are well supported." *Picture Show*

"Two U.S. names may help sell this British pic on both sides of the Atlantic, but basically it is a contrived meller which rates booking as a dualer...Leading roles are adequately played by Dennis O'Keefe and Coleen Gray..." *Variety*

The Flanagan Boy/US: Bad Blonde (1953) 81 mins (b&w)

"They called me BAD...spelled M-E-N!"

Hammer Films/Lippert Films; d: **Reginald Le Borg**; p: Anthony Hinds; screenplay: Guy Elmes, **Richard Landau;** from the novel by Max Catto; ph: Walter J Harvey; ed James Needs; ad: Wilfred Arnold; m: Ivor Slaney

Synopsis: Scheming millionaire's wife Barbara Payton seduces boxer Tony Wright to persuade him to murder her husband who is promoting the pugilist's comeback.

Cast: Barbara Payton (Lorna Vecchi), Tony Wright (Johnny Flanagan) Frederick Valk (Giuseppe Vecchi), Sid James (Sharkey), Marie Burke (Mother Vecchi) Selma Vaz (Mrs Corelli), Enzo Coticchia (Mr Corelli)

Milestones and Millstones: Reginald Le Borg, Richard Landau

Comment: Shocking and sleazy (for the time) with Hammer importing American director Le Borg to made the most of the melodramatic storyline—which he did.

Reviews: "Barbara Payton and manly Tony Wright keep the sordid story going. It's well worth a visit if you like strongish meat." *Picturegoer*

"Boxing, murder and romance intermingle...Barbara Payton gives a good performance." *Picture Show*

The House of the Arrow (1953) 73 mins (b&w)

"Doorway to Danger!" NOT SUITABLE FOR CHILDREN

Associated British Picture Corporation (APBC); d: Michael Anderson; p: Vaughan N Dean; screenplay: Edward Dryhurst; from the novel by A E W Mason; ph: Erwin Hillier; ed: Edward B Jarvis; ad: Terence Verity; m: Gerald Crossman

Synopsis: Celebrated French detective Oscar Homolka investigates the mysterious death of a wealthy widow in provincial France.

Cast: Oscar Homolka (Inspector Hanaud), Yvonne Furneaux (Betty Harlowe), Robert Urquhart (Jim Frobisher), Josephine Griffin (Anne Upcott), Harold Kasket (Boris Waberski), Anthony Nicholls (Jeremy Haslett), Pierre Lefevre (Thevenet), Jacques Cey (Giradot), Keith Pytott (Gaston)

Milestones and Millstones: Oscar Homolka

Comment: The third film version of Mason's novel works very well as a fast-paced thriller, making the most of its relatively short length and infusing neat humour into the growing suspense. Homolka is particularly effective.

Reviews: "... is given 'The Third Man' treatment—a blend of drama and sly humour—and the effect is stimulating...Homolka gives a masterly performance as the vain, confident detective..." *Picturegoer*

"Interest is sustained by the exciting developments and there is a surprise or two and a dramatic climax... Homolka's shrewd and clever performance... is most enjoyable and compensates largely for any deficiencies." *CEA Film Report*

The Limping Man (1953) 76 mins (b&w)

"RELENTLESS SUSPENSE!! the dragnet's out for him!"

Banner Films; d: Charles de la Tour (aka **Cy Enfield**); p: Donald Ginsberg; screenplay: Ian Stuart Black, Reginald Long; from the novel *Death on the Tideway* by Anthony Verney; ph: Jonah Jones; ed: Stanley Wills; ad: Cedric Dawe; m: Arthur Wilkinson

Synopsis: When former G.I. Lloyd Bridges visits London after six years to see his wartime girlfriend he becomes involved in a murder committed by a mysterious limping man.

Cast: Lloyd Bridges (Frank Prior), Moira Lister (Pauline French), Alan Wheatley (Inspector Braddock), Leslie Phillips (Detective Cameron), Hélène Cordet (Helene Castle), Andre Van Gyseghem (George), Tom Gill (Stage Manager), Bruce Beeby (Kendal Brown), Rachel Roberts (Barmaid), Lionel Blair (Dancer)

Milestones and Millstones: Lloyd Bridges, Cy Endfield

Comment: A neat, unpretentious B feature thriller that benefits strongly from Bridges's all-American charisma along with the competent storytelling and a (relatively) short running time.

Reviews: "Lloyd Bridges impresses ... incredible as the story seems, it's not entirely without thrills." *Picturegoer*

"Neatly acted with a suspenseful plot, it also has touches of romance and comedy." *Picture Show*

"This thriller is sufficiently full of mystery to hold the attention for most of its length. Bridges tends to underplay the legendary toughness of Americans in such circumstances." *Monthly Film Bulletin*

"The performances are adequate, the mood good and the pace leisurely British." *Variety*

The Man from Cairo/Dramma nella Kasbah/Avventura ad Algeri (1953) 81 min (b&w)

> *"EXPLODES WITH SIZZLING EXCITEMENT...UNEQUALED SUSPENSE FILMED WHERE IT HAPPENED!"*

Michaeldavid Productions/Societa Italiana Gestioni Manifestazioni Artistiche Italarte; d: Ray Enright; Edoardo Anton (Italian version); p: Bernard Luber, Livio Dall'Oglio; screenplay: Philip Stevenson, Janet Stevenson, Eugene Ling, Edoardo Anton, Ugo Velona; story: Ladislas Fodor; ph: Mario Albertelli; ed: Mario Serandrei; ad: Giulio Bongini; m: Renzo Rossellini

Synopsis: George Raft is mistaken for a detective by the French and sent to Algiers in search of $100,000,000 worth of gold stolen during WW2.

Cast: George Raft (Mike Canelli), Gianna Maria Canale (Lorraine Beloyan), Massimo Serato (Basil Constantine), Guido Celano (Emile Touchard), Irene Papas (Yvonne Lebeau), Alfredo Varelli (Professor. H.

M. Crespi), Leonardo Scavino (Police Captain Akhim Bey), Mino Doro (Major C Blanc)

Milestones and Millstones: George Raft

Comment: Raft, in the last film for which he received top billing, too often comes across like a good but not always perfect impersonation of himself in his cinema prime: the movie was shot in Italy and was director Enright's last movie.

"The plot has many complications and contains mystery and touch action, but there is no light relief... holds the interest well. Good entertainment...Raft is excellent." *CEA Film Report*

Mantrap/US: Man in Hiding (1953) 73 mins (b&w)

"When he comes out a city runs for cover!... an ex-sweetheart reaches for a gun..."

Hammer Film Productions; d: Terence Fisher; p: Michael Carerras, Alexander Paal; screenplay: Paul Tabori, Terence Fisher; from the novel *Queen in Danger* by Elleston Trevor; ph: Reginald Wyer; ed: James Needs; ad: J Elder Wills; m: Doreen Carwithen

Synopsis: A man escapes from prison after being found guilty of murder and goes after his wife who has changed her name, leaving lawyer Paul Henreid to save the day.

Cast: Paul Henreid (Hugo Bishop), Lois Maxwell (Thelma Speight/Tasman), Kieron Moore (Speight), Hugh Sinclair (Maurice Jerrard), Lloyd Lamble (Inspector Frisnay), Bill Travers (Victor Tasman), Mary Laura Wood (Susie) Kay Kendall (Vera Gorringe), Conrad Phillips (Barker), John Stuart (Doctor)

Milestones and Millstones: Paul Henreid

Comment: A British B film given a modicum of welcome pace by Fisher but marking yet a further decline in the career *Casablanca* (1942) star Henreid.

Reviews: "This is a heavy and dramatic picture, with an involved plot, which is confusing and difficult to follow... some tense situations, but scant light relief ... very moderate entertainment. Paul Henreid gives a sound and sincere performance." *CEA Film Report*

Personal Affair (1953) 82 mins (b&w)

"IT WAS TOO LATE TO RUN!"

Two Cities Films; d: Anthony Pelissier; ep: Earl St John; p: Anthony Darnborough; screenplay: Lesley Storm; from her play *The Day's Mischief*; ph: Reginald H Wyer; ed: Frederick Wilson; ad: Cedric Dawe; m: William Alwyn

Synopsis: Impulsive teenage pupil Glynis Johns disappears soon after being confronted by Gene Tierney over her infatuation with her teacher husband Leo Genn.

Cast: Gene Tierney (Kay Barlow), Leo Genn (Stephen Barlow), Glynis Johns (Barbara Vining), Walter Fitzgerald (Henry Vining), Pamela Brown (Evelyn), Megs Jenkins (Vi Vining), Michael Hordern (Headmaster), Thora Hird (Mrs Usher), Martin Boddey (Police Inspector), Nanette Newman (Sally)

Milestones and Millstones: Leo Genn

Comment: More stagey than convincing: (John Box, one of the four uncredited draughtsmen working on the film went on to win four Academy Awards for Best Art Direction and was nominated for two more).

Reviews: "For the most part, the going is too steady, the situation is kept too well in hand, everyone tries to be too chin-up and the scandal is too refined. It is an earnest and plausible study... But it doesn't develop much excitement. It is a decent, eventually tedious film." *New York Times*

"... Tierney is very good ...Genn convinces ... the plot is extremely well developed and tension is held to the end. It's a story that avoids the obvious." *Picturegoer*

Plaza Suite 605/US: Norman Conquest (1953) 75 mins (b&w)

"Excitement... and Suspense WILL BE YOURS WHEN YOU MEET...
Norman Conquest"

B & A Productions Limited; d: Bernard Knowles; p: Bertram Ostrer, Albert Fennell; screenplay: Bertram Ostrer, Albert Fennell, Bernard Knowles, Clifford Witting; based on the book *Dare-Devil Conquest* by

Berkeley Gray; ph: Eric Cross; ed: Clifford Boote; ad: John Elphick; m: Philip Green

Synopsis: Private detective Tom Conway is summoned to a hotel room where he is framed for murder but still succeeds in bringing a gang of smugglers to book.

Cast: Tom Conway (Norman Conquest), Eva Bartok (Nadina Rodin), Joy Shelton (Pixie Everard), Sid James (Superintendent Williams), Richard Wattis (Theodore Feather), Carl Jaffe (Boris Roff), Frederick Schiller (Ivan Burgin), Robert Adair (Baron von Henschel), Anton Diffring (Gregor)

Milestones and Millstones: Tom Conway

Comment: Passable but predictable bottom-of-the-bill thriller.

Reviews: "...a haphazard plot without a cliché out of place... Conway is the perfect amateur sleuth ... unsubstantial fare, but a showcase for its stars." *Picturegoer*

"An involved and indifferently made thriller; the actors give the impression that they have been there before." *Monthly Film Bulletin*

The Saint's Return/US: The Saint's Girl Friday (1953) 73 mins (b&w)

"THE SAINT MOVES IN Blondes...bullets and blackmail can't stop him!"

Hammer Film Production; d: **Seymour Friedman**; p: Anthony Hinds, Julian Lesser; screenplay: Allan Mackinnon; based on story by Leslie Charteris; ph: Walter J Harvey; ed: James Needs; ad: J Elder Wills; m: Ivor Slaney

Synopsis: Simon Templar, alias The Saint, arrives in England to help his girlfriend who had cabled for him help but he finds she has been her murdered and sets out to find the killers.

Cast: Louis Hayward (Simon Templar), Naomi Chance (Carol Denby) Sydney Tafler (Max Lennar), Charles Victor (Chief Insp. Claud Teal), Jane Carr (Kate Finch), Harold Lang (Jarvis), William Russell (Keith Merton, as Russell Enoch) Diana Dors (The Blonde in Lennar's Apartment) Fred Johnson (Irish Cassidy)

Milestones and Millstones: Seymour Friedman

Comment: Routine low-budget thriller with Hayward efficiently doing all required of him with ease and panache: future British film sex symbol Diana Dors features in a gratuitous (saucy for the time) sequence.

Reviews: "... at least this episode plays fair by picturegoers. You expect some mild mental gymnastics, a few red herrings with the conventional twist in the last reel, and you get these ... Hayward slips back into his Saint role with ease." *Picturegoer*

Spaceways (1953) 74 mins (b&w)

"Who rules the SPACE ISLANDS in the sky...rules the world!"

Hammer Films/Lippert Pictures; d: Terence Fisher; p: Michael Carreras; screenplay: **Richard H Landau**, Paul Tabori; from the radio play by Charles Eric Maine; ph: Reg Wyer; ed: Maurice Rootes; ad: J Elder Wills; visual special effect (vsfx): Les Bowie, Vic Margutti; m: Ivor Slaney

Synopsis: When scientist Howard Duff who works at a secret rocket base in England is accused of killing his unfaithful wife and her lover and sending their bodies into space in a satellite he has to go into space to prove his innocence.

Cast: Howard Duff (Dr Stephen Mitchell), Eva Bartok (Dr Lisa Frank), Alan Wheatley (Dr Smith), Philip Leaver (Professor Koepler), Michael Medwin (Dr Toby Andrews), Andrew Osbirb (Dr Philip Crenshaw), Cecile Chevreau (Vanessa Mitchell), Anthony Ireland (General Hayes), David Horne (Minister)

Milestones and Millstones: Richard H Landau

Comment: Another competently completed Fisher B made prior to his horror film breakthrough for Hammer with *The Curse of Frankenstein* (1957). More interesting for its director than for its storyline, this was Great Britain's first space adventure since 1936's *Things to Come*.

Reviews: "...the first British entry in the current cycle of science-fiction. And a pretty effective job it is, too ... the climax is exciting ... dramatically and sensationally enough to please most tastes. Howard Duff is very good ... it is, of course, a melodrama-and-hokum sandwich, but I found it worth a bite." *Picturegoer*

"Such a subject needs actionful treatment, which it doesn't get in this instance. Moreover, the two leading players are lifeless." *CEA Film Report*

"...comes off as a mild, talky and overlengthy melodrama ...script constantly betrays its radio play origin by running to long sides of static dialog." *Variety*

Street of Shadows/US: Shadow Man (1953) 84 mins (b&w)

"Every step he took led him to *MURDER!* and a woman!"

William Nassour Productions/ Merton Park Studios; d: Richard Vernon; p: **William Nassour,** William H Williams; screenplay: Richard Vernon; from the novel *The Creaking Chair* by Lawrence Meynell; ph: Phil Grindrod; ed: Geoffrey Muller; ad: George Haslam; m: Eric Spear

Synopsis: London pin able saloon owner Cesar Romero needs to clear himself when he is framed for murder.

Cast: Cesar Romero (Luigi), Kay Kendall (Barbara Gale), Edward Underdown (Insp. Johnstone), Victor Maddern (Limpy), Simone Silva (Angele Abbe), Fred Roberts (Constable Fred Roberts), Bill Travers (Nigel Langley), Robert Cawdron (Det. Sgt. Hadley), John Penrose (Gale), Eileen Way (Mrs Thoms)

Milestones and Millstones: Cesar Romero, William Nassour

Comment: Satisfactory second feature melodrama that tends to outstay its over-familiar welcome.

Reviews: "… complicated and very scrappy… manages to hold the interest. This is largely due to the excellent acting. There is an exciting climax. It is not a picture for the squeamish, but is good entertainment of its type. Cesar Romero gives a smooth and engaging portrayal." *CEA Film Report*

"Competently acted and directed." *Picture Show*

Three Steps to the Gallows/US: White Fire (1953) 81 mins (b&w)

"HER ONLY FLAW WAS A WEAKNESS FOR DIAMONDS…."

Tempean Films; d: John Gilling; p: Robert S Baker, Monty Berman; screenplay: John Gilling, Paul Erickson; ph: Monty Berman; ed: Marjorie Saunders; ad: Wilfred Arnold; m: Stanley Black

Synopsis: When American Scott Brady comes to London to look for his brother he finds he has three days to prove his brother, who is due to hang for murder, is innocent.

Cast: Scott Brady (Gregor Stevens), **Mary Castle** (Yvonne Durante), Gabrielle Brune (Lorna Dreyhurst), Ferdy Mayne (Mario Satargo), Colin Tapley (Arnold Winslow), John Blythe (Dave Leary), Michael Balfour (Carter), Lloyd Lamble (James Smith), Julian Somers (John Durante) Ballard Berkeley (Insp. Haley)

Milestones and Millstones: Scott Brady, Mary Castle

Comment: Well-chosen London locations add some substance to an otherwise standard second-feature suspenser.

Reviews: "A conventional thriller... Brady adequately fills the role of the American-in-Britain inevitable in this kind of story." *Monthly Film Bulletin*

"A passably fair 81 minutes of melodramatic complications are unspooled... A lively pace, stepped up quite a bit from the usual British tempo, helps carry it off and it has Scott Brady's name for the marquees in the lesser market." *Variety*

Dangerous Voyage/US: Terror Ship (1954) 72 mins (b&w)

"Make way for a Tornado of Excitement!"

Merton Park Studios; director and story by (d/story by): Vernon Sewell; p: William H Williams; screenplay: Julia Ward; ph: Josef Ambor; ed: Geoffrey Miller; m: Allan Gray

Synopsis: American pulp novelist William Lundigan finds inspiration for his next book when he investigates the mystery of a yacht found mysteriously drifting in the English Channel.

Cast: William Lundigan (Peter Duncan), Naomi Chance (Joan Drew), Vincent Ball (John Drew), Jean Lodge (Vivian Bolton), Kenneth Henry (Inspector Neal), Richard Stewart (Sergeant French), John Warwick (Carter) Beresford Egan (Hartnell), Frank Littlewood (Mr Martin), Armand Guinie (Fourneau)

Milestones and Millstones: William Lundigan

Comment: A storyline that features references to then contemporary concerns about nuclear warfare adds suspense to a plot-busy thriller.

Reviews: "8 marks as a second feature for the masses... interest is sustained with a murder, disappearances, motor-launch chase and a tense and thrilling climax... Lundigan gives a likeable performance." *CEA Film Report*

"...a pity, with such an intriguing and promising plot, that the action should lag behind ... good story material us watered down by indecisive direction Lundigan puts a star stamp on the cast list." *Picturegoer*

Devil's Point/US: Devil's Harbor (1954) 70 mins (b&w)

Charles Deane Productions; d: Montgomery Tully; producer and screenplay (p/screenplay): Charles Deane; ap: Desmond Kayton, Clive St George; ph: Geoffrey Faithfull; ed: Enid Mansell, Peter Seabourne; ad: Bert Davey

Synopsis: American Richard Arlen who operates a Thames barge becomes involved in crime and skullduggery when he comes across a mysterious parcel that has been dropped by drug smugglers.

Cast: Richard Arlen (John 'Captain' Martin), Greta Gynt (Peggy Mason), Donald Houston (Michael Mallard), Edwin Richfield (Daller), Michael Balfour (Bennett), Arnold Adrian (Mark), Mary Germaine (Margaret Lane), Sidney Bromley (Enson), Doreen Holiday (Waitress), Vincent Ball (Williams)

Milestones and Millstones: Richard Arlen

Comment: Unmemorable bottom half of a double bill with its American star patently nearing the end of his star career.

Reviews: "Second feature for uncritical audiences...story is complicated and the film very scraggy and disjointed; some of the incident is far-fetched and unconvincing and much of the dialogue is banal... Arlen gives a competent performance." *CEA Film Report*

"...best suited for fill-in bookings in the lesser situations... the basic plot idea furnished a good enough springboard for a program meller, but it falls apart in the script development." *Variety*

The Diamond/US: Diamond Wizard (1954) 83 mins (b&w)

Gibraltar Films Ltd; d: **Dennis O'Keefe**, Montgomery Tully; p: Steven Pallos; screenplay: John C Higgins, Jonathan Rix, aka Dennis O'Keefe;

from the novel *Rich is the Treasure* by Maurice Procter; ph: Arthur Graham; ed: Helga Cranston; ad: Denis Wreford; m: Matyas Seiber

Synopsis: American Treasury agent Dennis O'Keefe teams up with a Scotland Yard detective in London to track down crooks intending to create phony diamonds using money stolen from the US.

Cast: Dennis O'Keefe (Joe Dennison), Margaret Sheridan (Marline Miller), Philip Friend (Inspector McClaren), Alan Wheatley (Thompson Blake), Francis De Wolff (Yeo), Eric Berry (Hunziger), Michael Balfour (Hoxie) Gudrun Ure, as Ann Gudrun (Sergeant Smith), Paul Hardtmuth (Dr. Eric Miller), Cyril Chamberlain (Castle), Seymour Green (Lascelles)

Milestones and Millstones: Dennis O'Keefe

Comment: Enjoyable B-feature thriller, well cast. O'Keefe and his British colleagues work well together instead of the more usual USA-vs-Great Britain on-screen relationship: directed at an effectively fast pace. Shot but not exhibited in 3D.

Reviews: "Quite well-developed crime melodrama, with an exciting chase. It's well acted By Dennis O'Keefe ... Scotland Yard research detail is interesting and convincing." *Picturegoer*

"This is an actionful and dramatic picture it holds well, although there are many complications a pleasant performance... Sheridan makes an attractive and pleasing heroine." *CEA Film Report*

"O'Keefe tries his hand as director... and does fairly well for an initial effort." *Variety*

Diplomatic Passport (1954) 78 mins (b&w)

Rich & Rich Ltd; d: **Gene Martel**; p: **Burt Balaban**, Gene Martel; screenplay: Paul Tabori; ph: James Wilson; ed: Max Benedict; ad: John Elphick; m: Eric Spear

Synopsis: An American diplomat and his wife, Marsha Hunt, become involved with a gang of smugglers using the diplomat as an unwitting courier.

Cast: Marsha Hunt (June Andersen), Paul Carpenter (Ray Andersen), Henry Oscar (The Chief), Honor Blackman (Marcella), Marne Maitland (Philip), John Maclaren (Jack Gordon), Henry Longhurst (Jonathan, the waiter), John Welsh (US Embassy Official), John Bennett (André), John Boxer (Airline clerk)

Milestones and Millstones: Gene Martel, Burt Balaban

Comment: Carpenter has the most potent role as Hunt's diplomat husband, while she does what she can with her top-billed but frequently secondary role: forgettable.

Reviews: "As a straight thriller it just gets by—largely because if some good fighting sequences... Hunt and Paul Carpenter are both expert players, but fight a losing battle with makeshift material. The direction is slow-paced and the aimless plot has no punch." *Picturegoer*

Face the Music/US: The Black Glove (1954) 84 mins (b&w)

"CHILLING TERROR COMES WRAPPED IN THE BLACK GLOVE"

Hammer Films, in association with Lippert Films; d: Terrence Fisher; p: Michael Carreras; screenplay: Ernest Borneman; from his novel; ph: Walter J Harvey; ed: Maurice Rootes; ad: J Elder Wills; m: Kenny Baker, Ivor Slaney

Synopsis: American trumpet player Alex Nicol comes to London only to have to turn detective and hunt for the real killer after he is falsely accused of murdering a Spanish singer.

Cast: Alex Nicol (James Bradley), Eleanor Summerfield (Barbara Quigley), John Salew (Maxie Maguilies), Paul Carpenter (Johnny Sutherland), Geoffrey Keen (Maurie Green), Ann Hinslip (Maxine Halbard) Martin Boddey (Insp. Mulroney), Fred Johnson (Detective Sergeant Mulroney), Arthur Lane (Jeff Colt)

Milestones and Millstones: Alex Nichol

Comment: Not one of Fisher's finest films (*The Curse of Frankenstein* (1957) was some eight films in the future) but he makes the most of the low budget and thin screenplay to match.

Reviews: "Supporting star to Hollywood's Alex Nicol in this British thriller is London's Palladium Theatre ... the phoney atmosphere could have been excused if the story had a punch. But it's a slow-paced and obvious whodunit. Acting is good, particularly from Alex Nicol." *Picturegoer*

Five Days/US: Paid to Kill (1954) 75 mins (b&w)

"I'M THE GUY WHO PAID TO KILL...MYSELF!"

Hammer Films/Lippert Films: d: Montgomery Tully; p: Anthony Hinds; screenplay: Paul Tabori; ph: Walter J Harvey; ed: James Needs: ad: J Elder Wills; m: Ivor Slaney

Synopsis: Down-on-his-luck Dane Clark hires a hitman to kill him so that his family can have the insurance: but his luck changes and he faces a desperate race against time to prevent his own death.

Cast: Dane Clark (James Nevill), Paul Carpenter (Paul Kirby), Thea Gregory (Andrea Nevill) Cecile Chevreau (Joan), Anthony Forwood (Glanville), Howard Marion-Crawford (McGowan), Avis Scott (Eileen), Ross Hutchinson (Ingham), Peter Gawthorne (Bowman), Arnold Diamond (Perkins), Charles Hawtrey (Bill)

Milestones and Millstones: Dane Clark

Comment: A patently inexpensive, but moderately quite effective attempt at a second feature film noir.

Reviews: "This picture has an original plot... There is a surprising twist ad interest is well sustained... Clark gives a good performance." *CEA Film Report*

The Green Buddha/US: The Green Carnation (1954) 62 mins (b&w)

William N Boyle Productions; d: John Lemont: p: William N Boyle; screenplay: Paul Erickson; ph: Basil Emmott; ed: John Seabourne Jr; ad: John Stoll; m: Lambert Williamson

Synopsis: American charter pilot Wayne Morris becomes involved with the thieves who have stolen a priceless antique and rescues Mary Germaine along the way.

Cast: Wayne Morris (Gary Holden), Mary Germaine (Vivien Blake), Marcia Ashton (Susie), Mary Merrall (Mrs Rydon-Smith), Walter Rilla (Frank Olsen), Leslie Linder (Henry Marsh), Percy Herbert (Casey O'Rourke), Wolf Frees (Tony Scott), Kenneth Griffith (Nobby), Victor Platt (George De Carlo)

Milestones and Millstones: Wayne Morris

Comment: Morris plays fair with the material and the fairground climax gives the thriller a welcome boost.

Reviews: "Second feature for the masses... a highly improbable and complicated story... Morris is well cast as the hero." *CEA Film Report*

The House Across the Lake/US: Heatwave (1954) 68 mins (b&w)

"She's tempting...tantalizing...and cold-blooded!"

Hammer Films/Lippert Films; d/s: Ken Hughes; from his novel *High Wray*; p: Anthony Hinds; ph: Walter J Harvey; ed: James Needs; ad: J Elder Wills; m: Ivor Slaney

Synopsis: American writer Alex Nicol becomes dangerously enmeshed with a beautiful woman who is determined to dispose of her wealthy husband.

Cast: Alex Nicol (Mark Kendrick), **Hillary Brooke** (Carol Forrest), Sid James (Beverly Forrest), Susan Stephen (Andrea Forrest), Paul Carpenter (Vincent Gordon), Alan Wheatley (Insp. MacLennan), Peter Illing (Harry Stevens), Gordon McLeod (Doctor Emery), Joan Hickson (Mrs. Hardcastle)

Milestones and Millstones: Alex Nichol, Hillary Brooke

Comment: *The House Across the Lake* largely lacks 'Englishness', creating a similar atmosphere to many low-budget Hollywood films noir. It's slick, efficient and does not outstay its welcome.

Reviews: "...elegant entertainment. A British-made film with American stars, it captures the ease and escapism of the smoothest thrillers ... first-class script, direction and acting ... Brooke ... has knife-like thrust. Alex Nichol has the looks and humour of a young Franchot Tone. " *Picturegoer*

"The story is difficult to believe but holds the attention... moderate entertainment." *CEA Film Report*

Impulse (1954) 80 mins (b&w)

"IMPULSE ...with a woman like her it can lead to MURDER!"

Tempean Films; d: Charles de La Tour/**Cy Endfield** (uncredited); p: Robert S Baker, Monty Berman; screenplay: Jonathan Roach (aka Cy Endfield), Lawrence Huntingdon; story by: Robert S Baker, Carl Nystrom; ph: Jonah Jones; ed: Jack Slade; ad: C Wilfred Arnold; m: Stanley Black

Synopsis: When married estate agent Arthur Kennedy begins an affair with nightclub singer Constance Smith while his wife is away he lands in growing trouble with criminals.

Cast: Arthur Kennedy (Alan Curtis), Constance Smith (Lila), Joy Shelton (Elizabeth Curtis), Jack Allen (Freddie), James Carney (Jack Forrester), Cyril Chamberlain (Gray), Cameron Hall (Joe), Bruce Beeby (Harry Winters), Charles Lamb (Palmer), Sam Kydd (Ticket Inspector), Michael Balfour (Sailor)

Milestones and Millstones: Arthur Kennedy, Cy Endfield

Comment: A couple of minor plot twists help to keep you watching an otherwise standard B feature suspenser.

Reviews: "...second feature for the masses ...this is a conventional crime thriller with rather less action and excitement than usual ... Arthur Kennedy is good in the leading role; Constance Smith is well cast opposite him." *CEA Film Report*

Mask of Death/US: Race for Life (1954) 79 mins (b&w)

"WHERE EVERY CURVE CRIES *DANGER*... ONE WRONG MOVE SPELLS *DEATH!*"

Hammer Films; d: Terence Fisher; p: Mickey Delamar, ep: Michael Carreras; screenplay: **Richard H Landau**, Paul Tabori; based on the novel *The Last Race* by John Manchip White; ph: Walter J Harvey; ed: Bill Lenny; ad: J Eder Wills; m: Leonard Salzedo

Synopsis: Racing car driver Richard Conte rejoins the Italian Corsi team after Air Force service but, dogged by bad luck, his wife walks out on him, leaving Conte to prove himself behind the wheel.

Cast: Richard Conte (Peter Wells), **Mari Aldon** (Patricia Wells), Peter Illing (Tony Bellario), Alec Mango (Guido Rosetti), James Copeland (Johnny Jackson), George Coulouris ('Pic' Dallapiccola), Meredith Edwards (Laurence Gibson), Stirling Moss, Reg Parnell, John Cooper, Alan Brown' Geoffrey Taylor, Leslie Marr (themselves)

Milestones and Millstones: Richard Conte, Mari Aldon, Richard H Landau

Comment: Fisher's experience as a former editor generates useful pace for a slim story, filmed on location at Goodwood: suitable, well used stock footage and real-life racing car drivers add impact.

Reviews: "...story is slender and trite... good entertainment, especially for motor racing enthusiasts ... Conte gives a strong and dominating performance... Aldon...gives a sensitive performance." *CEA Film Report*

"...routine story bolstered somewhat by speed sequences... okay entry for minor double billing...the two stars struggle as best they can with cliché-filled roles but it's colorless acting at best." *Variety*

Murder by Proxy/US: Blackout (1954) 87 minutes (b&w)

"TRAPPED IN A NIGHT WITHOUT END!

Hammer Films; d: Terence Fisher; p: Michael Carreras; screenplay: **Richard H Landau;** based on the novel *Murder by Proxy, aka Gold Coast Nocturne* by Helen Nielsen; ph: Walter J Harvey; ed: Maurice Rootes; ad: J Elder Wills; m: Ivor Slaney

Synopsis: Down and out American in London Dane Clark accepts money to marry an heiress, ends up accused of murder and has to turn detective to clear himself.

Cast: Dane Clark (Casey Morrow), Belinda Lee (Phyllis Brunner), Betty AnnDavies (Alicia Brunner), Eleanor Summerfield (Maggie Doone), Andrew Osborn, (Lance Gordon), Harold Lang (Travis), Jill Melford (Miss Nardis), Alvys Mahen (Lita Huntley), Alfie Bass (Ernie) Michael Golden (Inspector Johnson)

Milestones and Millstones: Dane Clark, Richard H Landau

Comment: Routine imported-Hollywood star-led B film: the novel's original setting of Chicago adapts well enough the requirements of its transpanted-to-England *mise en scene*.

Reviews: "... a gabby, overlong, import from England... Condition of the supporting feature market is such currently that the film will have no trouble getting bookings, even though it offers scant measure of entertainment." *Variety*

River Beat (1954) 70 mins (b&w)

Insignia Films (Victor Hanbury Productions); d: Guy Green; ep: **Herman Cohen**; p: Victor Hanbury; screenplay: Rex Rienits; ph: Geoffrey Faithfull; ed: Peter Graham Scott; ad: John Stoll; m: Hubert Clifford

Synopsis: A London police Inspector investigating smugglers on the river Thames falls for Phyllis Kirk who may be involved with the racketeers.

Cast: Phyllis Kirk (Judy Roberts), John Bentley (Detective Inspector Dan Barker) Leonard White (Detective Sergeant Mack McLeod), Glyn Houston (Charlie Williamson), Patrick Jordan (Bert Fisher) Robert Ayres (Captain Watford), David Hurst (Paddy McClure), Charles Lloyd Pack (John Hendrick)

Milestones and Millstones: Phyllis Kirk, Herman Cohen

Comment: A strong, well-plotted and smartly characterised screenplay, good lead performances and well-paced direction add up to a gripping B feature with A film attributes. Cinematographer Peter Graham Scott subsequently turned to direction with such films as *The Headless Ghost* (1959), *The Pot Carriers* (1962) and *Mr Ten Per Cent* (1967), along with a body of television work.

Reviews: "Plenty of action and neat team work." *Picture Show*

The Scarlet Spear (1954) 87 mins (color)

> THE SCARLET SPEAR "Sacred Symbol of Manhood... of mystery and Murder!"

Charles Reynolds Productions (Present Day); d/s: George P Breakston, **C Ray Stahl**; p: Charles Reynolds; ap: Irene Breakston; ph: Bernard Davies; ed: John Shirley; m: Ivor Slaney

Synopsis: Reporter Martha Hyer, the wife of district officer Jim Morrison, helps her husband persuade a local African chief not to start a local war by disposing of a rival chief using a poisoned spear.

Cast: John Bentley (District Officer Jim T. Barneson), **Martha Hyer** (Christine), Morasi (Morasi, the chief's son), Yusef (Yusef, the head bearer), Farasi (Faraji, the second bearer)

Milestones and Millstones: Martha Hyer, C Ray Stahl

Comment: Some attractive, well-chosen Kenyan locations add valuable weight to a well-enough acted, if semi-standard, adventure story.

Reviews: "... taut, authentically staged Technicolor adventure ... Hyer has the grace of a gazelle. Personally, I thoroughly preferred this poor man's 'Where No Vultures Fly' and warmly recommend it to all action fans and youngsters." *Picturegoer*

"Adventure and action are uppermost, but there is also a nicely developed romantic interest and a few touches of humour ... excellent entertainment of its kind and possesses wide general appeal... Hyer makes a charming heroine." *CEA Film Report*

The Stranger Came Home/US: The Unholy Four (1954) 80 mins (b&w)

"What was the shock-SIN of... The Unholy Four"

Hammer Films/Lippert Films; d: Terence Fisher; p: Michael Carreras; screenplay: Michael Carreras; from the novel *The Stranger Came Home* by **George Sanders** (ghost: Leigh Brackett); ph: Walter J Harvey; ed: Bill Lenny; ad: J Elder Wills; m: Leonard Salzedo

Synopsis: A man thought to have died on a fishing trip to Portugal recovers from amnesia caused by being struck on the head and dumped overboard and comes home after four years seeking his assailant—and murders ensue...

Cast: Paulette Godard (Angie), William Sylvester (Philip Vickers), Patrick Holt (Job Crandall), Paul Carpenter (Bill Saul), Alvys Maben (Joan Merrill), Russell Napier (Inspector Treherne), Kay Callard (Jenny), Patricia Owens (Blonde), David King-Wood (Sessions), Jeremy Hawke (Police Sergeant Johnson)

Milestones and Millstones: Paulette Goddard, George Sanders

Comment: Average pre-horror Hammer programmer, passable but mainly notable for its star.

Reviews: "8 marks for the masses... the story is incredible, but the film has qualities popular with crime fiction fans. It develops a series of holding situations." *CEA Film Report*

"A third-rate British-made whodunit...A few more fly-by-nights like this Lippert presentation, produced and written by Michael Carreras (sic), and the still-shapely Miss Goddard may find herself collecting the pieces of a career." *The New York Times*

Stranger From Venus/US: Immediate Disaster (1954) 67 mins (b&w)

"FIRST CONTACT WILL BE MADE!"

Rich & Rich Ltd; d/p: **Burt Balaban**; p: **Gene Martel**, Roy Rich; screenplay: Hans Jacoby; story by: Desmond Leslie; ph: Kenneth Talbot; ed: Peter R Hunt; ad: John Elphick; m: Eric Spear

Synopsis: Alien Helmut Dantine arrives on Earth on a mission to help humans deal with atomic power but official interference and nascent romance with earthling Patricia Neal causes problems.

Cast: Patricia Neal (Susan North), **Helmut Dantine** (The Stranger), Derek Bond (Arthur Walker), Cyril Luckham (Dr. Meinard), Willoughby Gray (Tom Harding), Marigold Russell (Gretchen Harding), Arthur Young (scientist), Nigel Green (Second Police Officer), Graham Stuart (Police Chief Richards)

Milestones and Millstones: Patricia Neal, Helmut Dantine, Burt Balaban, Gene Martel

Comment: Remember *The Day the Earth Stood Still* (1951)? The makers of this average British B seem to have recalled its basic storyline, adding star Neal to the mixture: mild and only moderately interesting.

Reviews: "A leisurely moving science fiction-story, which is interesting if rather unexciting, apart from a tense climax in which a flying saucer figures... adequate acting and an exciting climax ... acceptable second feature entertainment." *CEA Film Report*

You Know What Sailors Are (1954) 89 mins (color)

"It's the most revealing comedy ever brought to blushing color by TECHNICOLOR!"

Group Film Productions Limited; d: Ken Annakin; ep: Earl St John; p: Peter Rogers, Julian Wintle; screenplay: Peter Rogers; from the novel *Sylvester* by Edward Hyams; ph: Reginald H Wyer; ed: Alfred Roome; ad: George Provis; m: Malcolm Arnold

Synopsis: A British Navy radar expert has problems when the 'weapon' he constructs while drunk on the deck of foreign destroyer belonging to Agararia becomes a genuine problem and not simply a prank.

Cast: Akim Tamiroff (President of Agraria), Donald Sinden (Lt. Sylvester Green), Sarah Lawson (Betty), Naunton Wayne (Captain Owbridge), Bill Kerr (Lt. Smart), Dora Bryan (Gladys), Martin Miller (Prof. Hyman Pfumbaum), Michael Shepley (Admiral), Michael Hordern (Capt. Hamilton), Bill Kerr (Lt. Smart), Ferdy Mayne (Stanislaus Voritz of Smorznigov) Peter Arne (Ahmed)

Milestones and Millstones: Akim Tamiroff

Comment: The storyline is rather less convincing than a *Carry On* comedy but sheer good spirits, light but right performances and plenty of easy-to-enjoy gags keep the comedy afloat and amusing.

Reviews: "An extravagant but highly amusing comedy which is played with gusto.... Akim Tamiroff is highly amusing." *CEA Film Report*

"Hilarious comedy extravaganza ...Sinden and Akim Tamiroff share the acting honours. Others go to the director, the script writer and the casting director for the bevy of beautiful girls." *Picture Show*

"As pure escapist entertainment it also deserves general showing in America, where they appreciate the British weakness for laughing at themselves." *Variety*

Barbados Quest/US: Murder on Approval (1955) 70 mins (b&w)

"IT'S CROWDED WITH EXCITEMENT AND SUSPENSE!"

The Barbour Corporation Limited; d: Bernard Knowles; p: Robert S Baker, Monty Berman; screenplay: Kenneth R Hayles; ph: Monty Berman; ed:

Jack Slade; ad: Wilfred Arnold; m: stock music

Synopsis: Private eye Tom Conway faces a slew of chicanery and murder when he is hired in London by an American to investigate the purchase of a rare Barbadian stamp that may be a counterfeit.

Cast: Tom Conway (Tom Martin), Delphi Lawrence (Jean Larson), Brian Worth (Geoffrey Blake), Michael Balfour (Barney), Campbell Cotts (Coburn) John Horsley (Insp. Taylor), Ronan O'Casey (Stefan Gordoni), Launce Maraschal (Everleigh), Colin Tapley (Lord Valchrist), Mayura (Yasmina)

Milestones and Millstones: Tom Conway

Comment: Lackluster on both sides of the camera: strictly a bland minor programmer.

Reviews: "This London-located meller is only so-so as entertainment and will just get by in lower-case programmer bookings ... direction is poorly paced and seldom builds to any thrills... none of the cast can do much with the stereotype characters." *Variety*

Before I Wake/US: Shadow of Fear (1955) 76 mins (b&w)

"If I die before I wake this note will reveal The Killer..."

Gibraltar Films Ltd/Roxbury Productions Inc.; d: **Albert S Rogell**; p: Charles Leeds, Steven Pallos; screenplay: **Brett Halliday** (as Hal Debrett), Robert Westerby; ph: Jack Asher; ad: Scott MacGregor; m: Leonard Salzedo

Synopsis: Mona Freeman travels to England to attend her parents' funeral and is targeted for death when she begins to suspect her stepmother may be a murderer.

Cast: Mona Freeman (April Haddon), Jean Kent (Florence Haddon), Maxwell Reed (Michael Elder), Hugh Miller (Mr Driscoll), Gretchen Franklin (Elsie), Frederick Leister (Dr Elder), Alexander Gauge (Police Sergeant), Josephine Middleton (Mrs Harrison), Frank Forsyth (Jack Storey) Stanley Van Beers (Harry)

Milestones and Millstones: Mona Freeman, Albert S Rogell

Comment: Freeman and Kent clearly enjoy themselves trying to upstage each other, enjoyment that is transmitted to the viewer while Rogell racks up commendable suspense despite the expected dénouement.

Reviews: "It's neat but naïve melodrama and definitely a woman's interest picture ... Moderately exciting entertainment." *Picturegoer*

"Better than average ... the premise has had a considerable workout in whodunit literature... the tension builds nicely." *Variety*

Breakaway (1955) 72 mins (b&w)

Cipa; d: Henry Cass; p: Robert S Baker, Monty Berman; screenplay: Norman Hudis; from a story by Manning O'Brine; ph: Monty Berman; ed: Anne Barker; ad: Norman G Arnold; m: Stanley Black, Ivor Slaney

Synopsis: Private eye Tom Conway goes on the trail of a kidnapped girl and the stolen formula for a method of preventing metal fatigue.

Cast: Tom Conway (Tom 'Duke' Martin), Michael Balfour (Barney), Honor Blackman (Paula Grant), Brian Worth (Johnny Matlock), Bruce Seton (Webb), Freddie Mills (Pat), Alexander Gauge (MacAllister), John Horsley: Michael Matlock), Paddy Webster (Diane Grant), John Colicos (First Kidnapper), Arthur Lowe (Mitchell)

Milestones and Millstones: Tom Conway

Comment: Uninvolving and illogical in places: screenwriter Hudis achieved fame for scripting the first six classic *Carry On* farces before making a successful career writing for television in the United States.

Reviews: "A neatly-made crime melodrama." *Picture Show*

Break in the Circle (1955) 87 mins (UK color) (US b&w)

"A MAN ON THE LOOKOUT FOR ADVENTURE...
AND A WOMAN ON THE LOOKOUT FOR TROUBLE!

Hammer Films; d/s: Val Guest; from the novel by Robin Estridge (as Philip Loraine); p: Michael Carreras, ap: Mickey Delamar; ph: Walter J Harvey; ed: Bill Lenny; ad: J Elder Wills; m: Doreen Carwithen

Synopsis: Professional smuggler Forrest Tucker is hired by a wealthy German industrialist to smuggle a brilliant Polish scientist out of Germany and escape to the West.   **Cast: Forrest Tucker** (Captain Morgan), Eva Bartok (Lisa), Reginald Beckwith (Dusty), Arnold Marle

(Professor Pal Kudnic), Marius Goring (Keller), Guy Middleton (Major Hobart), Eric Pohlmann (Emile), Fred Johnson (Chief Agent Farquarson) Reginald Beckwith (Daisy)
Milestones and Millstones: Forrest Tucker
Comment: Guest keeps the story moving briskly and makes the most of his own screenplay.
Reviews: "Exciting drama…well acted and told." *Picture Show*

Colonel March Investigates (1955) 70 min (b&w)

Criterion Films; d: Cy Enfield; p: Donald Ginsberg; screenplay: Leo Davies; from stories by Carter Dickson (John Dickson Carr); ph: Jonah Jones; ed: Stanley Willis; ad: George Paterson; m: John Lanchbery, Eric Robinson
Synopsis: Boris Karloff is Colonel March who heads Department of Queer Complaints at Scotland Yard and investigates two cases of murder and solves a bank robbery.
Cast: Boris Karloff (Colonel March), Ewan Roberts (Ames), Richard Wattis (Cabot), John Hewer (John Parrish), Sheila Burrell (Joan Forsythe), Anthony Forward (Jim Hartley), Patricia Owens (Betty Hartley), Ronald Leigh-Hunt (Mr Bowlder), Joan Sims (Marjorie Dawson) Dagmar Wynter (Francine Rapport)
Milestones and Millstones: Boris Karloff
Comment: A must for Karloff completists: otherwise average British TV production. Three enjoyable enough episodes (*Hot Money, Death In The Dressing Room, The New Invisible Man*) of the British small screen series released as a feature film.
Reviews: "Here's a case for the connoisseur of crime detection. It's a three part package film… Karloff takes the title role and his commanding performance sets the style for this absorbing excursion into the sinister, macabre and unexplainable, all tied up with a logical conclusion." *Picturegoer*

"…fair entertainment…Boris Karloff is well cast in the title role." *CEA Film Report*

Confession/The Deadliest Sin (1955) 74 mins (b&w)

"Behind these bars, an act of violence! Behind this door...
"THE DEADLIEST SIN!"

Anglo-Guild Productions; d: Ken Hughes; p: Alec C Snowden; ap: Nat Cohen, Stuart Levy; screenplay Ken Hughes; based on the play *Confession* by Don Martin; ph: Phil Grindrod; ed: Geoffrey Muller; ad: Harold Watson

Synopsis: Thieves fall out and gangster Sydney Chaplin, back in England from America, soon needs to murder a priest to prevent being implicated in a homicide.

Cast: Sydney Chaplin (Mike Nelson), Audrey Dalton (Louise Nelson), John Bentley (Inspector Kessler), Peter Hammond (Alan), John Welsh (Father Neil), Jefferson Clifford (Pop Nelson), Patrick Allen (Corey), Pat McGrath (Williams), Robert Raglan (Becklan), Richard Huggett (Young priest)

Milestones and Millstones: Sydney Chaplin

Comment: A slick, tense and well-made B thriller directed with good pace by Ken Hughes: the film, released with *Little Red Monkey* (1955) in the US, made money, proving the value of American stars in British second features.

Reviews: "...film is ably directed, every character is well acted and the script is an excellent one. Thus due interest is gripped from the start and maintained to the finish...Chaplin plays the sinister central character with great conviction." *CEA Film Report*

The Extra Day (1955) (color)

"HE ONLY HAD 12 HOURS TO FIND THEM!"

British Lion Film Corporation; d/s: William Fairchild; p: E M Smedley-Aston; ph: Arthur Grant; ed: Bernard Gribble; ad: Ray Simm; m: Philip Green

Synopsis: Disaster strikes a movie during production when the final reel of film is lost, leaving associate producer Richard Basehart trying to find the extras from the vital scene so that it can be reshot.

Cast: Richard Basehart (Joe Blake), Simone Simon (Michele Blanchard), George Baker (Steven Marlow), Josephine Griffin (Toni Howard), Colin Gordon (Sir George Howard), Lawrence Naismith (Kurt Vorn), Charles Victor (Bert), Sid James (Barney West), Joan Hickson (Mrs West)

Milestones and Millstones: Richard Basehart

Comment: Occasionally amusing riff on the (allegedly real but, speaking from experience, romanticised) lives of British film extras, as seen by filmmakers rather than by any actual extra who appears on screen. Glenda Jackson made her movie debut here as, naturally, an extra.

Reviews: "A quartet of cameos fit happily together...Basehart gives the pic some marquee value in the U.S. but its b.o. chances are not very bright...the story drags considerably...Basehart and Miss Simon do well enough with inadequate material." *Variety*

The Gilded Cage (1955) 77 mins

"Murder—FOR AN ART TREASURE!"

Tempean Films; d: John Gilling; p: Robert S Baker, Monty Berman; screenplay: Brock Williams; story by: Paul Erickson; ph: Monty Berman; ed: Jim Connock; ad: C Wilfred Arnold; m: Stanley Black

Synopsis: When Alex Nicol and his brother become involved in an art theft, the brother is framed by the crooks and arrested leaving Nicol to prove his innocence.

Cast: Alex Nicol (Steve Anderson), Michael Alexander (Harry Anderson), John Stuart (Harding), Elwyn Brook-Jones (Bruno), Ursula Howells (Brenda Lucas), Clifford Evans (Ken Aimes), Veronica Hurst (Marcia Farrell), Trevor Reid (Inspector Brace), John Stuart (Harding), Charles Wade (Sumarko)

Milestones and Millstones: Alex Nicol

Comment: Adequate but routine second feature for easily pleased audiences.

Reviews: "...a somewhat overcomplicated story ... it is, however, fairly exciting." *CEA Film Report*

Joe Macbeth (1955) 90 mins (b&w)

"The gun-blazing story of gangland's No.1 Killer! It's THAT story you've read about ... and what an exciting new movie it makes!"

Columbia Pictures Corporation/Film Locations; d/s: Ken Hughes; p: **Mike Frankovich**; ap: George Maynard; **Philip Yordan;** from the play *Macbeth* by William Shakesepeare; ph: Basil Emmott; ed: Peter Rolfe Johnson; pd: Alan Harris; m: Trevor Duncan

Synopsis: Ruth Roman incites her gangster husband Paul Douglas to murder the crime boss and take his place.

Cast: Paul Douglas (Joe MacBeth), **Ruth Roman** (Lily MacBeth), Bonar Colleano (Lennie), Grégoire Aslan (Duca 'The Duke), Sid James (Banky), Harry Green (Big Dutch), Walter Crisham (Angus), Kay Callard (Ruth), Robert Arden (Ross), George Margo (Second assassin), Bill Nagy (Marty)

Milestones and Millstones: Paul Douglas, Ruth Roman, Mike Frankovich, Philip Yordan

Comment: Independent producer Eugene Frenke considered Americanizing the Bard in1947 with Robert Cummings starring. In 1949 producer James Nasser wanted Lew Ayres and Shelley Winters. Mike Frankovich announced real-life husband and wife John Ireland and Joanne Dru as the infamous couple, roles that ultimately went to Douglas and Roman who worked hard failed to save an interesting but ultimately pointless project.

Reviews: "...a willful vulgarization of the material." *Monthly Film Bulletin*

"Well acted and directed." *Picture Show*

"The lead role makes substantial demands on Douglas, but he emerges with honorable distinction… Roman has the looks and talent to give a genuine veneer to her performance." *Variety*

Little Red Monkey/US: The Case of the Little Red Monkey
(1955) 71 mins (b&w)

"...a murder with only one clue...and that leading to a dead end—
and more murder!"

Merton Park Studios; d: Ken Hughes; p: Alec C Snowden; screenplay: James Eastwood, Ken Hughes; based on the television serial by Eric Maschwitz; ph: Josef Ambor; ed: Inman Hunter, Geoffrey Muller; ad: George Haslam; m: Trevor Duncan
   Synopsis: US State Department agent Richard Conte joins forces with a Scotland Yard investigator to find out who is killing leading atomic scientists in England, leaving a little red monkey as a clue.
   Cast: Richard Conte (Bill Locklin), Rona Anderson (Julia), Russell Napier (Supt. Harrington), Colin Gordon (Martin), Arnold Marle (Dushenko), Donald Bisset (Editor), John Horsley (Sgt. Gibson), Noel Johnson (Sgt. Hawkins), Bernard Rebel (Vinson), Colin Tapley (Sir Clive Raglan)
   Milestones and Millstones: Richard Conte
   Comment: Routine second-feature programmer that would have benefited considerably from a faster moving narrative and rather more suspense.
   Reviews: "Like many British-produced pictures, it lacks pace and is a routine entry in the program market...Conte... exhibits little of the dash and ingenuity such a part calls for." *Variety*
   "American actor Richard Conte is top-billed, primarily as a means to get the film into US theatres—a box office strategy frequently employed by director Ken Hughes." *The New York Times*

Portrait of Alison/US: Postmark For Danger (1955) 84 mins (b&w)

"DIAMONDS, DECEPTION AND DEATH"

Insignia Films; d; Guy Green; ep: Tony Owen; p: Frank Godwin; screenplay: Guy Green, Ken Hughes; based on the television serial *Portrait of Alison* by Francis Durbridge; ph: Wilkie Cooper; ed: Peter Taylor; ad: Ray Simm; m: John Veale

Synopsis: An investigative journalist and a woman die when their car plunges over a cliff and a Scotland Yard investigation involves actress Terry Moore, the dead man's two brothers, a murder and, eventually, a gang of smugglers.

Cast: Terry Moore (Alison Ford), Robert Beatty (Tim Forrester), William Sylvester (Dave Forrester), Geoffrey Keen (Inspector Colby), Josephine Griffin (Jill Stewart), Allan Cuthbertson (Henry Carmichael), Henry Oscar (John Smith), William Lucas (Reg Dorking), Terence Alexander (Fenby), Eric Corrie (Pilot)

Milestones and Millstones: Terry Moore

Comment: Armed with a proven storyline (from a successful television serial), Green creates a neat, complex and holding film noir containing most of the right ingredients to raise the thriller above its B feature origins.

Reviews: "Ingredients essential to the action are a beautiful strangulation victim (Josephine Green), an unusual charm bracelet, a curiously labelled bottle of Chianti, and a hastily sketched drawing on the back of a postcard." *New York Times*

"Briskly directed and well acted, with neat dialogue and varied settings." *Picture Show*

"As a British-lensed whodunit thriller, 'Postmark for Danger' averages out as a fair offering for the programmer market... Miss Moore, while contributing to the chances for domestic bookings, adds nothing to the performances... thesping is well taken care of by the British casters, all of whom do their work excellently." *Variety*

The Quatermass Xperiment/US: The Creeping Unknown
(1955) 82 min (b&w)

"YOU CAN'T ESCAPE IT! NOTHING CAN DESTROY IT!
IT'S COMING FOR YOU
from Space to wipe all Living Beings from the face of the Earth!"

Exclusive (Hammer Film Productions); d: Val Guest; p: Anthony Hinds, **Robert L Lippert** (uncredited); screenplay: **Richard Landau**, Val Guest; from the BBC TV play by Nigel Kneale; ph: Walter Harvey; ed: James Needs; ad: J Elder Wills; sfx: Les Bowie (Bowie Margutti, Roy Field, Ray Caple, uncredited); m: James Bernard

Synopsis: Scientist Professor Bernard Quatermass sets out to save mankind from an extraterrestrial that has killed two crew members of an experimental spacecraft and is transforming the survivor into an alien monster.

Cast: Brian Donlevy (Professor Bernard Quatermass); Jack Warner (Inspector Lomax); Margia Dean (Judith Carroon); Richard Wordsworth (Victor Carroon); David King Wood (Dr Gordon Briscoe); Thora Hird (Rosemary 'Rosie' Rigley); Lionel Jeffries (Blake); Gordon Jackson (TV Producer) Sam Kydd (Station Sergeant) Jane Asher (little girl with doll)

Milestones and Millstones: Brian Donlevy, Robert L Lippert, Richard Landau

Comment: This defiantly 'B' feature science fiction shocker marked Hammer Films' first foray into the profitable horror genre which, thanks to director Terence Fisher, Peter Cushing and Christopher Lee, brought the company international success.

American screenwriter Landau (replacing Nigel Kneale, writer of the classic BBC TV serial who was contracted to the BBC) shortened the original six half-hour part serial to a brisk 82 minutes. US box-office needs replaced British TV Quatermass Reginald Tate with Hollywood import Donlevy. Kneale, reportedly, was unhappy with this casting but nevertheless Donlevy reprised the role in the 1957 sequel *Quatermass II/ US: Enemy from Space.*

Slick, quick, delivering suitably nasty (for the time) shocks and shrieks: the make-up transformation of alien-infected astronaut Richard Wordsworth into a monster (Bowie employed entrails and (bovine) tripe to make the creature look more repellent) works well enough.

Reviews: "Realistic macabre 'creepie' whose spectacular treatment nevertheless gives plenty of human interest... It is very well acted by Brian Donlevy, Jack Warner and Richard Wordsworth." *Picture Show*

"... an extravagant piece of science fiction ... it merits rating as a reliable dualer on either side of the Atlantic. Production values are better than average for this type of picture ...unrelieved melodrama without any femme interest... Donlevy plays the scientist with a grim and ruthless conviction." *Variety*

"... comes closer to the horror film than most recent science fiction pictures...the monster proves ... more acceptably alarming than most of the Things of science fiction...moves at the pace of a smart thriller." *Monthly Film Bulletin*

The Secret (1955) 80 mins (color)

*"THE GAY HILARIOUS STORY OF A PROPER MISS…
who should have said "no" when she said "yes"!"*

Golden Era Film Distributors/Laureate; d: **Cy Enfield**: p: S Benjamin Fisz; screenplay: Cy Endfield; from the play by Robert Brenon; ph: Jack Asher; ed: Jack Slade; ad: Scott MacGregor; m: Phil Cardew

Synopsis: American in London Sam Wanamaker has to try to clear himself after he becomes the prime suspect in the murder of a woman diamond smuggler.

Cast: Sam Wanamaker (Nick Delaney), Mandy Miller (Katie Martin), André Morrell (Chief Inspector Blake), Marian Spencer (Aunt Doris), Jan Miller (Margaret), Richard O'Sullivan (John Martin), Wyndham Goldie (Dr Scott), Henry Caine (Superintendent), Aimée Delamain (Miss Lyons)

Milestones and Millstones: Sam Wanamaker, Cy Endfield

Comment: Slow and largely uninvolving.

Reviews: "The story is slight…fair entertainment for the easily satisfied… Wanamaker gives a competent performance in a not very thankful role." *CEA Film Report*

Secret Venture (1955) 70 mins (b&w)

William N Boyle Productions; d: **R G Springsteen**; p: William N Boyle; screenplay: Paul Erickson; add dial: Kenneth R Hayles; ph: Basil Emmott; ed: John Seabourne Sr; ad: John Stoll; m: Lambert Williamson

Synopsis: American Kent Taylor arrives in England, picks up the wrong briefcase at the airport and is targeted by foreign spies seeking the contents of the case.

Cast: Kent Taylor (Ted O'Hara), Jane Hylton (Joan Butler), Kathleen Byron (Renée l'Epinal). Karel Stepanek (Zelinsky), Frederick Valk (Otto Weber), Maurice Kaufmann (Dan Fleming), Martin Boddey (Squire Marlowe), Arthur Lane (Bob Hendon), Hugo Schuchster (Prof Henrik) John Boxer (Insp. Dalton)

Milestones and Millstones: Kent Taylor, R G Springsteen

Comment: Mercifully brisk: competently made, easy to forget.

Reviews: "Exciting mystery…a touch of romance and amusing dialogue are added to this fast-moving tale." *Picture Show*

Stolen Time/US: Blonde Blackmailer (1955) 69 mins (b&w)

"MAN BAIT! By day… Mr Fashion Model! By Night … the Racket Boss"

Charles Deane Productions; d/p/s: Charles Deane; ph: Geoffrey Faithfull; ed: Adam Dawson; ad: Bert Davey;

Synopsis: Richard Arlen gets out of jail after serving seven years for a murder he did not commit and sets out to clear his name.

Cast: Richard Arlen (Tony Pelassier), Susan Shaw (Carole), Constance Leigh (Marie), Vincent Ball (Johnson), Andrea Malandrinos (Papa), Clive St George (Harford), Richard Hearne (Inspector Martin), Alathia Siddons (Mama Pelassier), Howard Lang (Scotland Yard detective)

Milestones and Millstones: Richard Arlen

Comment: There is little to recommend it, apart from its (relatively) short running time.

Reviews: "Sub-standard melodrama. The plot is stereotyped and uneventfully worked out, with a climax no more than lukewarm…the acting is generally inexpert." *Monthly Film Bulletin*

The Atomic Man/Timeslip (1955) 76 mins (b&w)

"THIS was the deadliest secret of all The MAN with the RADIO-ACTIVE BRAIN!"

Merton Park Productions/Todon Productions; d: Ken Hughes; ep: Nat Cohen, Stuart Levy; p: Alec C Snowden; screenplay: Charles Eric Maine; from his novel *The Isotope Man*; ph: A T Dinsdale; ed: Geoffrey Muller; ad: George Haslam; m: Richard Taylor

Synopsis: When a man is found unconscious and radioactive, Gene Nelson sets out to track down his evil double who is threatening the world with destruction.

Cast: Gene Nelson (Mike Delaney), **Faith Domergue** (Jill Rabowski), Peter Arne (Dr. Stephen Rayner/Jarvis), Joseph Tomelty (Detective Inspector Cleary), Donald Gray (Robert Maitland), Vic Perry (Emmanuel Vasquo), Paul Hardtmuth (Dr. Bressler), Martin Wyldeck (Dr Preston)
Milestones and Millstones: Gene Nelson, Faith Domergue
Comment: Intriguing, effectively suspenseful science fiction gaining in impact from its setting in the atomic-haunted 1950s, well acted and directed at a suitably brisk pace to cover some of the more obvious plot-holes.
Reviews: "... fast-moving thriller ... some good surprise twists, so that it makes fast, gripping and amusing entertainment...effective cast headed by Gene Nelson (and)... Domergue." *CEA Film Report*

Third Party Risk/US: The Big Deadly Game (1955) 70 mins (b&w)

"Look ...BUT DON'T TOUCH! SHE'S...DEADLY GAME"

Hammer Films/Lippert Films; d: Daniel Birt; ep: Michael Carerras; p: Michael Dunbar; screenplay: Daniel Birt, Robert Dunbar; from the novel by Nicholas Bentley; ph Walter J Harvey; ed: James Needs; ad: J Elder Wills; m: Michael Krein
Synopsis: While American songwriter Lloyd Bridges is on vacation to Spain he becomes dangerously involved with a smuggling ring.
Cast: Lloyd Bridges (Philip Graham) Simone Silva (Mitzi), Finlay Currie (Mr Darius), Maureen Swanson (Lolita), Ferdy Mayne (Maxwell Carey), Peter Dyneley (Tony Roscoe), George Woodbridge (Inspector Goldfinch), Russell Waters (The Scientist), Roger Delgado (Gonzales), Mary Parker (Nancy)
Milestones and Millstones: Lloyd Bridges
Comment: Routine second feature noir but with a tad of added interest now because of its status as a precursor to the classic shockers that made Hammer Films famous.
Reviews: "There's little mystery, but plenty of moonshine, in this highly predictable Spanish-set plot." *Picturegoer*
"Though the leading ladies are forgettable, some excellent work is turned in by the male cast contingent, including British reliables Finlay Currie and Ferdy Mayne." *The New York Times*

Tiger By the Tail/US: Crossup (1955) 83 mins (b&w)

BANNERLINE *CRIME-BLAST!*

Tempean Films; d: John Gilling; p: Robert S Baker, Monty Berman; screenplay: John Gilling, **Willis Goldbeck**; based on the book *Never Come Back* by John Mair; ph: Eric Cross; ed: Jack Slade; ad C Wilfred Arnold; m: Stanley Black

Synopsis: American journalist Larry Parks sets out to expose a gang of counterfeiters in London and ends up being kidnapped by the crooks.

Cast: Larry Parks (John Desmond), Constance Smith (Jane Claymore), Donald Stewart (Macauly), Cyril Chamberlain (Foster), Ronan O'Casey (Nick), Alexander Gauge (Fitzgerald), Lisa Daniely (Anna Ray), Ronald Leigh-Hunt (Dr Scott), Joan Heal (Annabella), Thora Hird (Mary), Doris Hare (Nurse Brady)

Milestones and Millstones: Larry Parks, Willis Goldbeck

Comment: A sad come-down for Parks who, having starred as the legendary entertainer in *The Jolson Story* (1946) and *Jolson Sings Again* (1949), was blacklisted by the House Un-American Activities Committee, basically ending his movie career. He made only one more film, *Freud: The Secret Passion* (1962) after this clichéd and unmemorable minor thriller.

Reviews: "... a routine but quite arresting crime story... a good quota of action with some fairly exciting developments, and engaging romantic interest and some good touches of humour... the picture makes reliable second feature entertainment for the masses." *CEA Film Report*

Track the Man Down (1955) 75 mins (b&w)

William N Boyle Productions/Republic; d: **R G Springsteen**; p: William Boyle; screenplay: Paul Erickson; add dial; Kenneth R Hayles; ph: Basil Emmott; ed: John Seabourne Sr; ad: John Stoll; m: Lambert Williamson

Synopsis: A guard is killed during a robbery at a greyhound stadium and newspaperman Ken Taylor is drawn into the ensuing hostage situation.

Cast: Kent Taylor (Don Ford), Petula Clark (June Dennis), Rene Houston (Pat Sherwood), George Rose (Rick Lambert), Ursula Howells (Mary Dennis), Walter Rilla (Austin Melford), Lloyd Lamble (Inspector Barnett), Hugh Cameron (Reporter), Richard Molinas (Luis Remino).

Milestones and Millstones: Kent Taylor, R G Springsteen

Comment: Competent but otherwise professionally average: some interesting location shooting may add impact for American cinemagoers.

Reviews: "The picture, made on expanding suitcase lines, introduces romance, comedy, violence, and excitement into its extravagant plot on the reasonably safe assumption that one or the other will entertain the masses. Taylor plays Don as a very American newshawk, determined and brass-necked." *Today's Cinema*

"Dishevelled, romantic crime drama" *Picturegoer*

A Yank in Ermine (1955) 85 mins (color)

William Gell Productions; d: Gordon Parry; p: William J Gell; ap: Francis Searle; screenplay: John Paddy Carstairs, John Baines; from the novel *Solid! Said the Earl* by John Paddy Carstairs; ph: Arthur Grant; ed: Lito Carruthers; ad: Ray Simm; m: Stanley Black

Synopsis: American soldier Harold Lloyd Jr inherits the lordship of a British village.

Cast: Peter M. Thompson (Joe Turner), Noelle Middleton (Angela), **Harold Lloyd Jr** (Butch), Diana Decker (Gloria), Jon Pertwee (Slowburn), Reginald Beckwith (Kimp), Edward Chapman (Duke of Fontenham), Richard Wattis (Boone), Guy Middleton (Bertram), Jennifer Jayne (Enid), Sid James (Manager)

Milestones and Millstones: Peter M. Thompson, Harold Lloyd Jr

Comment: Possibly mildly amusing in 1955 but seen out of period the comedy seems laboured: regrettably, Harold Lloyd Jr proves the son doesn't always rise.

Reviews: "…good humoured satire directed at both British and American ways and several laughable moments; but the film is not quite as funny as might have been expected from the subject…brightly acted." *CEA Film Report*

Assignment Redhead/Million Dollar Manhunt (1956) 67 mins (b&w)

"NERVE-SHATTERING! Action-packed pursuit relentless as baying bloodhounds in the wild of night, with a curvaceous bombshell leading the chase!"

Butcher's Film Productions; d: Maclean Rogers; p: William G Chalmers; co-producer (co-p): **Richard Gordon, Charles F Vetter**; screenplay: w: Maclean Rogers; based on the novel *Requiem for a Redhead* by Lindsay Hardy; ph: Ernest Palmer: ed: Peter Mayhew; ad: John Stoll; m: Wilfred Burns

Synopsis: American major Richard Denning who is working for British intelligence goes after a murderous master criminal who comes to London from Berlin seeking a fortune in counterfeit cash.

Cast: Richard Denning (Major Gregory Keen), **Carole Mathews** (Hedy Bergner), Ronald Adam (Major Scammel/Dumetrius), Danny Green (Yotti Blum), Brian Worth (Captain Peter Ridgeway), Hugh Moxey (Sergeant Tom Coutts), Peter Swanwick (Paul Bonnet), Jan Holden (Sally Jennings), Elwyn Brooke-Jones (Digby Mitchel)

Milestones and Millstones: Richard Denning, Carole Mathews

Comment: Low budget, even lower impact second feature from prolific genre film director Maclean Rogers.

Reviews: "Double-crossing, car chase, fire and roof fall climax are also included. There is no light relief… Denning gives a sound performance… Matthews… is attractive." *CEA Film Report*

Fire Maidens from Outer Space/Fire Maidens of Outer Space (1956) 73 mins (b&w)

"SCIENCE FICTION'S GREATEST THRILL! MAIDENS WITHOUT MEN ON MYSTERY PLANET!"

Criterion Films; d/p/s and story by: **Cy Roth**; ap: George Fowler; ph: Ian D Struthers; ed: A.C.T. Clair (aka Lito Caruthers); ad: Scott McGregor

Synopsis: Astronauts on an expedition to the 13th moon of Jupiter discover 16 nubile women ruled by a patriarch and menaced by 'The Creature'.

Cast: Anthony Dexter (Luther Blair), Susan Shaw (Hestia), Paul Carpenter (Captain Larson), Harry Fowler (Anderson), Sydney Tafler (Dr Higgins), Jacqueline Curtiss (Duessa), Rodney Diak (Professor Stanhope), Owen Berry (Prasus), Jan Holden (Fire Maiden), Kim Parker (Fire Maiden)

Milestones and Millstones: Cy Roth, Anthony Dexter

Comment: So unbelievably awful it would be nigh on impossible to parody this science fiction calamity: acting, screenplay, direction and special effects are even more puerile than the title.

Reviews: "Even the most dedicated connoisseurs of the artless are likely to find this British attempt at science fiction something of a strain on their patience." *Monthly Film Bulletin*

"... a film that I nominate as the stupidest ever." *Picturegoer*

The Gamma People (1956) 76 mins (b&w)

"IS THIS YOUR FUTURE? MAD DICTATOR RULES COUNTRY WITH DEADLY GAMMA RAY!"

Warwick Film Productions; d: John Gilling; ep: **Irving Allen, Albert R Broccoli** p: John W Gossage; screenplay: John Gossage, John Gilling; story by: Louis Pollock, **Robert Aldrich** (uncredited); ph: Ted Moore; ed: Jack Slade; ad: John Box; m: George Melachrino

Synopsis: American newsman Paul Doulas is stranded in an isolated village behind the Iron Curtain and uncovers a dastardly plot by a mad scientist directed by a loony dictator to use gamma rays to transform youths into crazy mutants.

Cast: Paul Douglas (Mike Wilson), Eva Bartok (Paula Wendt), Leslie Phillips (Howard Meade), Walter Rilla (Boronski), Philip Leaver (Koerner), Martin Miller (Lochner), Michael Caridia (Hugo Wendt), Pauline Drewitt (Hedda Lochner). Jocelyn Lane (Anna), Olaf Pooley (Bikstein), Rosalie Crutchley (Frau Bickstein)

Milestones and Millstones: Paul Douglas, Irving Allen, Albert R Broccoli, Robert Aldrich

Comment: Never sure if it is science fiction, shocker, thriller or black comedy: cinematography is an asset. Production designer J Box went on to win Academy Awards for Art-Direction, Set-Direction for *Lawrence of Arabia* (1963), *Dr Zhivago* (1965), *Oliver!* (1969) and *Nicholas and Alexander* (1971).

Reviews: "Entertaining comedy thriller ... Paul Douglas does well ... well supported. Superb backgrounds and beautiful photography." *Picture Show*

"Exhibs packaging a twin horror how might find 'The Gamma People' a passable subject, but it has *little* merit otherwise… the performances is on a par with the script treatment and inept direction." *Variety*

The Gelignite Gang/US: The Dynamiters (1956) 74 mins (b&w)

"The Story of Killers Who Terrorized a City"

Cybex Film Productions Limited; d: Francis Searle; Terence Fisher (uncredited); p: Brandon Fleming, Geoffrey Goodheart; screenplay: Brandon Fleming; ph: Cedric Williams; ed: Douglas Myers; ad: John Elphick; m: Green Dragon Music Jerry Levy, song: *Soho Mamba* written and composed by Gene Crowley, performed by Simone Silva

Synopsis: Insurance investigator Wayne Morris goes after a gang of safecrackers who use dynamite to remove all evidence of their crimes.

Cast: Wayne Morris (Jimmy Baxter), Sandra Dorne (Sally Morton), Patrick Holt (John Rutherford), Eric Pohlmann (Mr Popoulis), Arthur Young (Pop Scobie), Lloyd Lamble (Detective-Inspector Felby), James Kenney (Chris Chapman), Hugh Miller (Mr Crosby), Simone Silva (Simone)

Milestones and Millstones: Wayne Morris

Comment: Morris works hard to endow the story with credible dramatic life: the most notable aspect of this otherwise routine thriller programmer is the uncredited contribution of Hammer hero Fisher.

Reviews: "…not particularly original and at times is far-fetched and incredible…one or two surprise twists and an element of tension and excitement…the stars are all capable." *CEA Film Report*

The High Terrace/US: High Terrace (1956) 69 mins (b&w)

"MYSTERY THAT CLUTCHES YOU LIKE A NIGHTMARE!"

Cipa; d: Henry Cass; p: Robert S Baker, Monty Berman; screenplay: Alfred Shaughnessy, Norman Hudis, Brock Williams; from a story by A T

Weisman; ph: Eric Cross; ed: Henry Richardson; ad: Arthur Lawson; m: Stanley Black

Synopsis: Suspects proliferate when American playwright Dale Robertson turns detective to find who murdered an unpopular stage producer in love with the actress who wanted to appear in Robertson's new play.

Cast: Dale Robertson (Bill Lang), Lois Maxwell (Stephanie Blake), Derek Bond (John Mansfield), Eric Pohlmann (Otto Kellner), Mary Laura Wood (Molly Kellner), Lionel Jeffries (Monkton), Jameson Clark (Detective Inspector MacKay), Carl Bernard (Jock Dunmow) Garard Green (Raymond White)

Milestones and Millstones: Dale Robertson

Comment: There are more than enough suspects to keep you involved even if the final dénouement is not quite as unexpected as the movie's makers might have hoped.

Reviews: "This British import is a taut, fairly well developed whodunit which rates as an okay entry. The Dale Robertson name may help… Cass's direction makes best use of suspenseful opportunities …Robertson is effective." *Variety*

The Hostage/A Place of Execution (1956) 80 mins (b&w)

Douglas Fairbanks Jr & Company/Westbridge; d: Harold Huth; p: Thomas Clyde; screenplay: Alfred Shaughnessy, based on his teleplay; ph: Brendan J Stafford, ed: Peter Pitt; ad: Harry White; m: Bretton Byrd

Synopsis: American airman Ron Randell is entangled in a plot to overthrow a South American president after rescuing the president's kidnapped daughter in London.

Cast: Ron Randell (Bill Trailer), Mary Parker (Rosa Gonzuelo), John Bailey (Dr Maine), Carl Jaffe (President Pablo Gonzuelo), Anne Blake (Mrs Steen), Cyril Luckham (British Minister Ferguson), Margaret Drummond (Madame Gonszuelo), Victor Brooks (Inspector Clifford), James Liggat (Sergeant Reid)

Milestones and Millstones: Ron Randell

Comment: Maintains a good pace until the last reel when the narrative loses pace and grip.

Reviews: "… a second feature for the masses…fairly good entertainment… Randell does well as a tough and resourceful hero." *CEA Film Report*

House of Secrets/US: Triple Deception (1956) 97 mins (color)

"AN EXCITING FAST MOVING SUSPENSE THRILLER"

The Rank Organisation; d: Guy Green; p: Julian Wintle, Vivian A Cox; screenplay: Robert Buchner, Bryan Forbes; from the novel *Storm Over Paris* by Sterling Noel; ph: Harry Waxman; ed: Sidney Hayers; ad: Alex Vetchinsky; m: Hubert Clifford

Synopsis: A British naval officer who is the double of a notorious counterfeiter who has, unknown to his accomplices been killed in a car accident, is sent undercover to bring the leader to justice.

Cast: Michael Craig (Larry Ellis/Steve Chancellor), Brenda de Banzie (Madame Isabella Ballu), **Barbara Bates** (Judy Anderson), Gérard Oury (Julius Pindar), Anton Diffring (Anton Lauderbach), Geoffrey Keen (Colonel Burleigh, CIA), David Kossoff (Henryk van de Heide, CIA), Julia Arnall (Diane Gilbert), Eugene Deckers (Vidal)

Milestones and Millstones: Barbara Bates

Comment: Unsubtle but firmly directed and featuring sufficient easy-on-the-intellect action and enthusiastic performances to maintain interest.

Reviews: "This is a very heavy and dramatic picture with no light relief... the plot is involved and has many complications, but the interest is well sustained...Barbara Bates is good." *CEA Film Report*

The Intimate Stranger/US: Finger of Guilt (1956) 95 mins (b&w)

"Women are Weapons and No Holds are Barred!"

Anglo Guild Productions/Merton Park Studios; d: **Joseph Losey** (as Joseph Walton), d/p: Alec C Snowden; ep: Tony Owen; w: Peter Howard (aka **Howard Koch**); ph: Gerald Gibbs; ed: Geoffrey Muller; ad: C Wilfred Arnold; m: Trevor Duncan

Synopsis: American filmmaker Richard Basehart, now in England after a Hollywood scandal, is blackmailed by a woman who claims to be his mistress and threatens his marriage and his career.

Cast: Richard Basehart (Reginald 'Reggie' Wilson), **Mary Murphy** (Evelyn Stewart), Constance Cummings (Kay Wallace), Roger Livesey

(Ben Case), Faith Brook (Lesley Wilson), Mervyn Johns (Ernest Chaple), Vernon Greeves (George Mearns), Andre Mikhelson (Steve Vadney), Joseph Losey (Director)

Milestones and Millstones: Richard Basehart, Mary Murphy, Joseph Losey, Howard Koch

Comment: Above-average second feature thriller—on both sides of the screen—and of added interest since it features blacklisted writer Howard and director Losey having to work under pseudonyms on a British B.

Reviews: "Intriguing and unusual mystery... Basehart... and the rest of the cast give fine performances and there is a surprise ending." *Picturegoer*

The Last Man to Hang? (1956) 79 minutes (b&w)

"THE LOVE TRIANGLE THAT BECAME A CIRCLE ... *of rope!*"

Association of Cinema Technicians A.C.T; d: Terence Fisher; p: John W Gossage; screenplay: Ivor Montagu, Max Trell, Maurice Elvey, Gerald Bullett; from Bullett's novel; ph: Desmond Dickinson; ed: Peter Taylor; ad: Allan Harris; m: John Wooldridge

Synopsis: Tom Conway is put on trial for the murder of his wife and only one member of the jury believes he is innocent.

Cast: Tom Conway (Sir Rodrick Strood), Elizabeth Sellars (Daphne Strood), Eunice Grayson (Elizabeth), Freda Jackson (Mrs Tucker), Hugh Latimer (Mark), Ronald Simpson (Dr Cartwright), Victor Maddern (Bonaker), Anthony Newley (Cyril Gaskin), Margaretta Scott (Mrs Cranshaw), Walter Hudd (The Judge)

Milestones and Millstones: Tom Conway

Comment: Despite the title, sadly lacks suspense.

Reviews: "This is the film that explodes one of the oldest screen theories... Murder trials *can* be dull- in fiction, anyway!" *Picturegoer*

"There is a twist ending to this unusual story which is well acted." *Picture Show*

The Man in the Road (1956) 83 mins (b&w)

"Would his captive mind betray his secret?"

Gibraltar Films Ltd; d: Lance Comfort; p: Charles A Leeds; screenplay: Guy Morgan; from the novel *He Was found in the Road* by Anthony Armstrong; ph: Stanley Pavey; ed: John Connock; ad: Eric Saw; m: Bruce Campbell

Synopsis: American Ella Raines helps a brilliant scientist who is suffering from amnesia and being hunted by Communist agents after a secret formula.

Cast: Derek Farr (Ivan Mason/Doctor James Paxton), **Ella Raines** (Rhona Ellison), Donald Wolfit (Professor Cattrell), Lisa Daniely (Nurse Mitz), Bruce Beeby (Doctor Manning), Russell Napier (Scotland Yard Supt. Davidson), Cyril Cusack (Dr Kelly), Frederick Piper (Inspector Hayman), Karel Stepanek (Dmitri Balinkev)

Milestones and Millstones: Ella Raines

Comment: Raines, cast for American audiences, is competent but relatively bland, the acting honours going to key British supporting players, notably Wolfit and Farr in an implausible but largely compelling thriller.

Reviews: "Suspenseful thriller… vey well acted, it is delightfully photographed amid countryside backgrounds." *Picture Show*

"7 ¾ marks for the unsophisticated." *CEA Film Report*

Passport to Treason (1956) 80 mins

"*Smashing* THROUGH A SPY RING! HE USED THE LAW OF BRUTAL MEN!"

Mid-Century Film Productions; d: Robert S Baker; p: Robert S Baker, Monty Berman; screenplay: Kenneth R Hayles, Norman Hudis; from the novel by Manning O'Brine; ph: Monty Berman; ed: Henry Richardson; ad: John Stoll; m: Stanley Black

Synopsis: Private eye Rod Cameron investigates the strange death of a friend and uncovers a peace organization that is the front for a crime syndicate.

Cast: Rod Cameron (Mike O'Kelly), Lois Maxwell (Diane Boyd), John Colicos: (Pietro), Clifford Evans (Orlando Syms), Ballard Berkeley (Inspector Thredgold), Marianne Stone ('Jonesy' Jones), Peter Illing (Giorgio Sacchi), Barbara Burke (Katrina), Andrew Faulds (Barrett), Trevor Reid (McCombe)

Milestones and Millstones: Rod Cameron

Comment: Watchable enough, although the combination of a by-numbers script and matching direction add up to nothing special.

Reviews: "Routine British whodunit, with only Rod Cameron's name to recommend it… storyline is blurry and frequently burdened by incomprehensible English accents …Cameron is sturdy in his role…" *Variety*

"Rod Cameron, the Western he-man, made this trip to England to star in this espionage melodrama set in London. Was his journey necessary? Yes! … his presence gives new vitality to stock situations." *Picturegoer*

Soho Incident /US: Spin a Dark Web (1956) 76 mins (b&w)

"SHE'LL ENSNARE YOU WITH HER KISSES…
ENTRAP YOU IN HER CRIMES!"

Film Locations/Frankovich Productions; d: Vernon Sewell; p: **Mike Frankovich**, George Maynard; screenplay: Ian Stuart Black, from the novel *Wide Boys Never Work* by Robert Westerby; ph: Basil Emmott; ed: Peter Rolfe Johnson; ad: Ken Adam; m: Robert Sharples

Synopsis: Faith Domergue, the sister of a local Sicilian mob boss, romances an ambitious Canadian in London and draws him into the gang's activities…

Cast: Faith Domergue (Bella Francesi), Lee Patterson (Jim Bankley), Rona Anderson (Betty Walker), Martin Benson (Rico Francesi), Robert Arden (Buddy), Joss Ambler (Tom Walker), Peter Hammond (Bill Walker), Peter Burton (Inspector Collis), Sam Kydd (Sam), Bernard Fox (Mcleod)

Milestones and Millstones: Faith Domergue, Mike Frankovich

Comment: Low-budget B hoping to ape Hollywood but lacking many necessary genre ingredients: brisk pace saves it: art director Ken Adam later designed key James Bond films and won Oscars for *Barry Lyndon* (1975) and 1995's *The Madness of King George*.

Reviews: "Exciting crime thriller... Plenty of action and romance." *Picture Show*

"As a gangster pic, it stirs up sufficient thriller entertainment for lowercase dates in the dual market. Faith Domergue heads the otherwise all British cast... with enough conviction to hold interest." *Variety*

The Weapon (1956) 77 mins (b&w)

"This Gun Talked...and four frightened people needed it—to live!

Periclean Productions Limited/Eros Films/Republic Productions; d: Val Guest, **Hal E Chester**; p: **Hal E Chester**, Frank Bevis, George Fowler, David Pelham; screenplay: **Fred Freiberger**; story: Hal E Chester, Fred Freiberger. ph: Reginald H Wyer; ed: Peter Rolfe Johnson; ad: John Stoll; m: James Stevens

Synopsis: A young boy finds a revolver used to murder of a US officer 10 years earlier, accidentally shoots another boy and is hunted by his mother Lizabeth Scott, US officer Steve Cochran—and the killer.

Cast: Steve Cochran (Mark Andrews), **Lizabeth Scott** (Elsa Jenner), George Cole (Joshua Henry), **Herbert Marshall** (Inspector Mackenzie), Nicole Maurey (Vivienne), Jon Whiteley (Erik), Laurence Naismith (Jamison), Dennis Shaw (Groggins), John Horsley (Johnson), Fred Johnson (Fitzsimmons)

Milestones and Millstones: Steve Cochran, Lizabeth Scott, Herbert Marshall, Hal E Chester, Fred Freiberger

Comment: Guest racks up commendable suspense on the way to a tense climax with useful contributions for the American market from Cochran and Scott and strong echoes of 1953's British movie *The Yellow Balloon*.

Reviews: "...a good, suspenseful melodrama... with familiar names of the cast toppers... acting is top rate ...direction... is another plus credit, keeping the suspense high and the performances entirely credible." *Variety*

"This is to some extent a conventional thriller but it has some unusual features... reliable fare for not too critical tastes. A good cast." *CEA Film Report*

Wicked as they Come (1956) 94 mins (b&w)

"What she wanted out of life…she got out of men!"

Film Locations/Frankovich Productions; d: Ken Hughes; p: Maxwell Setton; screenplay: Ken Hughes, Sigmund Miller, from the novel *Portrait in Smoke* by Bill Ballinger; ph: Basil Emmott; Max Benedict; ad: Don Ashton; m: Malcolm Arnold

Synopsis: Arlene Dahl rises from slum life in New York's Lower East Side by using men as stepping-stones and then pitilessly discarding them but finally her sins appear to have caught up with her.

Cast: Arlene Dahl (Kathleen 'Kathy' Allen, née Allenbourg), **Philip Carey** (Tim O'Bannion), **Herbert Marshall** (Stephen Collins), Michael Goodliffe (Larry Buckham) Ralph Truman (John Dowling), Sid James (Frank Allenbourg), David Kossoff (Sam Lewis), Faith Brook (Virginia Collins)

Milestones and Millstones: Arlene Dahl, Philip Carey, Herbert Marshall

Comment: Unexceptional film noir, mostly predictable and rather too often over the top: but still watchable for the key performances.

Reviews: "Good average entertainment material…pic supplies sufficient variation to maintain interest…Dahl looks sufficiently glamorous in an aloof manner to make her numerous conquests plausible." *Variety*

Women Without Men/Blonde Bait (1956) 71 mins (b&w)

"DANGEROUS DECOY IN A GAME OF MURDER!
She's a silken trap that waits in the dark"

Hammer Films; d: **Elmo Williams**; p: Anthony Hinds; screenplay: Val Guest, **Richard Landau**; story: Richard Landau; ph: Walter J Harvey, William Whitley; ed: Elmo Williams, James Needs; ad: John Elphick; m: Leonard Salzedo

Synopsis: The US State Department and Scotland Yard arrange for Beverly Michaels to escape from a British prison as bait to bring murderer Jim Davis to justice.

Cast: **Beverly Michaels** (Angie Booth), **Jim Davis** (Nick Randall) Joan Rice (Cleo), **Richard Travis** (Kent Foster), **Paul Cavanagh** (Inspector Hedges), Thora Hird (Granny), Avril Angers (Bessie), Joan Rice (Cleo), Hermione Baddeley (Grace), Gordon Jackson (Percy, **Harry Lauter** (US State Department Security Chief)

Milestones and Millstones: Beverly Michaels, Jim Davis, Richard Travis, Paul Cavanagh, Harry Lauter, Elmo Williams, Richard Landau

Comment: There were actually two films here, neither particularly notable except as a B film fit for the bottom of a double Bill. In Britain, the film was released as *Women Without Men*: in the United States, the version shown as *Blonde Bait* included additional footage featuring Hollywood actors Jim Davis, Richard Travis, Paul Cavanagh and Harry Lauter.

Reviews: ".. poor prospects indicated…offers an exploitative title but nothing more, an over-length below-par British entry strictly for lower-casing in the minor market." *Variety*

"It is agreeable entertainment. Beverly Michaels gives a competent performance." *CEA Film Report*

X: the Unknown (1956) 81 mins (b&w)

"It rises from 2000 miles beneath the earth to melt everything
in its path!
IT KILLS…BUT CANNOT BE KILLED!"

Hammer Film Productions; d: Leslie Norman, **Joseph Losey** (uncredited): ep: Michael Carreras; p: Anthony Hinds; screenplay/story/production manager: Jimmy Sangster; ph: Gerald Gibbs; ed: James Needs; sfx: Bowie Margutti, Jack Curtis; makeup/special effects makeup: Phil Leakey; m: James Bernard

Synopsis: Scientist Dr Adam Royston (Dean Jagger) leads the battle against a deadly extraterrestrial radioactive creature that rises from depths of the earth in Scotland.

Cast: Dean Jagger (Dr Adam Royston), Edward Chapman (John Elliott), Leo McKern (Inspector McGill), Anthony Newley (Corporal "Spider" Webb), Jameson Clark (Jack Harding), William Lucas (Peter Elliott), Peter Hammond (Lt Bannerman), Marianne Brauns (Zena), Ian Mac-

Naughton (Cpl Haggis), Michael Ripper (Sgt Harry Grimsdyke), John Harvey (Major Cartwright)

Milestones and Millstones: Dean Jagger, Joseph Losey

Comment: After their hit 1955 film of Nigel Kneale's cult BBC TV serial *The Quatermass Xperiment*, naturally Hammer sought a sequel. Kneale refused to allow another writer the use of the 'Quatermass' name. So first-time (and future Hammer regular) scenarist Jimmy Sangster simply named his scientist Dr Adam Royston.

Director Losey (working as Joseph Walton) began the film but American star Jagger refused to work with him since Losey had been blacklisted in Hollywood. British director Norman took over, although some footage shot by Losey was retained.

RKO provided half the budget but failed to distribute the film in the USA. Warner Bros finally distributed it eight months later.

Telling, for the period, special effects the flesh-melting sequences are particularly effective, adequately atmospheric cinematography and a brisk pace cause Hammer's second horror movie to hit hard.

Reviews: "…highly imaginative and fanciful meller with tense dramatic overtones… as in Britain, film needs shrewd and careful coupling for a double bill, but with suitable contrasting selection should register a study his in the US too." *Variety*

"Thrilling science fiction film, made with the cooperation of the War Office… it has an exciting and topical theme and is finely acted by Dean Jagger. Extravagant happenings are most plausibly presented." *Picture Show*

The Camp on Blood Island (1957) 82 mins (b&w)

"The Most Savage Drama of the World's Most Savage War!"

Hammer Film Productions; d: Val Guest; p: Anthony Hinds; screenplay: John Manchip White, Val Guest; from the novel by John Manchip White; ph: Jack Ashered; Bill Lenny; m: Gerard Schurmann

Synopsis: The sadistic commandant of a World War Two Japanese prison camp vows to kill all the Allied prisoners-of-war if Japan is defeated, leaving the prisoners to try and keep the news from him when the inevitable occurs.

Cast: André Morell (Colonel Lambert), Carl Möhner (Dutch), Walter Fitzgerald (Cyril Beattie), Edward Underdown (Maj. Dawes), **Phil Brown** (Lt. Bellamy), Barbara Shelley (Kate Keiller), Michael Goodliffe (Father Paul), Michael Gwynn (Tom Shields), Ronald Radd (Col. Yamamitsu), Jan Holden (Nurse)

Milestones and Millstones: Phil Brown

Comment: Sordid, sadistic and seriously graphic for the time, the reportedly "based on a true story" created considerable controversy which in turn created a strong box-office while Hammer's novelization of the screenplay also made money. Regrettably racist by today's standards.

Reviews: "There are as many holes in the film as there are in a fishing net. Yet it holds the attention mainly because of the frightful realization that such things did actually happen in the war. The dialog and situations have been devised on the very simple premise that all Japs are rats." *Variety*

The Crooked Sky (1957) 77 mins (b&w)

"BREATH TAKING! THE HEIGHTS OF SUSPENSE-ACTION!"

Luckwin Productions/Tudor Productions; d: Henry Cass; ep: Bill Luckwell; p: Henry Cass, Derek Winn; ap: **Richard Gordon, Charles F Vetter**; screenplay: Norman Hudis; story: Maclean Rogers, Lance Hargreaves (aka **Charles F Vetter**); ph: Phil Grindrod; ed: Peter Mayhew; ad: Harold Watson; m: Wilfred Burns

Synopsis: American sleuth Wayne Morris joins forces with Scotland Yard to bring a gang of counterfeiters to justice.

Cast: Wayne Morris (Mike Conlin), **Karin Booth** (Sandra), Anton Diffring (Fraser), Bruce Seton (Mac), Richard Shaw (Williams), Colette Bartrop (Benny), Seymour Green (Steve), Bill Brandon (Grange), Reginald Hearne (Smith), Frank Hawkins (Robson), Murray Kash (Lewis), Croupier (Jack Taylor)

Milestones and Millstones: Wayne Morris, Karin Booth, Richard Gordon, Charles F Vetter

Comment: Patently low-budget British B thriller with a subdued Morris adding mild spice as the Mike Hammer wannabe.

Reviews: "Credibility is not the strong point... the aerial background is not completely convincing but the acting is fairly well maintained... presenting a rather placid Wayne Morris." *CEA Film Report*

The Counterfeit Plan (1957) 80 mins (b&w)

"A PLAN TO SHAKE DOWN TWO CONTINENTS FOR $100,000,000!"

Merton Park Studios; d: Montgomery Tully; p: Alec C Snowden, **Richard Gordon**; co-p: **Charles F Vetter**; screenplay: James Eastwood; ph: Philip Grindrod; ed: Geoffrey Muller; ad: C Wilfred Arnold; m: Trevor Duncan

Synopsis: Escaped killer Zachary Scott flees from France to England where he forces a former forger to resume his criminal life.

Cast: Zachary Scott (Max Brant), **Peggie Castle** (Carole Bernard), Mervyn Johns (Louie Bernard), Sydney Tafler (Harry Flint), Lee Patterson (Duke), Eric Pohlmann (Frank Wandelman), Robert Arden (Bob Fenton), Chili Bouchier (Gerta), John Welsh (Police Inspector Grant), David Lodge (Sam Watson)

Milestones and Millstones: Zachary Scott, Peggie Castle, Richard Gordon, Charles F Vetter

Comment: Tully keeps the story moving fast over the several lacunae in the melodramatic plot. (*One Man's Secret* was the film's working title).

Reviews: "...British-made melodrama which provides suitable fare for the lower-case spot...Scott handles his lead chore excellently and Miss Castle is good." *Variety*

Date With Disaster (1957) 61 mins (b&w)

"A love hungry Rock and Roll babe...... who fired the spark to a violent adventure!"

Fortress Film Productions Limited; d: Charles Saunders; p: Guido Coen; screenplay and story: Brock Williams; ph: Brendan J Stafford; ed: Tom Simpson; ad: Herbert Smith; m: Reg Owen, Anthony Spurgin

Synopsis: Two partners in a garage, helped by a professional criminal, plan to steal £20,000 while senior partner Tom Drake is away—but the scheme goes wrong.

Cast: Tom Drake (Miles), William Hartnell (Tracy), Shirley Eaton (Sue), Maurice Kaufmann (Don), Michael Golden (Inspector Matthews), Richard Shaw (Ken), Charles Brodie (Charles), Deidre Mayne (Judy), Peter Fontaine (Sergeant Brace), John Drake (Constable Wilson), Hubert Hill (Policeman)

Milestones and Millstones: Tom Drake

Comment: Routine second feature: mercifully brief.

Reviews: "Few of the clichés known for the unpretentious crime thriller are omitted … on the whole it makes fair supporting entertainment for popular audiences." *CEA Film Report*

The End of the Line (1957) 66 mins (b&w)

> "A MURDEROUS plot … a Beautiful Dame, led to a Double Double-Cross at…THE END OF THE LINE"

Fortress Productions; d: Charles Saunders; p: Guido Coen; screenplay: Paul Erickson; ph: Walter J Harvey; ed: Tom Simpson; ad: Herbert Smith; m: Edwin Astley

Synopsis: American writer Alan Baxter is living in London where his wicked mistress frames him for murder.

Cast: Alan Baxter (Mike Selby), Barbara Shelley (Liliane Crawford), Ferdy Mayne (Edwards), Jennifer Jayne (Anne Bruce), Arthur Gomez (Arthur Crawford), Geoffrey Hibbert (Max Perrin), Jack Melford (Inspector Gates), Charles Clay (Henry Bruce), Harry Towb (Vince), Stella Bonheur (Mrs Edwards)

Milestones and Millstones: Alan Baxter

Comment: Nothing memorable: the preposterous plot initiates rather uninteresting performances.

Reviews: "…both played and presented in very much a run-of-the-mill fashion, most of the time against cramped-looking sets…decidedly moderate supporting entertainment." *CEA Film Report*

Escapement/US: The Electronic Monster (1957) 76 mins (b&w)

"THEY DEALT in DREAMS—and MURDER!"

Anglo-Guild Productions; d: Montgomery Tully; dream sequences director: David Paltenghi; ep: **Richard Gordon**; p: Alec C Snowden; co-p: **Charles F Vetter**; ap: Jim O'Connolly; screenplay: Charles Eric Maine, J McLaren Ross, from the novel *Escapement* by Charles Eric Maine; ph: Bert Mason; dream sequences cinematographer: Teddy Catford; ed: Geoffrey Muller; ad: Wilfred Arnold; electronic music; John Simmons

Synopsis: Insurance agent Rod Cameron investigates the mysterious death of a film star in the South of France and uncovers a sinister plot by a former Nazi using electronic dream therapy for evil ends.

Cast: Rod Cameron (Jeff Keenan), **Mary Murphy** (Ruth Vance), Peter Illing (Paul Zakon), Meredith Edwards (Dr Philip Maxwell), Kay Callard (Laura Maxwell), Carl Duering (Blore), Carl Jaffe (Dr Erich Hoff), Felix Felton (Commissaire), Larry Cross (Brad Somers), John McCarthy (Clark Denver)

Milestones and Millstones: Rod Cameron, Mary Murphy, Richard Gordon, Charles F Vetter

Comment: In 2010 Christopher Nolan used the same basic theme of invading people's dreams with *Inception*. Here, while Maine's concept is fascinating, the director reportedly had problems with the producer who wanted an 'X' (adults only) certificate: the result is science fiction hokum rather than riveting. Released as *Escapement* in the U.K. in 1958; released in the U.S. as *The Electronic Monster* in 1960.

Reviews: "… a solid production of semi-scientific hokum…holds the interest with a nearly credible mixture of drama and original nonsense. It will amuse and at the same time thrill." *CEA Film Report*

"… is a modest thriller designed as a second feature… the presence of two American artists, Rod Cameron and Mary Murphy, is likely to make it an acceptable entry for most U.S. houses." *Variety*

The Flesh is Weak (1957) 88 mins (b&w)

"THE NEWEST HEADLINES ON THE OLDEST PROFESSION!"

Raymond Stross Productions; d: Don Chaffey; p: Raymond Stross; screenplay: Lee Vance; story by: Deborah Bedford; ph: G Massy-Collier; ed: Charles Hasse; ad: John Stoll; m: Tristram Cary
   Synopsis: Pimp John Derek exploits vulnerable young women and lures them into becoming prostitutes in London.
   Cast: John Derek (Tony Giani), Milly Vitale (Marissa Cooper), William Franklyn (Lloyd Buxton), Martin Benson (Angelo Giani), Freda Jackson (Trixie), Norman Wooland (Inspector Kingcombe), Harold Lang (Harry), Patricia Jessel (Millie), John Paul (Sergeant Franks), Shirley Anne Field (Susan)
   Milestones and Millstones: John Derek
   Comment: The theme of prostitution, still relevant today, was considered highly exploitative in the 1950s and earned *The Flesh is Weak* substantial critical opprobrium on its release. By today's standards, however, it simply seems tame and tawdry.
   Reviews: "It is difficult to know what producer Raymond Stross had in mind…as a social document, it makes only the mildest impact…as entertainment it is rather mediocre stuff…Vitale…and …Derek… are convincing enough." *Variety*

Grip of the Strangler/The Haunted Strangler (1958) 78 mins (b&w)

"KING OF THE MONSTERS! Their wild beauty marked them for death by… THE HAUNTED STRANGLER"

Amalgamated Productions; d: Robert Day; p: John Croydon, **Richard Gordon**, **Charles F Vetter**; screenplay: John C Cooper, Jan Read; from Read's story *Stranglehold*; ph: Lionel Banes; ed: Peter Mayhew; ad: John Elphick; sfx: Les Bowie; m: Buxton Orr
   Synopsis: When writer Boris Karloff investigates the execution of The Haymarket Strangler 20 years previously he becomes possessed by the killer's spirit and follows in his murderous footsteps.

Cast: Boris Karloff (James Rankin), Jean Kent (Cora Seth), Elizabeth Allan (Mrs. Rankin), Anthony Dawson (Detective Superintendent Burk), Very Day (Pearl), Tim Turner (Kenneth McColl), Diane Aubrey (Lily), Leslie Perrins (Prison Governor), Max Brimmel (Turnkey), Jessica Cairns (Asylum maid)

Milestones and Millstones: Boris Karloff, Richard Gordon, Charles F Vetter

Comment: Karloff's gothic charisma more than compensates for a familiar horror movie storyline that is unexpectedly nasty for the period.

Reviews: "… moments of macabre suspense and the atmosphere of the period is well conveyed…Karloff makes the most of his fiendish role, twisting his face to spine-chilling ugliness and generally being suitably horrific." *CEA Film Report*

"Boris Karloff's back and Metro's got him…There are, to say the least, interesting touches, full-blooded scenes and a cute little rat who nibbles contentedly at a rather handsome skull." *Variety*

Hour of Decision (1957) 81 mins (b&w)

"TIME RAN OUT for the MAN ALL WOMEN HATED!"

Tempean Films; d: C M Pennington-Richards; p: Monty Berman; screenplay: Norman Hudis; based on the novel *Murder in Mayfair* by Frederic Goldsmith; ph: Stanley Pavey; ed: Douglas Myers; ad: Arthur Lawson; m: Stanley Black

Synopsis: American journalist Jeff Morrow turns detective to solve the murder of an unpleasant newspaper columnist and to clear his wife who is one of the suspects.

Cast: Jeff Morrow (Joe Saunders), Hazel Court (Margaret Saunders/Peggy), Anthony Dawson (Gary Bax), Mary Laura Wood (Olive Bax), Alan Gifford (J. Foster Green), Carl Bernard (Inspector Gower), Lionel Jeffries (Albert Mayne), Anthony Snell (Andrew Crest), Vanda Godsell (Eileen Chadwick)

Milestones and Millstones: Jeff Morrow

Comment: There are no really unexpected surprises, but the Agatha Christie-style climax with Our Hero unmasking the perpetrator at the climax works well.

Reviews: "This tidy little whodunnit may not break the mould, but it packs in more than its fair share of surprises. Here the obligatory Hollywood star-on-the-skids is Jeff Morrow." *Radio Times*

Kill Her Gently (1957) 75 mins (b&w)

"She's the only wife I have so… KILL HER *Gently!*"

Fortress Film Productions Ltd; d: Charles Saunders; p: Guido Coen; screenplay; Paul Erickson; ph: Walter J Harveyed, Margery Saunders; ad: Harry White; m: Edwin Astley
  Synopsis: Escaped convicts Marc Lawrence and George Mikell are picked up by a motorist: he then puts pressure on them to murder his wife for him.
  Cast: Griffith Jones (Jeff Martin), Maureen Connell (Kay Martin), **Marc Lawrence** (William Connors), George Mikell (Lars Swenson), Shay Gorman (Dr Jimmy Landers), Marianne Brauns (Rania), Frank Hawkins (Inspector Raglan), John Gaylord (Truck driver), Roger Avon (Constable Brown)
  Milestones and Millstones: Marc Lawrence
  Comment: Brisk, atmospheric and competent but with a clichéd storyline that is a tad too familiar.
  Reviews: "..a British-made melodrama that will have to do for double-bill fare, at least in this country…." *Variety*

Kill Me Tomorrow (1957) 80 mins (b&w)

"MURDER FLAWLESS AS THE DIAMOND! BUT…"

Delta (Francis Searle Productions); d: Terence Fisher; p: Francs Searle; co-p: **Richard Gordon**; screenplay: Robert Falconer, Manning O'Brine (aka Paddy Manning O'Brine); ph: Geoffrey Faithfull; ed: Ann Chegwidden; ad: Bernard Robinson; m: Temple Abady
  Synopsis: After losing his wife and his job, hard-drinking reporter Edmond O'Brien needs money for an operation for his son but when he goes to ask for his job back he finds his former boss has been murdered.

Cast: Pat O'Brien (Bart Crosbie), Lois Maxwell (Jill Brook), George Coulouris (Heinz Webber), Wensley Pithey (Inspector Lane), Tommy Steele (as himself), Freddie Mills (Waxy Lister), Ronald Adam (Mr Brook), Robert Brown (Steve Ryan), Richard Pasco (Dr Fisher), April Olrich (Bella Braganza)

Milestones and Millstones: Pat O'Brien, Richard Gordon

Comment: Firm direction makes the most of O'Brien and the conventional screenplay to deliver a taut, if low-spirited, second feature thriller. Maxwell achieved fame playing 'Miss Moneypenny" to Sean Connery's James Bond in 1962's *Dr No* and subsequent 007 movies. Pop star Tommy Steele (*Finian's Rainbow* 1968) made his film debut playing himself.

Reviews: "Conventional crime story... acceptable is unexciting entertainment and is well acted by a cast headed by Pat O'Brien." *CEA Film Report*

"Warner Bros rarely pushed leads roles Pat Obrien's way. Even so, it's hard to fathom why he cross the Atlantic for the starring role in this farfetched B-movie." *Radio Times*

Lady of Vengeance (1957) 73 mins (b&w)

"A SHOCKING WOMAN...A SHOCKER OF A MOVIE...
One of the screen's most suspenseful stories of total love...
total fury...total destruction!"

Princess Productions Corporation/Rich & Rich Ltd; d: **Burt Balaban**; p: Burt Balaban, Bernard Donnenfeld; screenplay, story by: **Irve Tunick**; ph: Ian Struthers; ed: Eric Boyd-Perkins; ad: Harry White; m; Phil Cardew

Synopsis: Wealthy newspaper publisher Dennis O'Keefe seeks violent vengeance against the man responsible for the suicide of his ward.

Cast: Dennis O'Keefe (William T Marshall), Ann Sears (Katie Whiteside), Anton Diffring (Karnak), Patrick Barr (Inspector Madden), Vernon Greeves (Larry Shaw), Eileen Elton (Melissa), Frederick Schiller (Schtegel), G H Mulcaster (Bennett), Gerald Case (Hawley), Jack McNaughton (Coroner)

Milestones and Millstones: Dennis O'Keefe, Burt Balaban, Irve Tunick

Comment: Dreary and slow moving—and far too frequently, even despite relatively the short running time.

Reviews: "Far-fetched and very unconvincing mystery melodrama... with the additional drawback of acting that is generally weak... mild supporting entertainment for easy-gong audiences." *CEA Film Report*

"Burdened with a contrived and confusing plot, import carries small appeal for American audiences... a dull entry, ponderously and often amateurishly produced and of a genre that went out many years ago on screen." *Variety*

Man From Tangier/US: Thunder Over Tangier (1957) 66 mins (b&w)

"INVITATION TO DANGER...DESIRE...AND DEATH!!!!"

Butcher's Film Service; d: Lance Comfort; p: W G Chalmers; screenplay: Paddy Manning O'Brine; ph: Geoffrey Faithfull; ed: Peter Mayhew; ad: John Stoll; m: Wilfred Burns

Synopsis: When movie stuntman Robert Hutton accidentally puts on the wrong raincoat he becomes involved with crooks operating passport and forgery rackets

Cast: Robert Hutton (Chuck Collins), Lisa Gastoni (Michele), Martin Benson (Voss), Derek Sydney (Darracq), Jack Allen (Rex), Leonard Sachs (Heinrich), Robert Raglan (Inspector Meredith), Harold Berens (Sammy), Emerton Court (Armstrong), Richard Shaw (Johnny), Michael Balfour (Spade Murphy)

Milestones and Millstones: Robert Hutton

Comment: Action rather than logical and/or credible story telling is the driving force of a brisk programmer that more or less justifies its relatively brief running time.

Reviews: "The picture's asset is the fairly well sustained action which should secure the interest of indulgent audiences... it is put over with vigour by a cast which notably includes Robert Hutton..." *CEA Film Report*

The Man Without a Body (1957) 80 mins (b&w)

"A diabolical dream come true!"

Filmplays Ltd; d: **W Lee Wilder**, Charles Saunders; p: Guido Coen; screenplay: William Grote; ph: Brendan Stafford; ed: Tom Simpson; ad: Harry White; m: Robert Elms

Synopsis: There are horrifying consequences when a surgeon revives the head of Nostradamus and grafts it onto a colleague suffering from a brain tumour.

Cast: Robert Hutton (Dr. Phil R. Merritt), George Coulouris (Karl Brussard), Julia Arnall (Jean Cramer), Nadja Regin (Odette Vernet), Sheldon Lawrence (Dr. Lew Waldenhouse), Peter Copley (Leslie), Michael Golden (Michel de Notre Dame (Nostradamus), Norman Shelley (Dr Alexander), Tony Quinn (Burton)

Milestones and Millstones: Robert Hutton, W Lee Wilder

Comment: Ludicrous and laughable but impressive, too, for the amazing ability of the players to keep straight faces in the face of such escalating drivel. Bizarrely, the film received funding from the National Film Finance Corporation (NFCC) which was set up in the United Kingdom help fund British moviemakers: hence the direction credit for Englishman Charles Saunders in order to qualify for NFFC help. A career low for character actor Coulouris, who had appeared in *Citizen Kane* (1941).

Reviews: "a full-blooded horror film…wildly extravagant and becoming increasingly absurd… good entertainment for the right audiences." *CEA Film Report*

"… the few laughs in the wrong place should not prevent it from throwing a scare into the industrial ninepennies." *Kine Weekly*

Night of the Demon/US: Curse of the Demon (1957) 95 mins (b&w)

"DEMONS! MONSTERS FROM HELL! You Will Actually SEE Them on the Screen!"

Columbia Pictures Corporation/Sabre Film Production; d: **Jacques Tourneur**; p: **Hal E Chester**, Frank Beavis; screenplay: Charles Bennett, Hal E Chester, **Cy Enfield** (uncredited); based on the story *Casting the Runes* by M R James; ph: Ted Scaife; ed: Michael Gordon; ad: Ken Adam; sfx: George Blackwell, S D Onions, Wally Veevers, Bryan Langley; m: Clifton Parker

Synopsis: American psychologist Dana Andrews goes up againat a satanic cult leader who summons a demon to dispose of his enemies.

Cast: Dana Andrews (John Holden), Peggy Cummins (Joanna Harrington), Niall MacGinnis (Doctor Karswell), Maurice Denham (Professor Harrington), Athene Seyler (Mrs. Karswell), Liam Redmond (Mark O'Brien), Reginald Beckwith (Mr. Meek), Ewan Roberts (Lloyd Williamson), Peter Elliott (Kurmar)

Milestones and Millstones: Dana Andrews, Jacques Tourneur, Hal E Chester, Cy Endfield

Comment: Tourneur's finest film after his RKO classics is a great British horror movie, atmospheric and chilling and surviving the less-than-credible demon inserted (reportedly against the wishes of star and director) to give the shocker a visual boost. Columbia changed the title to *Curse of the Demon* and cut the running time to 81 minutes for the film's American release.

Reviews: "Really creepy horror film... the monstrous Fire Demon is spectacularly spine-chilling, the performances are good from the stars who are well supported by an excellent cast." *Picture Show*

"At last—the monster shocker grows up. Sounds impossible but here's a crude-creature story tailored into an adult, glossy thriller." *Picturegoer*

"Technically it's a reasonably competent job, but the story and the dialog have an old-fashioned ring which wavers uncertainly between the melodramatic and the ludicrous... Andrews wanders through this trivial piece with a stiff upper lip." *Variety*

No Road Back (1957) 83 mins (b&w)

"A TIGRESS OF CRIME IN THE NIGHT-CLUB JUNGLE!
With the crimson stain of murder on a fortune in stolen gems!

Gibraltar Films Ltd; d: Montgomery Tully; p: Steve Pallos, Charles Leeds; screenplay: Charles Leeds, Montgomery Tully; from the play *Madame Tic Tac* by Falkland L Carey and Philip Weathers; ph: Lionel Banes; ed: Jim Connock; ad: John Stoll; m: John Veale

Synopsis: A blind and deaf woman dedicates her life and sacrifices all for her no-good son Skip Homeier who gets involved with criminals who set out to frame him for a robbery.

Cast: Skip Homeier (John Railton), Paul Carpenter (Clem Hayes), Patricia Dainton (Beth), Norman Wooland (Inspector Harris), Margaret Rawlings (Mrs Railton), Eleanor Summerfield (Marguerite), Alfie Bass (Rudge Harvey), Sean Connery (Spike), Robert Brown (Sergeant Brooks), Philip Ray (Garage man)

Milestones and Millstones: Skip Homeier

Comment: Former child star Homeier is adequate in this minor second feature: the acting honours belong firmly to Rawlings as his blind and deaf mother. The film marks the feature film debut of future James Bond, Sean Connery, who does nothing here to mark him as a potential future megastar.

Reviews: "Skip Homeier makes his British screen bow…it's a typical, if unconvincing, crime meller…Homeier plays the young medico in a refreshing way." *Variety*

Nowhere to Go (1957) 89 mins

MGM/Ealing Films, A Michael Balcon Production; d: Seth Holt, Basil Dearden (uncredited); p: Michael Balcon, Eric Williams; screenplay: Seth Holt, Kenneth Tynan; based on the novel by Donald Mackenzie; ph: Paul Beeson; ed: Harry Aldous; pd: Peter Proud; ad: Alan Withy; m: Dizzy Reece

Synopsis: George Nader escapes from prison after swindling a wealthy woman but is double-crossed by an old friend when he sets out to collect his ill-gotten gains.

Cast: George Nader (Paul Gregory), Maggie Smith (Bridget Howard), Bernard Lee (Vic Sloane), Geoffrey Keen (Inspector Scott), **Bessie Love** (Harriet P Jefferson), Harry H Corbett (Sullivan), Andree Melly (Rosa), Howard Marion Crawford (Cameron), Lionel Jeffries (Pet Shop Clerk)

Milestones and Millstones: George Nader, Bessie Love

Comment: Reece's jazz score makes it rather more mock Hollywood noir than traditional Ealing but while essentially bleak and bitter, it is never tedious. Nader does well (playing a Canadian to explain his accent)

and Smith is passable in her first leading role. Former editor Holt does well in his directorial debut.

Reviews: "Not very eventful, only remotely plausible, and not always meticulously clear… should nonetheless appeal to crime drama addicts whose approach to their screen fare is not highly critical… the portrayal is smooth enough." *CEA Film Report*

Operation Murder (1957) 66 mins (b&w)

"No clues… no way of catching the man with the perfect alibi!"

Danziger Productions Ltd; d: Ernest Morris; p: **Edward J Danziger, Harry Lee Danziger**; screenplay: Brian Clemens; ph: James Wilson; ed: Anne Barker; ad: George Beech; m: Edwin Astley

Synopsis: Surgeon Tom Conway and a colleague plan and execute a potentially profitable murder but their luck runs out.

Cast: Tom Conway (Dr Wayne), Patrick Holt (Dr Bowen), Sandra Dorne (Pat Wayne), John Stone (Inspector Price), Virginia Kelley (Julia), Rosamund John (Head Nurse), Frank Hawkins (Sergeant Vine), Robert Ayres (Larry Vinton), Gilbert Winfield (Garage attendant), Timothy Fitzgerald (Harry Bright)

Milestones and Millstones: Tom Conway, Edward J Danziger, Harry Lee Danziger

Comment: Dull and uninvolving, even at its relatively short running time. Unreleased in the US until 1959.

Reviews: "Looking rather spent, Tom Conway walks through the British programmer." *ALLMOVIE*

"A surprisingly ridiculous story from the usually brisk thriller director." *TV Guide*

Sail Into Danger/El Aventurero (1957) 72 mins (b&w)

Patria Films; d: Richard Gascón, Kenneth Hume; p: Steven Pallos; screenplay: Kenneth Hume; ph: Phil Grindrod; ed: Edward Jeffries; m: Ivor Slaney

Synopsis: When hoods force American ex-smuggler Dennis O'Keefe to sail them from Barcelona to Tangiers and his son is killed, O'Keefe seeks violent vengeance.

Cast: Dennis O'Keefe (Steve Ryman), Kathleen Ryan (Lena), James Hayter (Monty), Ana Luisa Peluffo (Josafina), Pedro de Córdoba (Luis), Barta Berry (Emil), Félix de Pomés (Inspector Gomez), John Bull (Angel)

Milestones and Millstones: Dennis O'Keefe

Comment: Brisk, well plotted and just the right length: O'Keefe took over direction when scenarist/director Kenneth Hume died during the shooting of the film.

Reviews: "Intriguing crime melodrama ... well acted with a spectacular climax, this film will thrills most audiences." *Picture Show*

Morning Call/The Strange Case of Dr. Manning (1957) 75 mins

"MISSING...OR MURDERED!"

Republic Pictures/Winwell; d: Arthur Crabtree; ep: John Bash; p: Alfred Strauss, Derek Winn, Bill Luckwell; screenplay: Bill Luckwell, Paul Tabori, Tom Waldron; story: Leo Townsend; ph: Walter J Harvey; ed: John Ferris; ad: John Stoll; m: John Bath

Synopsis: Private detective Ron Randell joins the police to track down a kidnapped doctor in London.

Cast: Greta Gynt (Annette Manning), **Ron Randell** (Nick Logan), Garard Green (Gil Stevens), Bruce Seton (Inspector Brown), Peter Fontaine (Fred Barnes), Virginia Keiley (Vera Clark), Robert Raglan (Plainclothesman), John Watson (Plainclothesman), Brian Sunners (Freddie), Wally Patch (Wally)

Milestones and Millstones: Ron Randell

Comment: Apparently unhappy with the screenplay, originally cast George Raft quit and costar Bella Darvi also vanished to be replaced by Randell and Gynt in a patchy programmer that understandably raised little interest with distributors.

Reviews: "...the actual plot, of course, is a routine and familiar one... but capable treatment helps to make it acceptable supporting entertainment for the masses. Ron Randell is well cast." *CEA Film Report*

That Woman Opposite/US: City After Midnight (1957) 85 mins (b&w)

"LOVE, MURDER AND BLACKMAILARE ROOMATES IN THE... CITY AFTER MIDNIGHT"

William Gell Productions; d/s: Compton Bennett; from the novel *The Emperor's Snuffbox* by John Dickson Carr; p: William J Gell; ph: Lionel Banes; ed: Bill Lewthwaite; ad: John Stoll; m: Stanley Black

Synopsis: Private eye Dan O'Herlihy investigates the murder of an antique dealer in London.

Cast: Phyllis Kirk (Eve Atwood), **Dan O'Herlihy** (Dermot Kinross), William Franklyn (Ned Atwood), Jack Watling (Toby Lawes), Wilfrid Hyde-White (Sir Maurice Lawes), Petula Clark (Janice Lawes), Guido Lorraine (Aristide Goron), Margaret Withers (Lady Helena Lawes), Tita Dane (Marie Latour)

Milestones and Millstones: Phyllis Kirk, Dan O'Herlihy

Comment: Efficiently done, with a killer who is not immediately obvious.

Reviews: "At last, a British thriller with class. Not just because it boasts two better than average Hollywood stars, but because here's a gloss that usually comes with an import label." *Picturegoer*

"Story is a bit complex, and difficult to transfer to the screen in simple terms... Kirk sustains the strong emotional role as the suspect... O'Herlihy balances easily." *Variety*

The Traitor/US: The Accursed (1957) 78 mins (b&w)

"From the Files of the World's Most Fabulous SECRET SOCIETY! 1958'S SENSATIONAL SPY SHOCKER!"

E J Fancey Productions/Fantur Films; d: Michael McCarthy; p: E J Fancey; screenplay: Michael McCarthy; ph: Bert Mason; ed: Monica Kimick; ad: Herbert Smith; m: Jackie Brown

Synopsis: Survivors of a WW2 resistance group meet at a country house to find out who betrayed their leader to the Nazis. Murders follow and US Intelligence Officer Robert Bray sets out to unmask the killer.

Cast: Donald Wolfit (Colonel Charles Price), **Robert Bray** (Major Shane), Jane Griffiths (Vicki Toller), Carl Jaffe (Professor Stefan Toller), Anton Diffring (Joseph Brezina), Christopher Lee (Doctor Neumann), Oscar Quitak (Thomas Rilke), Karel Stepanek (Mayor Friederich Sudermann), Rupert Davies (Butler)

Milestones and Millstones: Robert Bray

Comment: Wolfit wolfs down the scenery with gusto, as usual, rendering the other players into second place in the process. The 'Old Dark House' setting adds atmosphere. *The Accursed* was not released in the United States until 1960.

Reviews: "The developments are intriguing, successfully keeping the audience guessing until the end when there is a surprising and ironic denouement." *CEA Film Report*

West of Suez/US: The Fighting Wildcats (1957) 85 mins (b&w)

Winwell Productions/Amalgamated Productions; d: Arthur Crabtree; exec p: **Richard Gordon,** co-p **Charles F Vetter**; p: Kay Luckwell, Derek Winn; screenplay: Norman Hudis; original story: Lance Hargreaves (aka **Charles F Vetter**), Norman Hudis; ph: Walter J Harvey; ed: Peter Mayhew; ad: John Stoll, Wilfred Burns

Synopsis: American adventurer Keefe Brasselle is hired in London to assassinate an Arab leader who advocates peace but the project goes awry.

Cast: Keefe Brasselle (Brett Manders), Kay Callard (Pat), Karel Stepanek (Langford), Ursula Howells (Eileen), Richard Shaw (Cross), Bruce Seton (Major Osborne), Harry Fowler (Tommy), Sheldon Lawrence (Jeff), Alex Gallier (Ibrahim Sayed), Maya Koumani (Men Hassa)

Milestones and Millstones: Keefe Brasselle, Richard Gordon, Charles F Vetter

Comment: The Middle Eastern plotline has more contemporary significance now than it had when this ultimately innocuous but competently made British B was first released in 1957.

Reviews: "Fast moving and action-filled crime story of popular appeal... Brasselle and Kay Callard are well co-starred." *CEA Film Report*

Corridors of Blood (1958) 86 mins (b&w)

"HIS NEWEST AND MOST FRIGHTENING ROLE! BORIS KARLOFF *TOPS IN TERROR!*"

Amalgamated Productions; d: Robert Day; p: **Richard Gordon, Charles F Vetter,** John Croydon, Peter Mayhew; screenplay: Jean Scott Rogers; ph: Geoffrey Faithfull; ed: Peter Mayhew; ad: Anthony Masters; m: Buxton Orr

Synopsis: 19th century surgeon Boris Karloff's search for ways of alleviating pain in patients causes him to become an opiate addict and fall foul of a gang of murderous grave robbers.

Cast: Boris Karloff (Dr Thomas Bolton), **Betta St John** (Susan), Finlay Currie (Superintendent Matheson), Francis Matthews (Jonathan Bolton), Adrienne Corri (Rachel), Francis De Wolff (Black Ben), Christopher Lee (Resurrection Joe), Frank Pettingell (Mr Blount), Carl Bernard (Ned, The Crow)

Milestones and Millstones: Boris Karloff, Betta St John, Richard Gordon, Charles F Vetter

Comment: Even minus monstrous makeup, Karloff is convincingly chilling in this dark and rather unnervingly credible shocker. *Corridors of Blood* had to wait five years before being released in New York in 1963.

Reviews: "Robust clinical melodrama...assiduously courts sensation seekers." *Kine Weekly*

Death Over My Shoulder (1958) 89 mins (b&w)

Vicar; d: Arthur Crabtree; p: Nat Miller, Frank Bevis, Burt Pugach; screenplay: Norman Hudis; story by: Alyce Canfield; ph: Walter J Harvey; ed: Seymour Logie; ad: Herbert Smith; m: Douglas Gamley

Synopsis: American private eye Keefe Brasselle strikes a bargain with a London gangster to have him killed so that the insurance will pay for an operation on his small son.

Cast: Keefe Brasselle (Jack Regan), Bonar Colleano (Joe Longo), Jill Adams (Evelyn Connors), **Arlene DeMarco** (Julie), Charles Farrell (Shiv Maitland), Al Mulock (Brainy Peterson), Sonia Dresdel (Miss Upton), Peter Swanwick (Nick Dayton)

Milestones and Millstones: Keefe Brasselle, Arlene DeMarco

Comment: Little going for it: dull and sluggish: Brasselle's sinking career sinks further.

Reviews: "It is an inferior, in-artistic production which affords only moderate entertainment for the easily pleased...Brasselle makes a rather flabby hero." *CEA Film Report*

Family Doctor/Prescription for Murder/US: RX: Murder
(1958) 89 mins (b&w)

"His patients loved him ... to their murdered day!!!"

Templar Film Studios; d: Derek N Twist; p: John W Gossage; screenplay: Derek N Twist, John W Gossage; based on the novel *The Deeds of Dr. Deadcert* by Joan Fleming; ph: Arthur Grant; ed: Desmond Saunders; ad: Elven Webb; m: John Wooldridge

Synopsis: American doctor Rick Jason turns detective and investigates the deaths of three wives of another doctor in an English seaside resort.

Cast: Rick Jason (Jethro), Lisa Gastoni (Kitty Mortlock), Marius Goring (Dr Dysert), Mary Merrall (Miss Bettyhill), Vida Hope (Louise), Nicholas Hannen (Colonel), Kynaston Reeves (Mr Sparrow), Avice Landone (Mrs Mortlock), Frederick Leister (Dr Alexander), Patrick Waddington (Sir George Watson), Noel Hood (Lady Watson)

Milestones and Millstones: Rick Jason

Comment: Average programmer that features supporting players who are largely superior to their material and prove it by attempting to upstage each other and the star whenever they have a chance.

Reviews: "As mystery thrillers go, this is an agreeable enough specimen though not in any way outstanding...Jason revealing a likeable personality in the role of the American." *CEA Film Report*

"Little stellar or dramatic impact in this routine drama that suffers from sluggish writing and direction...Jason, making his British debut, gives a pleasant, relaxed performance...although he has little opportunity to do more than saunter through his stint." *Variety*

Fiend Without a Face (1958) 74 mins (b&w)

"NEW HORRORS! MAD SCIENCE SPAWNS EVIL FIENDS!
... *Taking form before your horrified eyes!*"

Producers Associates, Amalgamated Productions; d: Arthur Crabtree; p: John Croydon, **Richard Gordon**, **Charles F Vetter**, Ronald Kinnock; screenplay: **Herbert J Leder**; original story by Amelia Reynolds; ph: Lionel Banes; ed: Richard Q McNaughton; ad: John Elphick; sfx: Peter Neilson, Karl-Ludwig Ruppel, Flo Nordhoff; m: Buxton Orr

Synopsis: US Air Force Major Marshall Thompson investigates bizarre deaths at an air base in Canada caused by invisible atomic monsters created by an experimenting scientist.

Cast: Marshall Thompson (Major Jeff Cummings), Kynaston Reeves (Professor R. E. Walgate), Michael Balfour (Sergeant Kasper), Kim Parker (Barbara Griselle), Terry Kilburn (Captain Al Chester), Gil Winfield (Captain Warren, M.D.), Shane Cordell (Nurse), Stanley Maxted (Colonel G. Butler)

Milestones and Millstones: Marshall Thompson, Richard Gordon, Charles F Vetter

Comment: The credibly realized (for the period) attacking airborne human brains give this crisp low-budget science fiction shocker a welcome terror-boost.

Reviews: "... some not too horrifying moments and a lot of dialogue... story is mostly slow-moving and takes a long time to get under way." *CEA Film Report*

Floods of Fear (1958) 82 mins (b&w)

"*SUSPENSE* ROARS FROM THE PAGES OF THE SAT. EVE. POST *SERIAL!*"

The Rank Organisation; d: Charles Crichton; p: Earl St John, Sydney Box, David Deutsch; screenplay: Charles Crichton, Vivienne Knight; based on the novel by John and Ward Hawkins; ph: Christopher Challis; ed: Peter Bezencenet; ad: Cedric Dawe; m: Alan Rawsthorne

Synopsis: The Humboldt River bursts its banks and wrongly convicted killer Howard Keel, a fellow prisoner and their guard are swept away and end up in a flooded house with a terrified woman.

Cast: Harold (Howard) Keel (Donovan), Anne Heywood (Elizabeth Matthews), Cyril Cusack (Sharkey), Harry H Corbett (Jack Murphy), Eddie Byrne (Sheriff), John Phillips (Dr Matthews), Mark Baker (Watchman), James Dyrenforth (Mayor), Peter Madden (Banker), Guy Kingsley Pointer Deputy Sheriff)

Milestones and Millstones: Howard Keel

Comment: The dénouement may be predictable enough but Crichton and his actors, notably Keel (still billed here as Harold) keep you watching: the boldly recreated (for the period) American background comes off as unexpectedly convincing.

Reviews: "…it's a brilliant production job. The American setting is completely believable, a major feat for a British film." *Picturegoer*

"… one of Britain's most determined attempts to woo the U.S. market. Not only does it have Howard Keel as its male star, but the meller is unabashedly set in the U.S.… Keel…gives a robust display, combining virility with a surprising gentleness." *Variety*

High Hell (1958) 87 mins (b&w)

"Actually Filmed in the World's Most Rugged Mountains"

Princess Production Company/Rich & Rich Ltd; d: **Burt Balaban**; p: Burt Balaban, **Arthur Mayer**; screenplay: **Irve Tunick**; based on the novel *High Cage* by Steve Frazee; ph: James Wilson; ed: Eric Boyd-Perkins; ad: Frank White; m: Phil Cardew

Synopsis: Dangerous tensions arise when snow traps gold miner John Derek, his estranged wife Elaine Stewart and her would-be lover high in the Canadian Rockies.

Cast: John Derek (Craig Rhodes), **Elaine Stewart** (Lenore Davidson), Patrick Allen (Luke Fulgham), Jerold Wells (Spence), Al Mulock (Al Davidson), Rodney Burke (Danny Rhodes), Colin Croft (Malvern), Nicholas Stuart (Mob Leader)

Milestones and Millstones: John Derek, Elaine Stewart, Burt Balaban, Arthur Mayer, Irve Tunick

Comment: Dull drama—location shooting in Switzerland does little to alleviate narrative/dramatic tedium.

Reviews: "There is little drama or thrill or even incident…the leading players in this tedious to-do comprise John Derek … and Elaine Stewart… neither player being given much chance of distinction." *CEA Film Report*

A Question of Adultery (UK 1958/USA 1959) 86 mins (b&w)

Connaught Place; d: Don Chaffey; p: Raymond Stross, Victor Lyndon; screenplay: Ann Edwards, Denis Freeman; based on the play *A Breach of Marriage* by Dan Sutherland; ph: Stephen Dade; ed: Peter Tanner; ad: John Stoll; m: Philip Green

Synopsis: Left sterile after an accident, Julie London and her husband agree on artificial insemination to have a child and they go to a Swiss clinic. Their relationship shatters and a jury has to decide whether she has committed adultery.

Cast: Julie London (Mary Loring), Anthony Steel (Mark Loring), Basil Sydney (Sir John Loring), Donald Houston (Mr Jacobus), Anton Diffring (Carl Dieter), Andrew Cruikshank (Dr Cameron), Conrad Phillips (Mario), Kynaston Reeves (Judge), Frank Thring (Mr Stanley), Mary Mackenzie (Nurse Parsons)

Milestones and Millstones: Julie London

Comment: An attempt at a mass-market exploitation drama that soon sags before collapsing completely.

Reviews: "It emerges as a stodgy, novelettish affair which dodges the vital issue with a contrived, soggy ending…may well attract the curious. But those expecting to be shocked will be disappointed…London brings grace and charm to her difficult part." *Variety*

"With Julie London enacting the central role with husky-voiced sincerity, the longsuffering heroine is at least attractive." *The New York Times*

"…as a serious or even dramatic commentary on modern sex ethics or marriage, then, the film is something of a misfire." *CEA Film Report*

The Secret Man (1958) 78 mins (b&w)

Producers Associates/Amalgamated Productions; d: Ronald Kinnoch; p: Ronald Kinnoch, **Richard Gordon, Charles F Vetter**; screenplay: Tony O'Grady (Brian Clemens), Ronald Kinnoch; from a story by O'Grady/Clemens; ph: Geoffrey Faithfull; ed: Peter Mayhew; ad: William Constable; m: Albert Elms

Synopsis: Canadian physicist Marshall Thompson helps the authorities to apprehend the leader of a spy ring in England.

Cast: Marshall Thompson (Dr Cliff Mitchell), John Loder (Major Anderson), Anne Aubrey (Jill Warren), Magda Miller (Ruth), John Stuart (Dr Warren), Henry Oscar (John Manning), Murray Cash (Waldo), Michael Mellinger (Tony Norwood), Robert MacKenzie (Charles), Tom Bowman (Sergeant Dale)

Milestones and Millstones: Marshall Thompson, Richard Gordon, Charles F Vetter

Comment: Kinnoch makes good use of the relatively short running time, blending lively action and mystery—and then pulling off the 'surprise ending' very effectively.

Reviews: "Swordplay, brawn, brains, the lot are used to produce a breezy enjoyable entertainment which will be a winner with children and, in any case provides jolly good clean fun for everyone." *Picture Show*

"The cast really does its stuff and the surprise ending is sprung in spectacular circumstances. The film, realistically staged, not only keeps you guessing, but also carries quite a kick for its modest size." *Picturegoer*

The Snorkel (1958) 74 mins (b&w)

"TEEN-AGE GIRL…VS. KILLER-WITH-A GIMMICK!"

Clarion Films/Hammer Films; d: Guy Green; p: Michael Carreras, Anthony Nelson-Keys; screenplay: Jimmy Sangster, Peter Myers; story by: Anthony Dawson; ph: Jack Asher; ed: James Needs, Bill Lenny; ad: John Stoll; m: Francis Chagrin

Synopsis: A young girl suspects that her stepfather killed her mother, sets out to prove it and becomes the target for the killer.

Cast: Peter Van Eyck (Paul Decker), **Betta St John** (Jean Edwards), Mandy Miller (Candy Brown), Grégoire Aslan (The Inspector), William Franklyn (Wilson), Marie Burke (Daily Woman), Irene Prador (French woman), Henri Vidon (Italian Gardener), Robert Rietti (Station Sergeant), David Ritch (Hotel Clerk)

Milestones and Millstones: Betta St John

Comment: Hammer minus a monster creates some effective moments but not enough while Van Eyck is unfortunately less menacing than he should be, resulting in concomitant dilution of suspense.

Reviews: "Hammer Films apparently has become proficient in the manufacture of motion pictures that are not greatly distinguished but that nonetheless manage to be more absorbing than the usual low-budget program film..." *The New York Times*

"Adequate for twin bills...has an intriguing gimmick as to the clue to its murder mystery plot and some moments of suspense and horror, but lackadaisical direction and unresourceful screen writing prevent the film from being continuously engrossing." *Variety*

Spy in the Sky! (1958) 75 mins (b&w)

"SECRET AGENTS OF THE SATELLITE ERA!"

Allied Artists/W Lee Wilder Productions; d/p: **W Lee Wilder**; screenplay: **Myles Wilder**; based on the novel *Counterspy Express* by A S Fleischman; ph: Walter J Harvey; ed: Lien d'Oliveyea, Loet Roozekrans; ad: Nico Van Baarle; m: Hugo de Groot:

Synopsis: Women distract American Intelligence agent Steve Brodie as he battles a Soviet spy ring when he tries to locate a missing German scientist in Europe

Cast: Steve Brodie (Vic Cabot), Sandra Francis (Eve Brandisi), George Coulouris (Colonel Benedict), Andrea Domburg (Alexandrine Duvivier), Bob De Lange (Sidney Jardine), Hans Tiemeyer (Dr Fritz Keller aka Hans Krass), Herbert Curiel (Pepi Vidor), Dity Oorhuis (Fritzi), Leon Dorian (Agent Maxwell)

Milestones and Millstones: Steve Brodie, W Lee Wilder, Myles Wilder

Comment: Minor British-Spanish-B film co-production, directed in dreary television movie style.

Reviews: "Poorly and cheaply made espionage thriller. Low grade filler on twin-bills … The cast performs adequately … very little advantage is taken of the foreign location." *Variety*

The Strange Awakening/US: Female Fiends (1958) 69 mins (b&w)

"THEIR MOTIVE GREED! THEIR METHOD MURDER!"

Merton Park Studios; d: Montgomery Tully; p: Alec C Snowden, Jim O'Connolly, Nat Cohen, Stuart Levy; screenplay; McLaren Ross; based on the novel *Puzzle for Friends* by Patrick Quentin; ph: Philip Grindrod; ed: Geoffrey Muller; ad: Wilfred Arnold, Ray Simm; stock music

Synopsis: Lex Barker loses his memory in the South of France and wakes up to find he has a sinister new 'family', is the heir to a fortune and caught up in crime.

Cast: Lex Barker (Peter Chance), Carole Mathews (Selena Friend), Lisa Gastoni (Marny Friend), Nora Swinburne (Mrs Friend), Peter Dyneley (Dr Rene Normand), Joe Robinson (Sven), Malou Pamtera (Isabella), Richard Molinas (Louis), John Serret (Commissaire Sagain), Yvonne Andre (Nun)

Milestones and Millstones: Lex Barker

Comment: Acceptable second-feature melodrama: B film specialist Tully makes the most of the relatively short running time to create an effective atmosphere of mystery and unease.

Reviews: "… a romantic crime melodrama which has many surprising twists" *Picture Show*

"An intriguing story…is the main asset of this quite well made mystery story…the characters are well drawn and the acting, though hardly in any way remarkable, is capable enough… Lex Barker does not entirely convince… but in general does well in a difficult role…" *CEA Film Report*

Cosmic Monsters (1958) 75 mins (b&w)

"MAN AND ALIEN UNITE TO COMBAT THE MOST INSIDIOUS PERILTHE UNIVERSEHAS EVER KNOWN!"

Artistes Alliance Limited; d: Gilbert Gunn; p: John Bash, George Maynard; screenplay: Paul Ryder; based on the novel by René Ray; ph: Josef Ambor; ed: Francis Bieber; ad: Bernard Sarron; m: Robert Sharples

Synopsis: A scientist experimenting in a small British laboratory creates huge killer insects—and also attracts a visitor from space.

Cast: Forrest Tucker (Gil Graham), Gaby Andre (Michele Dupont), Martin Benson (Smith), Wyndham Goldie (Brigadier Cartwright), Alec Mango (Dr. Laird), Hugh Latimer (Jimmy Murray), Geoffrey Chater (Gerard Wilson), Patricia Sinclair (Helen Forsyth), Dandy Nichols (Mrs. Tucker)

Milestones and Millstones: Forrest Tucker

Comment: With only moderate movie magic affordable to create the killer insects and a visitor-from-space storyline all-too reminiscent of *The Day the Earth Stood Still* (1951), a minor offering whose title that is more effective than the movie itself.

Reviews: "A genuine science fiction theme is in evidence here, but unfortunately its treatment achieves the ludicrous rather than the thrilling… early promise is speedily swamped in a mass of irrelevant detail, vague characterisations and inept dialogue." *CEA Film Report*

"Yet another entry in the pseudo science-fiction stakes…it is a singularly uninspired potboiler." *Variety*

The Trollenberg Terror/US: The Crawling Eye (1958) 84 mins (b&w)

"The nightmare terror of the slithering eye "

Tempean Films; d: Quentin Lawrence; p: Robert S Baker. Monty Berman; screenplay: Jimmy Sangster; from the TV serial by Peter Kay; ph: Monty Berman; ed: Henry Richardson; ad: Duncan Sutherland; sfx: Les Bowie; m: Stanley Black

Synopsis: Hideous alien creatures invade a remote mountain resort in Switzerland.

Cast: Forrest Tucker (Alan Brooks), Janet Munro (Anne Pilgrim), Jennifer Jayne (Sarah Pilgrim), Warren Mitchell (Professor Crevett), Laurence Payne (Philip Truscott), Andrew Faulds (Brett), Stuart Sanders (Dewhurst), Frederick Schiller (Klein)

Milestones and Millstones: Forrest Tucker

Comment: Lawrence, who had directed the original six-half hour episode television serial, does well considering a patently low-budget and keeps tension and shocks on a high enough level. Payne was in the TV series and camera operator Desmond Davis went on to direct such films as *The Girl With Green Eyes* (1964) and *Clash of The Titans* (1981).

Reviews: "Several sequences...are genuinely alarming, although much more could have been made of the dramatic sequences...gives the impression of having been shot and edited in a great hurry." *Monthly Film Bulletin*

"...is a likely candidate for big b.o. honors in the science fiction realm... taut screenplay extracts the most from the situations and is helped by strong acting from a solid cast. Tucker tackles the problem with commendable lack of histrionics." *Variety*

The Bandit of Zhobe (1959) 80 mins (color)

"Ruthless! Riotous! Romantic! She hated his violence…
but she sought him out!"

Warwick Film Productions; d: John Gilling; **Albert R Broccoli, Irving Allen**, Harold Huth; screenplay: John Gilling; story by: **Richard Maibaum**; ph: Ted Moore; ed: Bert Rule; ad: Duncan Sutherland; m: Kenneth V Jones

Synopsis: Bandit Victor Mature goes on the rampage in British India because he wrongly believes the British have killed his family.

Cast: Victor Mature (Kasim Khan), Anne Aubrey (Zena Crowley), Anthony Newley (Corporal Stokes), Norman Wooland (Major Crowley), Dermot Walsh (Captain Saunders), Walter Gotell (Azhad), Paul Stassino (Hatti), Murray Kash (Zecco), Sean Kelly (Lieutenant Wylie), Denis Shaw (Hussu)

Milestones and Millstones: Victor Mature, Albert R Broccoli, Irving Allen, Richard Maibaum

Comment: Essentially a B feature Western in all but its 'Indian' setting featuring plenty of action to disguise the lack of logic and Anthony Newley's embarrassing comic interpolations.

Reviews: "7¾ marks as usable action fare for unsophisticated audiences...a blood and thunder drama... a gory tale." *CEA Film Report*

Behemoth The Sea Monster/US: The Mighty Behemoth
(1959) 72 mins (b&w)

"THE BIGGEST THING SINCE TIME BEGAN!"

Artistes Alliance Ltd/Diamond Pictures Corp; d: **Eugène Lourié**, Douglas Hickox; p: **David Diamond**, Ted Lloyd: screenplay: Daniel Hyatt (aka Daniel James), Eugène Lourié; story by: Robert Abel, Alan Adler, Daniel James; ph: Desmond Davis, Ken Hodges; ed: Lee Doig; sfx, Pete Peterson, Jack Rabin, Louis DeWitt, Irving Block, Phil Kellison; ad: Eugène Lourié; m: Edwin Astley

Synopsis: Marine biologist Gene Evans is proved right when the giant marine creature he predicted would be created by radioactivity caused by atomic tests emerges from the ocean and attacks London.

Cast: Gene Evans (Steve Karnes), André Morell (Professor James Bickford), John Turner (John), Leigh Madison (Jean Trevethan), Jack MacGowran (Paleontologist Dr. Sampson), Maurice Kaufmann (Mini-submarine Officer), Henri Vidon (Thomas Trevethan), Leonard Sachs (Scientist)

Milestones and Millstones: Gene Evans, Eugène Lourié, Willis O'Brien

Comment: Featuring live action sequences filmed in Britain and very satisfactory special effects shot in Hollywood (O'Brien had worked on the original *King Kong* in 1933) this lively monster movie boldly went where Hollywood had gone before, notably 1953's *The Beast from 20,000 Fathoms*.

Reviews: "... modestly made, routine science-fiction yarn which cannot be regarded as more that a useful dualer for average audiences... Douglas Hickox and Eugene Lourié can be complimented for playing the film seriously and not for laughs." *Variety*

"Well, fancy that! Now Britain is beating Hollywood at its own game in the undersea monster market. Of course, the plot of this yarn is just as barmy... the solution is reached after bags of excitement and suspense." *Picturegoer*

"Rather better terror melodrama than usual." *Picture Show*

First Man Into Space (1959) 77 mins (b&w)

"THE PICTURE THAT LEAPS AHEAD OF THE HEADLINES!"

Amalgamated Productions; d: Robert Day; p: John Croydon, **Charles F Vetter, Jr, Richard Gordon**; screenplay: John C Cooper (John Croydon) Lance Z Hargreaves (Charles F Vetter); story by: **Wyatt Ordung**; ph: Geoffrey Faithfull; ed: Peter Mayhew; ad: Denys Pavitt; m: Buxton Orr

Synopsis: A pilot becomes the first man to fly into space, is exposed to cosmic rays and seems to have vanished when his rocket returns to Earth—and his brother Marshall Thompson fears the worst when a bloodthirsty creature strikes...

Cast: Marshall Thompson (Commander Charles Ernest Prescott), Marla Landi (Tia Francesca), Bill Edwards (Lieutenant Dan Milton Prescott) Robert Ayres (Captain Ben Richards), Bill Nagy (Police Chief Wilson), Carl Jaffe (Doctor Paul von Essen), Roger Delgado (Mexican Consul), Richard Shaw (Witney)

Milestones and Millstones: Marshall Thompson, Charles F Vetter, Jr, Richard Gordon, Wyatt Ordung

Comment: Better than average (for the period) science fiction/monster-on-the-loose B feature thriller.

Reviews: "... a good entry in the exploitation class... excitement and some genuine horror. It is generally well made and suffers only from a tendency to get cosmic in philosophy as well as in geography...The cast performs acceptably and is generally successful in employing American accents." *Variety*

"Treatment is both tense and polished, special effects are well above average (with the make-up department having contributed a splendid job, and it is all backed up by earnest and natural acting." *CEA Film Report*

Horrors of the Black Museum (1959) 95 mins (color)

"IT ACTUALLY PUTS YOU IN THE PICTURE!" HYPNOVISTA"

Carmel Productions/Merton Park Studios; d: Arthur Crabtree; p: **Samuel Z Arkoff, Herman Cohen**, Jack Greenwood; screenplay: Herman Cohen, **Aben Kandel**; ph: Desmond Dickinson; ed: Geoffrey Muller; ad: C Wilfred Arnold; m: Gerard Schurmann

Synopsis: A crime journalist in London hypnotizes his assistant Rick to commit the grisly crimes he needs to write about for his next book.

Cast: Michael Gough (Edmond Bancroft), June Cunningham (*Joan Berkley*), Graham Curnow (Rick), Shirley Anne Field (Angela Banks), Geoffrey Keen (Superintendent Graham), Gerald Anderson (Dr Ballan), John Warwick (Inspector Lodge), Beatrice Varley (Aggie), Austin Trevor (Commissioner Wayne)

Milestones and Millstones: Samuel Z Arkoff, Herman Cohen, Aben Kandel

Comment: Nasty for its time, the film's success with horror movie fans helped generate Gough's subsequent career in genre films.

Reviews: "... potentially big, despite—or perhaps because of—the fact that it panders to bad tastes...the film vends horror in its most nauseating form for the sake of slaking a thirst for gore." *Variety*

"For those who want gory fare, there is blood everywhere, but the picture has little else to offer...despite all its defects, the picture should satisfy those who demand blood-curdling entertainment." *CEA Film Report*

Idle on Parade/US: Idol on Parade (1959) 88 min (b&w)

Warwick Film Productions; d: John Gilling; p: **Irving Allen, Albert R Broccoli** ap: Harold Huth; screenplay: John Antrobus; based on the novel *Idle on Parade* by William Camp; ph: Ted Moore; ed: Bert Rule; visual sfx: Vic Margutti, ad: Ray Simm; m: Bill Shepherd

Synopsis: When pop star Anthony Newley is drafted into the army for National Service he contrives to continue his recording career.

Cast: William Bendix (Sergeant Major Lush), Anthony Newley (Jeep Jackson), Anne Aubrey (Caroline), Lionel Jeffries (Bertie), Sid

James (Herbie), David Lodge (Shorty), Dilys Laye (Renee), William Kendall (Commanding Officer), Bernie Winters (Joseph Jackson), Harry Fowler (Ron)

Milestones and Millstones: William Bendix, Irving Allen, Albert R Broccoli

Comment: A low-budget comedy-musical based on William Camp's 1958 novel which was inspired by Elvis Presley's induction into the US Army: Newley sings five songs, one of which, *I've Waited for So Long*, became a hit and brought him stardom. Bendix deserved praise for keeping a straight face in face of the broad farce.

Reviews: "… pure corn, a series of ore-or-less related situations and gags…an unambitious film which will garner enough yocks to keep the b.o. clicking merrily." *Variety*

"… topical enough for comedy entertainment … the material of this picture is just not up to the mark, and for much of the time is decidedly unfunny…Bendix has poor material." *CEA Film Report*

Model for Murder (1959) 73 mins (b&w)

"SUSPENSE! when a glamorous model meets MURDER!"

Jack Parsons Productions (Parroch); d: Terry Bishop; p: Jack Parson , Robert Dunbar; screenplay: Terry Bishop, Robert Dunbar; from a story by Peter Fraser; ph: Peter Hennessey; ed: Helga Cranston; m: William Davies

Synopsis: American sailor Keith Andes is on leave in London when he is unwittingly involved in the theft of valuable jewelry.

Cast: Keith Andes (David Martens), Hazel Court (Sally Meadows), Jean Aubrey (Annabelle Meadows), Michael Gough (Kingsley Beauchamp), Julia Arnall (Diana Leigh), Patricia Jessel (Mme Dupont), Peter Hammond (George)

Milestones and Millstones: Keith Andes

Comment: Nothing special: efficient enough time-passer but ultimately rather ordinary.

Reviews: "While at no time completely convincing, the strong point of the picture is that it moves quickly and vivaciously… hero manfully done by Keith Andes." *CEA Film Report*

"...it oft-times breeds an atmosphere of sex that's as powerful as anything to emanate from British studios. The trouble ... is that it presents the love stuff in the course of a story that, one feels, could almost have been drummed up for that purpose alone...Bendix, too make a hit." *Variety*

The Stranglers of Bombay (1959) 80 mins

"THIS IS TRUE! THIS IS REAL! THIS ACTUALLY HAPPENED! MURDER CULT TERROR IN EXOTIC ASIA"

Hammer Films, in association with Kenneth Hyman; d: Terence Fisher; p: Michael Carerras, Anthony Hinds, Anthony Nelson Keys, Kenneth Hyman; screenplay: **David Z Goodman**; ph: Arthur Grant; ed: Alfred Cox; ad: Bernard Robinson; m: James Bernard

Synopsis: A British army captain in 1830s colonialist India investigates a murderous cult of Thugee killers.

Cast: Guy Rolfe (Captain Harry Lewis), Jan Holden (Mary Lewis), Andrew Cruikshank (Colonel Henderson), George Pastell (High Priest of Kali), Marne Maitland (Patel Shari), Paul Stassino (Lieutenant Silver), Allan Cuthbertson (Captain Christopher Connaught-Smith), Michael Nightingale (Sidney Flood)

Milestones and Millstones: David Zelag Goodman

Comment: Fisher creates a potent meld of gruesome terror and historical melodrama without the studios by now usual brash colour cinematography. The film shot in 'Stranglescope' marked the director's first wide screen movie: location shooting included, improbably, a quarry in the English countryside.

Reviews: "...a straightforward melodrama...it lacks star value and slick writing, but Terence Fisher has done a good directing job." *Variety*

"What might have been a framework of real history inspiring an unusual plot has handled with little imagination or coherence." *CEA Film Report*

Too Young to Love (1959) 88 mins (b&w)

"THE STORY THAT PEELS BARE THE RAW EMOTIONS OF TODAY'S GENERATION"

Welbeck Films Ltd; d: Muriel Box; p: Sydney Box, Herbert Smith; screenplay: Muriel Box, Sidney Box; based on the play *Pick-Up Girl* by Elsa Shelley; ph: Gerald Gibbs; ed: Jean Barker; ad: George Provis; m: Bruce Montgomery

Synopsis: New York judge Thomas Mitchell hears the case of a neglected teenage girl arrested after being caught in bed with a man more than twice her age.

Cast: Pauline Hahn (Elizabeth Collins), Joan Miller (Mrs Collins), Austin Willis (Mr Collins), Vivian Matalon (Larry Webster), Jess Conrad (Peter Martin), Sheila Gallagher (Ruby Lockwood), Alan Gifford (Mr Elliott), Miki Iveria (Mrs. Martin), **Bessie Love** (Mrs Busch) **Thomas Mitchell** (Judge Bentley)

Milestones and Millstones: Bessie Love, Thomas Mitchell

Comment: Filmed in Britain, set in New York: while the play had made waves in the theater, the film ultimately comes across as stagey and moralistic while over-reliance on courtroom scenes adds tedium.

Reviews: "Shows its stage pedigree only too clearly, being wordy and static... sincere but it never moves. The producer must thank Mitchell in the main that the picture is gripping." *Variety*

"...the American setting—rarely attempted in a British picture—has been wisely preserve; except for some minor roles, it is well acted, some lapses of accent being excusable." *CEA Film Report*

Whirlpool (1959) 95 minutes (color)

"CAN A MAN MAKE A WOMAN DO THINGS SHE DOESN'T WANT TO?"

The Rank Organisation; d: **Lewis Allen**; p: Sam Lomberg, George Pitcher; screenplay: Lawrence P Bachman, Marcel Stellman; based on the novel *The Lorelei* by Lawrence P Bachman; ph: Geoffrey Unsworth; ed: Russell Lloyd; ad: Jack Maxsted; m: Ron Goodwin

Synopsis: The former girlfriend of a German fugitive takes refuge with the captain and crew of a boat on the river Rhine.

Cast: Juliette Gréco (Lora), O.W. Fischer (Rolph), Marius Goring (Georg), Muriel Pavlow (Dina), William Sylvester (Herman), Richard Palmer (Derek), Lily Kann (Mrs Steen), Peter Illing (Braun), Geoffrey Bayldon (Wendell), Harold Kasket (Stiebel), Victor Brooks (Bootsman), Arthur Howell (Pilot)

Milestones and Millstones: Lewis Allen

Comment: Location filming in Germany fails to add much impact to a lackluster programmer.

Reviews: "… a major disappointment, with flat performances, uninspired direction and stilted dialog and situations… more urgent direction and brisker editing might have helped out." *Variety*

The 1960s

*"I don't try to guess what a million people will like.
It's hard enough to know what I like"*
— *John Huston*

Bluebeard's Ten Honeymoons/Bluebeard's 10 Honeymoons
(1960) 92 mins (b&w)

"THE MAN WITH THE DO-IT-YOURSELF MURDER KIT!"

Anglo Allied; d: **W Lee Wilder**; p: Roy Parkinson; screenplay: **Myles Wilder**; ph: Stephen Dade; ed: Tom Simpson; ad: Paul Sherriff; m: Albert Elms

Synopsis: Landru revisited: a homicidal husband turns to multiple murders to keep his mistress happy.

Cast: George Sanders (Henri Landru), **Corinne Calvet** (Odette), Jean Kent (Guillin), Patricia Roc (Dueaux), Greta Gynt (Jeanette), Ingrid Haffner (Giselle), Ian Fleming (Lawyer), Peter Illing (Lefevre), Sheldon Lawrence (Pepi), Jack Melford (Concierge), Maxine Audley (Cynthia)

Milestones and Millstones: George Sanders, Corinne Calvet, W Lee Wilder, Myles Wilder

Comment: Sanders, far better than the material he has to work with is barely the sole reason to watch this otherwise messy mix of moods and embarrassing attempts at black comedy.

Reviews: "This is a dull, preposterous yarn…drags tremendously, is acted only adequately, is written in clichés and directed with no sense of drama… Sanders…wanders through the proceedings…" *Variety*

"Treated in banal and uninspired fashion so that whether played for laughs or horror it fails on both counts…Sanders gives a standard performance of polished urbanity…." *CEA Film Report*

The Body Stealers (1960) 91 minutes (color)

"CAN THE EARTH SURVIVE AGAINST THE ALIENS FROM OUTER SPACE?"

Tigon Pictures/Sagittarius Productions; d: Gerry Levy; p: Tony Tenser; screenplay and story by: Michael St Clair; revised screenplay: Gerry Levy; ph: John Coquillon; ed: Howard Lanning; sfx: Tom Wadden; m: Reg Tilsley

Synopsis: Parachutists who disappear in mid-air turn out to be being snatched by aliens who intend to use them to repopulate their dying world.

Cast: George Sanders (General Armstrong), Maurice Evans (Dr Matthews), Patrick Allen (Bob Megan), Neil Connery (Jim Radford), Hilary Heath (Julie Slade), Robert Flemyng (Wing Commander Baldwin), Lorna Wilde (Lorna), Allan Cuthbertson (Hindsmith), Michael Culver (Lieutenant Bailes)

Milestones and Millstones: George Sanders

Comment: Tedious and tepid science fiction, made on a patently low budget: the alien spacecraft is borrowed footage of a Dalek saucer first featured in the 1966 movie *Daleks: Invasion Earth 2150 A.D.* Where his father Sean achieved stardom as James Bond, his son Neil made only 11 screen appearances before quitting film and operating a plaster business in Glasgow.

Reviews: "… a moderate level of excitement and suspense. Patches of weak dialogue and generally unimpressive acting are not likely to bother the majority of fans… acceptable unsophisticated offering of its kind." *CEA Film Report*

"Science fiction has never been the forte of British film-makers and The Body Stealers (nee Thin Air, a much better title) proves to be no exception to the rule." *Films and Filming*

It Takes a Thief (1960) 101 mins (b&w)

"THE FABULOUS JAYNE A TERRIFIC DRAW
IN ANY SITUATION"

Alexandra; d/s: John Gilling; p: John Temple-Smith; ph: Gordon Dines; ed: Alan Osbiston, John Victor-Smith; ad: Jim Morahan, Tom Morahan; m: William McGuffie

Synopsis: Ringleader Jayne Mansfield and her gang hunt for hidden loot from a failed heist that was stashed away in London by her now jailed boyfriend.

Cast: Jayne Mansfield (Billy), Anthony Quayle (Jim), Carl Möhner (Kristy), Peter Reynolds (Buddy), Barbara Mullen (Ma Piper), Robert Brown (Bob Crowther), Dermot Walsh (Detective Sergeant Willis), Patrick Holt (Max), Edward Judd (Detective Sergeant Gittens), John Bennett (Spider)

Milestones and Millstones: Jayne Mansfield

Comment: Slipshod plotting and uninspired editing combine to deliver a dull and not very thrilling thriller that relies more on its star than on its content.

Reviews: "… fairly conventional…it isn't easy to see why Miss Mansfield should have elected to stay on in Britain to appear in this film." *Variety*

Circus of Horrors (1960) 88 mins (color)

"SPECTACULAR TOWERING TERROR One man's lust…made men into beasts, stripped women of their souls! For even stranger thrills he turned the greatest show on earth in a…
CIRCUS OF HORRORS!"

Lynx Films Ltd; d: Sidney Hayers; p: **Samuel Z Arkoff**, Leslie Parkyn, Julian Wintle, Norman Priggen; screenplay: **George Baxt**: ph: Douglas Slocombe; ed: Reginald Mills, Sidney Hayers; ad: Jack Shampan; m: Muir Matheson, Franz Reizenstein

Synopsis: A deranged plastic surgeon flees to France after horribly disfiguring a woman during a botched operation and ends up running a circus as a cover for subsequent sinister surgery.

Cast: Anton Diffring (Dr Rossiter, aka Dr Bernard Schueler), Erika Remberg (Elissa Caro), Yvonne Monlaur (Nicole Vanet), Donald Pleasence (Vanet), Jane Hylton (Angela), Kenneth Griffith (Martin), Conrad Phillips (Inspector Arthur Ames), Jack Gwillim (Superintendent Andrews)

Milestones and Millstones: Samuel Z Arkoff, George Baxt

Comment: Over the top and all the more bloodily entertaining for it with filming in a genuine circus (Billy Smart's Circus) adding glamour to the recurrent innate nastiness (for the period) on display.

Reviews: "… aptly titled… replete with blood and gore in the best 'Dracula' tradition… hardly suitable for moppets, it has a wealth of exploitable values which could lure teenagers." *Variety*

"With such a blood-strewn story, it is surprising that this film contains relatively few really horrific sequences… the introduction of a man in gorilla's clothing strikes a naïve note and makes a corny climax." *CEA Film Report*

The City of the Dead/US: Horror Hotel (1960) 78 mins (b&w)

"THE THRILLS—THE CHILLS—OF WITCHCRAFT TODAY"

Vulcan; d: John Moxey; p: **Max Rosenberg, Milton Subotsky**, Donald Taylor, Seymour S Dorner; screenplay: George Baxt; story by: Milton Subotsky; ph: Desmond Dickinson; ed: John Pomeroy; ad: John Blezard; m: Douglas Gamley

Synopsis: When her professor recommends student Venetia Stevenson to go Massachusetts to research into witchcraft she ends up in the hands of murderous Satanists.

Cast: Denis Lotis (Richard Barlow), Christopher Lee (Alan Driscoll), **Betta St John** (Patricia Russell), Patricia Jessel (Elizabeth Selwyn/Mrs Newless), Tom Naylor (Bill Maitland), **Venetia Stevenson** (Nan Barlow), Ann Beach (Lottie), Norman MacGowran (Reverend Russell), Fred Johnson (The Elder)

Milestones and Millstones: Betta St John, Venetia Stevenson, Max J Rosenberg, Milton Subotsky

Comment: Moxey (who later directed what was briefly the most watched TV movie *Kolchak: The Night Stalker* in 1974) makes effective use of in-studio shooting, well supported by moody monochrome cinematography to create a mounting atmosphere of unease and, possibly prior to *Psycho* (1960), disposing of his 'leading lady' Stevenson unexpectedly early. No masterpiece but still impressive.

Reviews: " ..most of the familiar ingredients of traditional spooky horror films are present- camera gloom, sinister close-ups, swirling ground mist, thunder, trapdoors, disappearances, a dumb servitor and general Satanic assumptions." *CEA Film Report*

"…extraordinarily good chiller … One of the few horror films of the period which still has the power to frighten, *"Horror Hotel"* is required viewing for genre fans. " *New York Times*

Faces in the Dark (1960) 84 mins

A Penington Eady Production; d: David Eady; p: Jon Penington; screenplay: Ephraim Logan, John Tully; based on the novel *Les Visages De L'Ombre* by Pierre Boileau and Thomas Narcejac; ph: Ken Hodges; ed: Oswald Hafenrichter; ad: Antony Masters; m: Mikis Theodorakis

Synopsis: When his wife, business partner and brother John Ireland take an inventor blinded in a laboratory experiment to a remote cottage to recover he starts to suspect dirty business is afoot.

Cast: John Gregson (Richard Hammond), Mai Zetterling (Christiane Hammond), **John Ireland** (Max Hammond), Michael Denison (David Merton), Tony Wright (Clem), Nanette Newman (Miss Hopkins), Valerie Taylor (Miss Hopkins), Ronald Bartrop (French doctor), John Serrett (French Surgeon)

Milestones and Millstones: John Ireland

Comment: The key characters are all essentially dislikeable which robs the "drive him crazy" storyline of much of its potential impact; director David Eady's uninteresting storytelling style does not improve impact either.

Reviews: "This novelettish tale is not without a surface ingenuity but it has been allowed to get out of hand…the ending is unsatisfying, rounding off a largely baffling tale which leaves loose ends never cleared up." *CEA Film Report*

Moment of Danger/Malaga (1960) 97 mins (b&w)

"THE GIRL THEY CALLED TROUBLE"

Cavalcade Films Limited; d: **Lazlo Benedek**; p: Thomas Clyde; screenplay: David Osborn, **Donald Ogden Stewart**; based on the novel *The Scent of Danger* by Donald MacKenzie; ph: Desmond Dickinson; ed: Gerald Turney-Smith; ad: Harry White, Pamela Cornell; m: Matyas Seiber

Synopsis: Thief Edmond Purdom abandons girlfriend Dorothy Dandridge after he and locksmith Trevor Howard steal some jewels, then she and Howard join forces to get even with Purdom.

Cast: Trevor Howard (John Bain), Dorothy Dandridge (Gianna), **Edmond Purdom** (Peter Carran), Michael Hordern (Inspector Farrell), Paul Stassino (Juan Montoya), John Bailey (Cecil), Alfred Burke (Shapley), Peter Illing (Pawnbroker), Martin Boddey (Sir John Middleburgh), Helen Goss (Lady Middleburgh)

Milestones and Millstones: Lazlo Benedek, Edmond Purdom, Donald Ogden Stewart

Comment: Dandridge (in one of her last films) and Howard are excellent but the film is tepid as a thriller and unpersuasive as a romance.

Reviews: "… it becomes increasingly slow-moving and talkative, with little action; the whole thing sags and there is little build-up to the climax with remains singularly unexciting… striking performances from Trevor Howard and Dorothy Dandridge." *CEA Film Report*

The Damned/US: These Are The Damned (1961) 87 mins (b&w)

"CHILDREN OF ICE AND DARKNESS… THEY ARE THE LURKING, UNSEEN EVIL YOU DARE NOT FACE ALONE!"

Hammer Film Productions; d: **Joseph Losey**; ep: Michael Carreras; p: Anthony Hinds; Anthony Nelson Keys; screenplay: Evan Jones; from the novel *The Children of Light* by H L Lawrence; ph: Arthur Grant; ed: Reginald Mills; pd: Bernard Robinson; ad: Don Mingaye; sfx: Les Bowie; m: James Bernard

Synopsis: American tourist Macdonald Carey tries to escape a gang of Teddy Boy bikers in an English seaside town and ends up in a military base where radioactive children are being groomed for survival after an atomic war.

Cast: Macdonald Carey (Simon Wells), Shirley Anne Field (Joan), Viveca Lindfors (Freya Neilson), Alexander Knox (Bernard), Oliver Reed (King), Walter Gotell (Major Holland), James Villiers (Captain Gregory), Tom Kempinski (Ted), Kenneth Cope (Sid), Barbara Everest (Miss Lamont)

Milestones and Millstones: Macdonald Carey, Joseph Losey

Comment: Not released in Britain until 1963, with cuts demanded by the Censor, and not released (again cut) in the United States in 1965. By then Hammer were celebrated for horror: this overly pretentious science fiction thriller has its moments but its near-iconic status is as much due to its iconic director as to its content. Its unique attribute is that it is the nearest Hammer got to make an art movie, even, as here, by accident.

Reviews: "Unusual combination of science-fiction and teenage hoodlum entertainment, this emerges as neither one thing nor the other…the mystery, while well built-up and intriguing, is most unsatisfactorily explained, while the "shock" ending is inconclusive." *CEA Film Report*

Gorgo (1961) 78 mins (color)

"LIKE NOTHING YOU'VE EVER SEEN BEFORE!"

King Brothers Productions; d: **Eugène Lourié**; ep: **Frank King, Maurice King**; p: **Herman King**, Wilfred Eades; ap: James Leicester; screenplay and story by: Robert L Richards (aka John Loring), Daniel James (aka Daniel Hyatt); ph: Freddie Young; ed: Eric Boyd-Perkins; ad: Elliott Scott: sfx: Tom Howard; m: Angelo Lavagnino

Synopsis: A giant monster is captured off the Irish coast and sold as a fairground exhibit in London—but its much larger and angry mother turns up and causes chaos.

Cast: Bill Travers (Joe Ryan), William Sylvester (Sam Slade), Vincent Winter (Sean). Christopher Rhodes (McCartin), Bruce Seton (Professor Flaherty), Joseph O'Connor (Professor Hendricks), Martin Benson (Dorkin), Barry Keegan (1st mate), Dervis Ward (bo'sun), Basil Dignam (Admiral Brooks)

Milestones and Millstones: Eugène Lourié, Frank King, Herman King, Maurice King

Comment: *Godzilla*? Is this vigorous monster-mangles-a big-city homage to the famed Japanese giant lizard or simply audience-aimed exploitation second feature fodder? Either way, it delivers the goods excitingly enough for genre fans.

Reviews: "...pretty darn good. For awesome technical wizardry and the boiling crescendo of its climax—the most hair-raising close-up of metropolitan panic we've ever seen on film, this is probably the best outright monster shocker since "King Kong"." *New York Times*

"... as a piece of "monster' hokum the entertainment rests on the spectacle angle... Unsophisticated fans of this kind of fare are provided with plenty to watch." *CEA Film Report*

A Matter of WHO (1961) 90 mins (b&w)

"Another hilarious comedy film from the producers of "The Mouse That Roared."

Foray; d: Don Chaffey; p: William Shenson, Milton Holmes; screenplay: Milton Holmes, Harold Buchman; adapted by Patricia Lee from her article co-written with Paul Dickinson; ph: Erwin Hillier; ed: Frank Clarke; sfx: Tom Howard; ad: Eliot Scott; m: Edwin Astley

Synopsis: A British World Health Organization "germ detective" sets out to track down the source of a deadly virus.

Cast: Terry-Thomas (Archibald Bannister), Sonja Ziemann (Michele), **Alex Nicol** (Kennedy), Richard Briers (Jamieson), Honor Blackman (Sister Bryan), Carol White (Beryl), Guy Deghy (Ivonovitch), Clive Morton (Hatfield), Martin Benson (Rahman), Geoffrey Keen (Foster), The John Barry Seven (Band)

Milestones and Millstones: Alex Nicol

Comment: The subject—a smallpox epidemic—is hardly obvious comic material, and Terry-Thomas is somewhat miscast as a 'germ detective'. Nicol plays the token British B film American as well as possible under the circumstances.

Reviews: "... tends to rely too much on dialogue rather than dramatic action... Undemanding tastes might, however, find it reasonably entertaining." *CEA Film Report*

"it does not add up as an entry likely to have much popular appeal... Nicol plays a bewildered but determined American oil man with a firm touch." *Variety*

Murder She Said (1961) 87 mins (b&w)

SEE THE STRANGE CASE OF THE STRANGLER-KILLER ON THE NIGHT EXPRESS!

MGM/George H Brown Productions; d: George Pollock; p: George H Brown; screenplay: David Pursall, Jack Seddon; adapted by David D Osborn from the novel *4.50 From Paddington* by Agatha Christie; ph: Geoffrey Faithfull; ed: Ernest Walter; sfx: Tom Howard; ad: Harry White; m: Ron Goodwin

Synopsis: Spinster Margaret Rutherford witnesses a murder from a passing train and turns sleuth to find the killer when the police refuse to believe her.

Cast: Margaret Rutherford (Miss Jane Marple), **Arthur Kennedy** (Dr Paul Quimper), Muriel Pavlow (Emma Ackenthorpe), James Robertson Justice (Ackenthorpe), Thorley Walters (Cedric Ackenthorpe), Conrad Phillips (Harold Ackenthorpe), Joan Hickson (Mrs Kidder), Stringer Davis (Mr Jim Stringer)

Milestones and Millstones: Arthur Kennedy

Comment: Perfect as Agatha Christie's celebrated amateur sleuth Miss Marple, character actress Rutherford achieved stardom in this engaging murder mystery and reprised the role in sequels *Murder at the Gallop* (1963), *Murder Most Foul* (1964) and the same year's *Murder Ahoy!* MGM added Hollywood actor Kennedy to *Murder She Said*: the sequels did not need one.

Reviews: "...warm, cheerful and funny results ...this modest whodunit comes off as a thoroughly satisfying and suspenseful diversion..." *New York Times*

"Rather wordy whodunit...Enough red herrings to satisfy the average murder mystery addict." *Variety*

"... fair suspense marches hand-in-hand with modest thrill to maintain interest down to the capably handled surprise climax." *CEA Film Report*

Return of a Stranger (1961) 63 mins (b&w)

Danziger Productions Ltd; d: Max Varnel; p: Edward J Danziger, Harry Lee Danziger, Brian Taylor; screenplay: Brian Clemens; ph: Walter J Harvey; ed: L Spencer Reeve; ad Norman G Arnold: m: Bill LeSage

Synopsis: The serene lives of John Ireland and his wife are transformed into a living nightmare when a mysterious man begins to stalk their every move.

Cast: John Ireland (John Allen), Susan Stephen (Pam Allen), Cyril Shaps (Homer Trent), Timothy Beaton (Tommy Allen), Patrick McAlinney (Whittaker), Kevin Stoney (Wayne), Ian Fleming (Meecham), Raymond Rollett (Somerset), Frederick Piper (Fred), Martin Carthy (Lift boy), Ray Austin (Police Sergeant)

Milestones and Millstones: John Ireland

Comment: Eminently forgettable: it feels longer than its relatively short running time.

Reviews: "Creepy yet risible Brian Clemens scripted quota-quickie thriller from low-budget specialists the Danziger Brothers." *Britmovie*

The Unstoppable Man (1961) 68 mins (b&w)

"RAW COURAGE...RAGING ACTION THE BLISTERING BLAZING STORY OF THE UNSTOPPABLE MAN"

Argo Film Productions; d: Terry Bishop; p: John Pellatt; screenplay: Alun Falconer, Paddy Manning O'Brine, Terry Bishop; from the novel *Amateur in Violence* by Michael Gilbert; ph: Arthur Grant; ed: Anthony Gibbs; ad: Anthony Masters; m: William McGuffie

Synopsis: When Industrialist Cameron Mitchell is told by Scotland Yard not to interfere after his son is kidnapped he puts his own rescue plan into action.

Cast: Cameron Mitchell (James Kennedy), Marius Goring (Inspector Hazelrigg), Harry H Corbett (Feis), Lois Maxwell (Helen Kennedy), Denis Gilmore (Jimmy Kennedy), Humphrey Lestocq (Sergeant Plummer), Ann Sears (Pat Delaney), Timothy Bateson (Rocky), Kenneth Cope (Benny)

Milestones and Millstones: Cameron Mitchell

Comment: Cameron adds useful star power to a brisk B film which features some effective action sequences.

Reviews: "This fanciful but decidedly ingenious slant on the kidnapping racket bowls briskly along and maintains an interest throughout… the animated climax rounds off an unpretentious but thoroughly acceptable second feature." *CEA Film Report*

Visa to Canton/US: Passport to Chine (1961) 75 mins (color)

"GO-FOR-BROKE YANK BLASTS THE BAMBOO CURTAIN!"

Hammer Film Productions/Swallow Films; d: Michael Carreras; p: Michael Carreras, Anthony Nelson Keys; screenplay: Gordon Wellesley; ph: Arthur Grant: ed: Alfred Cox, James Needs; ad: Bernard Robinson, Thomas Goswell; m: Edwin Astley

Synopsis: The US government sends former World War Two pilot Richard Basehart as a spy to Communist China where he reluctantly helps a Chinese woman's search for her missing son.

Cast: Richard Basehart (Don Benton), Lisa Gastoni (Lola Sanchez), Athene Seyler (Mao Tai Tai), Eric Pohlmann (Ivono Kong), Alan Gifford (Charles Orme), Bernard Cribbins (Pereira), Burt Kwouk (Jimmy), Hedger Wallace (Inspector Taylor), Marne Maitland (Han Po), Milton Reid (Bodyguard)

Milestones and Millstones: Richard Basehart

Comment: By 1961 Hammer was established as the new cinematic House of Horror: this routine thriller was very much an American star-led B film. Carreras, who was making only his second feature film as director, never really made the most of star, cast or material.

Reviews: "…gradually settles down to a vague though not uninteresting spy thriller… Despite the confusing mystery, there us a fair amount if tension though little exciting action." *CEA Film Report*

Taste of Fear/US: Scream of Fear (1961) 81 mins (b&w)

"THE MOTION PICTURE SHOCKER OF THE YEAR!"

Hammer Films/Falcon Films; d: Seth Holt; ep: Michael Carreras; p/screenplay: Jimmy Sangster; ph: Douglas Slocombe; ed: Eric Boyd-Perkins; pd: Bernard Robinson; ad: Thomas Goswell; sfx: Les Bowie, Ian Scoones; m: Clifton Parker

Synopsis: Wheelchair-bound Susan Strasberg is told her father is away but starts to see his corpse when she goes to live on the estate of her widowed stepmother in the South of France.

Cast: Susan Strasberg (Penny Appleby), Ronald Lewis (Bob), Ann Todd (Jane Appleby), Christopher Lee (Dr Gerraed), John Serret (Inspector Legrand), Leonard Sachs (Spratt), Anne Blake (Marie), Fred Johnson (Father)

Milestones and Millstones: Susan Strasberg

Comment: Hammer regular Sangster's neat, homage-laden screenplay, his insistence on filming monochrome and Holt's crisp direction deliver a slick, satisfying psychological thriller with Lee for added impact: a deserved hit for Hammer.

Reviews: "Ingenious and frequently baffling tale fully achieves its purpose of mystery, suspense and thrills... the prevailing atmosphere of brooding menace us admirably maintained and the climax is plausible enough even though if not entirely convincing." *CEA Film Report*

"The script can be shot to pieces for contrived plausibility but the overall effect, which is to keep audiences on edge, is well achieved...Strasberg... gives a useful performance of bewilderment, fear and near craziness." *Variety*

The Treasure of Monte Cristo/US: The Secret of Monte Cristo (1961) 95 mins (color)

"HE FOLLOWED A MYSTERY MAP TO TERROR
AND TREASURE!"

Mid Century Film Productions; d/p: Robert S Baker, Monty Berman; screenplay: Leon Griffiths; ph: Robert S Baker ed: John Jympson; ad: Allan Harris; m: Clifton Parker

Synopsis: 19th century soldier Rory Calhoun becomes involved in danger when he is hired to escort a man and his daughter in search of a fabled treasure.

Cast: Rory Calhoun (Captain Adam Corbett), Patricia Bredin (Pauline), John Gregson (Renato), Peter Arne (Boldoni), Sam Kydd (Albert), Ian Hunter (Colonel Jackson), David Davies (Van Ryman), Francis Matthews (Louis Auclair), Tutte Lemkov (Gino), George Street (Innkeeper)

Milestones and Millstones: Rory Calhoun

Comment: Action, not intellect, drives this by-numbers swashbuckling programmer.

Reviews: "… becomes increasingly absurd and peopled by mechanical characters, but it serves as a peg on which to hang a mass of action padding…in the old adventure serial spirit of schoolboy days." *CEA Film Report*

The Devil's Agent (1962) 77 mins (b&w)

Eichberg Film/Bavaria Filmkunst/Central Cinema Company Film/Emmett Dalton Productions; d: John Paddy Carstairs; ep: Artur Brauner; p: Emmett Dalton; screenplay: Robert Westerby, John Paddy Carstairs (uncredited); from the novel *Im Namen des Teufels* by Hans Habe; ph: Gerald Gibbs; ed: Tom Simpson; ad: Tony Inglis; m: Philip Green

Synopsis: US Intelligence agent MacDonald Carey turns a man staying with an old friend in the Soviet zone into a double agent and sends him to Budapest to gather information.

Cast: Peter van Eyck (Droste), Marianne Koch (Nora), Christopher Lee (Baron von Staub), **Macdonald Carey** (Mr Smith), Albert Lieven (Inspector Huebring), Billie Whitelaw (Piroska), David Knight (Father Zambory), Marius Goring (General Greenhahn), Helen Cherry (Countess Cosimano), Eric Pohlmann (Bloch)

Milestones and Millstones: Macdonald Carey

Comment: Irish locations add little of interest to an otherwise tedious minor second feature thriller most relevant for Christopher Lee completists.

Reviews: "A ragged and episodic affair, which no sooner gets going on one thing than it switches to another, this I now way lives up to the promise of its cast which, for a B picture, is formidable." *Monthly Film Bulletin*

The Iron Maiden/US: The Swingin' Maiden (1962) 98 mins (color)

Peter Rogers Productions; d: Gerald Thomas; p: Peter Rogers: ap: Frank Bevis; screenplay: Vivian Cox, Leslie Bricusse; story by: Harold Brooke, Kay Bannerman; ph: Alan Hume; ed: Archie Ludski; ad: Carmen Dillon; m: Eric Rogers

Synopsis: A British aircraft designer's passion for traction engines and his initial relationship with the daughter of American airline owner Alan Hale Jr, almost wrecks a business deal with the Americans.

Cast: Michael Craig (Jack Hopkins), **Ann Helm** (Kathy Fisher), **Jeff Donnell** (Miriam Fisher), **Alan Hale Jr** (Paul Fisher), Noel Purcell (Admiral Sir Digby Trevelyan), Cecil Parker (Sir Giles Thompson), Roland Culver (Lord Upshott). Joan Sims (Nellie Trotter), John Standing (Humphrey Gore-Brown), Jim Dale (Bill)

Milestones and Millstones: Alan Hale Jr, Jeff Donnell, Ann Helm

Comment: Solid, not particularly amusing comedy from director Rogers and producer Thomas of *Carry On* comedies fame (*Carry On* regulars Jim Dale and Joan Sims are featured).

Reviews: "Some veteran British actors help make the best of a flimsy plot, but the gleaming traction engines steal the show." *Monthly Film Bulletin*

"… an amusing comedy which could have benefited from a wittier script…the three Americans are newish and welcome faces to British audiences." *Variety*

Night of the Eagle/Burn, Witch, Burn (1962) 92 mins (b&w)

> "DON'T SEE THIS PICTURE Unless you can withstand the emotional shock of a lifetime!"

Independent Artists; d: Sidney Hayers; ep: Leslie Parkyn, Julian Wintle; p: **Samuel Z Arkoff**, Albert Fennell; screenplay: **Charles Beaumont, Richard Matheson, George Baxt**; based on the novel *Conjure my Wife* by Fritz Lieber; ph: Reginald Wyer; ed: Ralph Sheldon; ad: Jack Shampan; m: William Alwyn

Synopsis: Thing go horribly wrong for the college professor who learns his wife Betsy Blair has been practicing witchcraft and makes her burn her magical paraphernalia.

Cast: Peter Wyngarde (Norman Taylor), **Betsy Blair** (Tansy Taylor), Margaret Johnston (Flora Carr), Anthony Nicholls (Harvey Sawtelle), Colin Gordon (Lindsay Carr), Kathleen Byron (Evelyn Sawtelle), Reginald Beckwith (Harold Gunnison), Norman Bird (Doctor), Judith Stott (Margaret Abbott)

Milestones and Millstones: Betsy Blair, Samuel Z Arkoff, Charles Beaumont, Richard Matheson, George Baxt

Comment: An over-melodramatic, over-talkative screenplay reduces some of the eerie impact of this competently directed remake of the 1944 Fritz Lieber-based chiller *Weird Woman*.

Reviews: "There is little visually to terrify in this film which relies more on suggestion and sometimes verges on the unintentionally comical." *CEA Film Report*

"Not much of a movie but it goes to show what can happened in a community that fails to pay its teachers a living wage." *Time*

The Pirates of Blood River (1962) 87 mins (color)

"RANSACKING A LOST TROPIC ISLAND... FOR A FABULOUS IDOL OF GOLD!"

Hammer Films; d: John Gilling; ep: Michael Carreras; p Anthony Nelson Keys; screenplay: John Gilling, John Hunter, Anthony Nelson Keys; from a story by Jimmy Sangster; ph: Arthur Grant; ed: Eric Boyd-Perkins; pd: Bernard Robinson; ad: Don Mingaye; sfx: Les Bowie; m: Gary Hughes

Synopsis: Ruthless pirates in search of hidden treasure attack a Huguenot penal colony and kidnap Huguenot Kerwin Matthews to force him to lead them to his village.

Cast: Kerwin Mathews (Jonathon Standing), **Glenn Corbett** (Henry), Christopher Lee (Captain LaRoche), Peter Arne (Pirate Hench), Marla Landi (Bess Standing), Desmond Llewellyn (Tom Blackthorne), Oliver Reed (Pirate Brocaire), Andrew Keir (Jason Standing), Michael Ripper (Pirate Jack)

Milestones and Millstones: Kerwin Mathews, Glenn Corbett

Comment: Serviceable action swashbuckler for youngsters: Lee clearly enjoys himself by playing a human rather than a monster for a change and sensibly makes his evil pirate larger than life. Llewellyn, later famous as James Bond's gadget maker, appears in a supporting role.

Reviews: "…wastes little time on dramatic nuance or romantic mush; instead stresses visual adventure elements all the way, which should make it a special favourite with the muppet brigade, male division…Mathews… engineers another solid swashbuckling performance…forcefully directed." *Variety*

Stranglehold (1962) 73 mins (b&w)

Argo Film Productions; d: Lawrence Huntingdon: p: Jack Lamont, David Henley; screenplay: Guy Elmes, Joy Garrison; ph: S.D. Onions, Ceni Davis; ed: Peter Weatherley; ad: Duncan Sutherland; m: Eric Spear

Synopsis: Actor Macdonald Carey becomes so obsessed with gangster roles that he comes to believe he murdered a young woman.

Cast: Macdonald Carey (Bill Morrison), Barbara Shelley (Chris Morrison), Phillip Friend (Steffan), Nadja Regin (Lilli), Leonard Sachs (The Dutchman), Mark Loerering (Jimmy Morrison), Susan Shaw (Actress), Josephine Brown (Grace)

Milestones and Millstones: Macdonald Carey

Comment: A misfire: while the screenplay possesses some minor merits, neither the actors nor the director manage to make anything much of it.

Reviews: "… so unconvincing in its succession of coincidences and improbabilities that it becomes almost disarming… the hero is an American actor—who seems to make all his films in this country." *Monthly Film Bulletin*

"There is no mystery… instead we have an involved and incredible melodrama… it does not seem a very entertaining film, although its conventional action may make it acceptable for undemanding tastes." *CEA Film Report*

The Bay of St Michel/US: Operation Mermaid (1963) DVD: Pattern for Plunder 90 mins (b&w)

"A VOYAGE OF RAPE and MURDER AS FIVE ADVENTURERS LUST FOR BURIED TREASURE"

Acropolis Film/Alfa Studios S.A. Athens; d: John Ainsworth; p: John Ainsworth, Marion Gering; ap: John Brason; assistant p (Greece): Nassos Christides; screenplay: Christopher Davis; ph: Stephen Dade; ed: Tristam Cones; ad: Duncan Sutherland; m: Johnny Douglas

Synopsis: Keenan Wynn leads a group of fellow ex-WW2 soldiers on a hunt for lost Nazi treasure.

Cast: Keenan Wynn (Nick Rawlings), Mai Zetterling (Helene Breton), Ronald Howard (Bill Webb), Rona Anderson (Pru Lawson), Trader Faulkner (Dave Newton), Victor Beaumont (Man), Michael Peake (Captain Starkey), Rudolph Offenbach (Fr. Laurent), Paul Bogdan (General Von Kiesling)

Milestones and Millstones: Keenan Wynn

Comment: Snappy direction moves the story along fast enough to make the implausible but incident-filled story justify its running time.

Reviews: "Like many Secret Service yarns, this has a familiar magaziney quality and tends to lack plausibility, but it certainly bowls along briskly with plenty of incident and some touches of tension." *CEA Film Report*

Children of the Damned (1963) 90 mins

"BEWARE THE EYES THAT PARALYZE!!! ALL-NEW SUSPENSE SHOCKER…
… even more eerie and unearthly than "Village of the Damned"!

Laurence P Bachman Productions/Metro-Goldwyn-Mayer British Studios; d: **Anton M Leader**; p: Laurence P Bachman; ap: Ben Arbeid: screenplay: John Briley; from the novel *The Midwich Cuckoos* by John Wyndham; ph: Davis Boulton; ed: Ernest Walter; sfx: Tom Howard; ad: Eliot Scott; m: Ron Goodwin

Synopsis: Scientists bring six children born at different places around the world with bizarrely high intelligence and special powers to London with unexpected consequences.

Cast: Ian Hendry (Colonel. Tom Lewellyn), Alan Badel (Dr. David Neville), Barbara Ferris (Susan Eliot), Alfred Burke (Colin Webster), Patrick Wymark (Commander), Martin Miller (Professor Gruber), Sheila Allen (Diana Looran), Ralph Michael (Defence Minister), Harold Goldblatt (Professor Gruber)

Milestones and Millstones: Anton M Leader

Comment: The creepy child protagonists owe everything to John Wyndham's original extraterrestrial creations: as written and portrayed, they give the sequel enough eerie science fiction/horror flavour to help maintain interest.

Reviews: "Like most sequels...isn't nearly as good as its predecessor...what weakens this sequels the fact that, unlike the original, it is burdened with a "message"...Anton Leader's lethargic direction doesn't help any." *Variety*

"... a dull, pretentious successor to that marvelous little chiller of several seasons ago, "Village of the Damned." What a comedown... Hamstrung by a lusterless script, Anton M. Leader's dection is hardly inspired." *New York Times*

The Cool Mikado (1963) 81 mins (color)

Gilbert & Sullivan Operas; d: Michael Winner; p: Harold Baim; screenplay: Michael Winner; adaptation by: Maurice Browning; from the libretto of the operetta *The Mikado* by W S Gilbert; additional material: Robert White, Lew Schwartz; ph: Denis Ayling, Martin Curtis; ed: Frank Gilpin; ad: Derrick Barrington; m: Arthur Sullivan

Synopsis: Classic Gilbert and Sullivan comic operetta is heartlessly parodied in modern dress.

Cast: Frankie Howerd (Ko-Ko Flintridge), **Stubby Kaye** (Judge Herbert Mikado /Charlie Hotfleisch), Mike Winters (Mike), Bernie Winters (Bernie), Tommy Cooper (Poo-Bah, Private Eye), Dennis Price (Ronald Fortescue), Peter Barkworth (Fanshaw), Burt Kwouk (Art School Teacher), Lionel Blair (Nanki), Pete Murray (Man in Boudoir), Tsai Chin (Pitty-Sing)

Milestones and Millstones: Stubby Kaye

Comment: The whining noise on the soundtrack was probably made by Gilbert and Sullivan spinning in their graves: witless waste of film stock for G&S devotees and not much better for anyone seeking a good movie either.

Reviews: "It will make Gilbert and Sullivan fans squirm, but even for the uncritical and easily pleased audiences, it is rather feeble musical comedy entertainment." *CEA Film Report*

Maniac/US: The Maniac (1963) 86 mins (b&w)

"The maniac stalks his wife…his daughter…their lover!"

Hammer Films; d: Michael Carreras; p/screenplay: Jimmy Sangster; ph: Wilkie Cooper; ed: Tom Simpson; pd: Bernard Robinson; ad: Edward Carrick; m: Stanley Back

Synopsis: Down-and out-American painter Kerwin Mathews is stranded in France where he is persuaded by a Frenchwoman to help her murderer husband to escape from prison.

Cast: Kerwin Mathews (Jeff Farrell), Nadia Gray (Eve Beynat), Donald Houston (Henri), Liliane Brousse (Annette Beynat), George Pastell (Inspector Etienne), Arnold Diamond (Janiello), Norman Bird (Salon), Justine Lord (Grace), Jerold Wells (Giles), André Maranne (Voice of Salon)

Milestones and Millstones: Kerwin Mathews

Comment: Leaden direction by Michael Carreras hardly helps this Hammer B film psychological thriller: the climax is taut but a tad too late to make it a genre great.

Reviews: "An incredible confusing and unappealing melodrama…a product of England's usually reliable Hammer Films…Michael Carreras directed, although there's not much evidence of it." *Variety*

"Cut-to-pattern Hammer gangster thriller…already let down by inferior playing (Kerwin Matthews is a wooden hero…)… finally and decisively trampled into dim mediocrity by the direction of Michael Carreras, with its marked absence of film sense." *Monthly Film Bulletin*

The Old Dark House (1963) 86 mins (b&w & color)

"The murder mystery with a difference: YOU DIE LAUGHING!"

Columbia Pictures Corporation/William Castle Productions/Hammer Films; d: **William Castle**; p: William Castle, Anthony Hinds; Donna Holloway: screenplay: Robert Dillon; from the book *The Old Dark House* by J B Priestley; ph: Arthur Grant: ed: James Needs; sfx: Les Bowie; ad: Bernard Robinson: m: Benjamin Frankel

Synopsis: American car dealer Tom Poston, who works in London, delivers a car to an old family mansion and lands up in trouble with the living and the dead.

Cast: Tom Poston (Tom Penderel), Robert Morley (Roderick Femm), Janette Scott (Cecily Femm), Joyce Grenfell (Agatha Femm), Mervyn Johns (Potiphar Femm), Fenella Fielding (Morgana Femm), Peter Bull (Caspar/Jasper Femm), Danny Greeen (Morgan Femm), John Harvey (Club Receptionist)

Milestones and Millstones: William Castle, Tom Poston

Comment: Major disservice to the 1932 Karloff classic: deservedly forgettable remake is less a remake as a witless assault, neither scary nor funny, despite Hammer founder Michael Carreras stating "It will take the mickey out of horror pictures in a most original and entertainingly way."

Reviews: "…a laboriously arch and broad blend of humor and the creeps. It still leaves the old J.B. Priestley property as defunct as a doornail. Even a picturesque cast…can't rejuvenate it." *New York Times*

"Anyone hoping for something even fractionally as enjoyable as James Whale's *Old Dark House* will be sadly disappointed… this comedy-shocker is abysmal, repeat abysmal, from beginning to end." *Monthly Film Bulletin*

The Sicilians (1963) 70 mins (b&w)

Butcher's Film Service; d: Ernest Morris; p: John J Phillips, Ronald Liles; screenplay: Ronald Liles, Reginald Hearne; ph: Geoffrey Faithfull; ed: Henry Richardson; ad: Harry White; m: Johnny Gregory

Synopsis: American Embassy aide in London Robert Hutton and a Scotland Yard Inspector join forces to rescue the kidnapped son of a Mafioso.

Cast: Robert Hutton (Calvin Adams), Reginald Marsh (Inspector Webb), Ursula Howells (Madame Perrault), Alex Scott (Henri Perrault), Susan Denny (Carole), Robert Ayres (Angelo Di Marco), Eric Pohlmann (Inspector Bressin), Patricia Hayes (Airplane passenger), Warren Mitchell (O'Leary)

Milestones and Millstones: Robert Hutton

Comment: Nothing much to remember: a British B movie that is well enough made but mediocre.

Reviews: "A mundane piece of direction flatly directed and unconvincingly scripted." *Monthly Film Bulletin*

Siege of the Saxons (1963) 85 mins (color)

"SAXON LEGIONS STORM THE FLAMING WALLS OF KING ARTHUR'S CAMELOT"

Columbia Pictures/Ameran; d: **Nathan Juran**; p: **Charles H Schneer**, Jud Kinberg; screenplay: Jud Kinberg; John Kohn; ph: Wilkie Cooper, Jack Mills; ed: Maurice Rootes; ad: Bill Constable; m: Laurie Johnson

Synopsis: King Arthur is recovering from an illness but does not know his host is in league with the Saxons who want to seize power.

Cast: Janette Scott (Katherine), Ronald Lewis (Robert Marshall), Ronald Howard (Edmund of Cornwall), Mark Dignam (King Arthur), John Laurie (Merlin), Jerome Willis (The Limping Man), Charles Lloyd-Pack (Blacksmith), Peter Mason (Young Priest)

Milestones and Millstones: Nathan Juran, Charles H Schneer

Comment: A low-budget star-free second feature historical swashbuckler that looks better than it deserves because costumes and props from other more expensive Columbia films, *The Black Knight* (1954) and 1963's *Sword of Lancelot*, were reused to beef up the production.

Reviews: "… Constantly hampered by flat direction and cramped settings. The film rarely makes the most of its opportunities." *Monthly Film Bulletin*

"Presented as a straight action adventure film is not intended to be quite as comic as it often turns out to be…the team has come up with about every cliché invented for this type of film. Nathan Juran directed serviceably but with little imagination." *Variety*

Station Six-Sahara (1963) 99 mins (b&w)

Only one woman and five longing, desperate men...!
A story as violent and searing as the desert sun!"

CCC Films London/CCC Filmkunst; d: Seth Holt: ep: Gene Kutowski, Artur Brauner; p: Victor Lyndon; screenplay: Bryan Forbes, Brian Clemens; based on the play *Men Without a Past* by Jean Martet: ph: Gerald Gibbs; ed: Alastair McIntire; ad: Jack Stephens; m: Ron Grainer

Synopsis: Sexy Carroll Baker sets the men's pulses racing when she turns up at an oil station in the Sahara Desert.

Cast: Carroll Baker (Catherine), Peter Van Eyck (Kramer), Ian Bannen (Fletcher), Denholm Elliott (Macey), Hansjörg Felmy (Martin), Mario Adorf (Santos), **William 'Biff' McGuire** (Jimmy), Harry Baird (Sailor)

Milestones and Millstones: Carroll Baker, William 'Biff' McGuire

Comment: Sex sells and director Holt (later to become a minor auteur among fashionable film lovers and trendy reviewers) skillfully uses Baker to serve up as much sexual titillation as the then current censors would allow.

Reviews: "What started as murderous irony soon turns into a steamy farce that couldn't matter less. The purring Miss Baker seems perfectly at home in No Man's Land but she has managed to seduce the picture as well." *New York Times*

"... for once in a British film some real erotic tension is palpable on the screen." *The Times*

"... a tough slam-bang script... at least this is filming with the courage of its own clichés." *Monthly Film Bulletin*

The Curse of the Mummy's Tomb (1964) 81 mins (color)

"HALF-BONE, HALF-BANDAGE, AND ALL
BLOOD-CURDLING HORROR!"

Hammer Film Productions/Swallow Productions Ltd; d/p: Michael Carreras; ap: William Hill; screenplay: Henry Younger (aka Michael Carreras); ph: Otto Heller; ed: Eric Boyd-Perkins; pd: Bernard Robinson; m: Carlo Martelli

Synopsis: An ancient Egyptian mummy brought to London in his sarcophagus by an American showman is woken up and goes on a bandaged rampage.

Cast: Terence Morgan (Adam Beauchamp), Ronald Howard (John Bray), **Fred Clark** (Alexander King), Jeanne Roland (Annett Dubois), George Pastell (Hashmi Bey), Jack Gwillim (Sir Giles Dalrymple), John Paul (Inspector Mackenzie), Dickie Owen (The Mummy), Michael Ripper (Achmed)

Milestones and Millstones: Fred Clark

Comment: Michael Carreras was no Fisher and, even covered with bandages, Dickie Owen's Undead Egyptian failed to reach the heights of Christopher Lee in Hammer's 1959 classic *The Mummy*.

Reviews: "... just the usual old bundle of rags on two lumbering legs...some of the incident is ridiculous... however the sewer finale has a moderate grandeur." *Monthly Film Bulletin*

"...modest and rather slapdash horror pic...mediocre thesping and direction, obvious backcloths, ponderous dialog...a below-average make this a below-average entry from the Hammer horror stable...the liveliest performance comes from Fred Clark." *Variety*

Victim Five/Code 7, Victim 5 (1964) 89 mins (color)

"A very special agent with a code that means...
He Can Go All the Way!"

Towers of London Productions; d: Robert Lynn; p: Harry Alan Towers, Skip Steloff; screenplay: Peter Yeldham; story by: Peter Welbeck (aka Harry Alan Towers); ph: Nicolas Roeg; ed: John Trumper; m: Johnny Douglas

Synopsis: Private detective Lex Barker joins the local police to track down a murderer in Cape Town.

Cast: Lex Barker (Steve Martin), Ronald Fraser (Inspector Dickie Lean), Ann Smyrner (Helga Swenson), Véronique Vendell (Gina), Walter Rilla (Wexler), Dietmar Schönherr (Dr. Paul Bryson), Percy Sieff (George Anderson), Gustel Gundelach (Hans Kramer), Gert Van Den Berg (Vanberger), Howard Davis (Rawlings)

Milestones and Millstones: Lex Barker

Comment: A typical trashy Towers programmer, this attempt to cash in on 007 is a routine thrills-suspense-action offering whose South African locations make it seem a tad more interesting than it actually is.

Reviews: "Still another "takeoff" on the successful James Bond films, this British produced but South African filmed variation has enough action and scenic beauty to enable it to do well in the thriller market…biggest drawback…is the casting of Lex Barker." *Variety*

Devil Doll (1964) 81 mins (b&w)

"WHAT IS THE STRANGE, TERRIFYING EVIL SECRET OF THE DUMMY… AND WHY IS IT LOCKED IN A CAGE EVERY NIGHT?"

Galaworldfilmproductions/Gordon Films; d: Lindsay Shonteff; ep: **Richard Gordon**; p: Kenneth Rive, Lindsay Shonteff; screenplay: George Bentley (aka Ronald Kinnoch), Lance Z Hargreaves (aka **Charles F Vetter**); story by: Frederick E Smith; ph; Gerald Gibbs; ed: Ernest Bullingham; pd: Stan Shield

Synopsis: Ventriloquist-hypnotist Bryant Halliday traps a human soul in his malevolent dummy Hugo and embarks on an orgy of evil.

Cast: Bryant Halliday (The Great Vorelli), William Sylvester (Mark English), Yvonne Romain (Marianne), Sandra Dorne (Vorelli's assistant Magda), Karel Stepanek (Dr Heller), Francis De Wolff (Dr Keisling), Norah Nicholson (Aunt Eve), Philip Ray (Uncle Walter), Alan Gifford (Bob Garrett), Heidi Erich (Grace)

Milestones and Millstones: Bryant Halliday, Richard Gordon

Comment: Yet another 'evil mannequin' shocker (cf Tod Browning in 1939) and a not very good one: the original story, published in 1951 in *London Mystery Magazine*, earned the author £10. Original director Sidney Furie got a better offer and sensibly passed the project on to his fellow-Canadian Shonteff.

Reviews: "…few horrific moments and its weirdness is of a mild order. Its lack of conviction or excitement is a drawback, the acting is not particularly impressive, and the pace is slow with much dialogue and little action." *CEA Film Report*

The Earth Dies Screaming (1964) 62 mins (b&w)

"Who…Or What Were They…Who Tried To Wipe All Living Creatures Off The Face of The Earth?"

Lippert Films; d: Terence Fisher; p: **Robert J Lippert**, Jack Parsons; screenplay: Henry Cross; ph: Arthur Lavis; ed: Robert Winter; ad: George Provis; m: Elizabeth Lutyens
   Synopsis: When aliens invade the earth, their human kills return from the dead as zombies.
   Cast: Willard Parker (Jeff Nolan), Virginia Field (Peggy), Dennis Price (Taggart), Dennis Price (Quinn Taggart), Thorley Walters (Edgar Otis), Vanda Godsell (Violet Courtland), David Spenser (Mel), Anna Palk (Lorna)
   Milestones and Millstones: Willard Parker, Robert J Lippert
   Comment: Fisher's days as an editor pay off well, delivering more undead terror than his minimal budget and short shooting schedule deserve and beating George A Romero to the zombie punch by several years. Contemporary reviewers disagreed since Fisher had yet to achieve auteur status.
   Reviews: "This is rather juvenile nonsense and it takes a little too long getting to the real excitement, but it will get by in most situations." *Kine Weekly*
   "After an effective opening, this tale of the survivors of a catastrophic attack by aliens develops lamely… might get by as a second for uncritical audiences." *CEA Film Report*

East of Sudan (1964) 85 mins (color)

"You Live Every Terror Known to Man…When You Dare to Cross…
EAST OF SUDAN"

Columbia Pictures/Ameran; d/p: **Nathan Juran**; ep: **Charles H Schneer**; screenplay: **Jud Kinberg**; ph: Wilkie Cooper; ed: Ernest Hosler; sfx: Ted Samuels; ad: Lionel Couch; m: Laurie Johnson
   Synopsis: A British soldier helps an emir's daughter and her governess escape to safety during the Mahdist insurrection in 19th century Anglo-Egyptian Sudan.

Cast: Anthony Quayle (Private Richard Baker), Sylvia Syms (Miss Margaret Woodville), Derek Fowlds (Murchison), Johnny Sekka (Kimrasi), Jenny Agutter (Asua), Derek Blomfield (Second Major), Harold Coyne (Major Harris), Desmond Davies (Aide), Edward Ellis (Arab), Joseph Layode (Gondoko)

Milestones and Millstones: Nathan Juran, Charles H Schneer, Judd Kinberg

Comment: Good cinematography and energetic action footage, some borrowed from other films, helps make this second feature offering very watchable.

Reviews: "Plenty of action in this workmanlike dualer...much of the effect of the pic is lost because of its obvious studio setting the easygoing cinema patron will not worry unduly, however..." *Variety*

"Shamelessly unoriginal hokum... Nathan Juran could direct this sort of thing blindfold, and for once would have appear to have done so." *Monthly Film Bulletin*

The Eyes of Annie Jones (1964) 73 mins (b&w)

"Eyes so young... yet they knew man's every passion and crime!"

Parroch-McCallum/Associated Producers; d: **Reginald Le Borg**; p:Jack Parsons, Neil McCallum; screenplay: Henry Slesar, Louis Vittes; ph: Peter Hennessey; ed: Robert Winter; ad: George Provis; m: Buxton Orr

Synopsis: A murder results after a wealthy man is kidnapped and her aunt gets a young girl with ESP powers to help foil the abductors.

Cast: Richard Conte (David Wheeler), Franesca Annis (Annie Jones), Joyce Carey (Aunt Helen), Myrtle Reed (Carol Wheeler), Shay Gorman (Lucas), Victor Brooks (Sergeant Henry), Jean Lodge (Geraldine Wheeler), Alan Haines (Constable Marlowe), Mark Dignam (Orphanage director)

Milestones and Millstones: Richard Conte, Reginald Le Borg

Comment: A sleepwalking girl with extrasensory powers is an offbeat subject but rather too much leaden direction leaves the film firmly in the 'routine B Feature' slot.

Reviews: "...odd little detective thriller compensates with some rather good characterisation, and, on the whole, rather good acting...

unfortunately, the film is hamstring throughout by uninspired direction." *Monthly Film Bulletin*

"The characters in this mystery tale are not stereotypes and are made plausible by the acting… holds the attention well and contains some mild suspense." *CEA Film Report*

The Horror of it All (1964) 75 mins (b&w)

"THE ZANIEST BUNCH OF GHOULS TO HAUNT A HOUSE!"
"Just sit back and Howl at the Chill of it all!!"

Lippert Pictures; d: Terence Fisher; p: **Robert Lippert**, Margia Dean; screenplay: Ray Russell; ph: Arthur Lavis; ed: Robert Winter; ad: Harry White; m: Douglas Gamley; song: *The Horror of It All*, words and music by Pat Boone

Synopsis: American Pat Boone meets up with mystery and murder when he goes to his English girlfriend's grim family mansion to ask for her hand in marriage.

Cast: Pat Boone (John Robinson), Erica Rogers (Cynthia Marley), Dennis Price (Cornwallis Marley), Andre Melly (Natalie Marley), Valentine Dyall (Reginald Marley), Archie Duncan (Muldoon Marley), Eric Chitty (Grandpa Marley), Jack Bligh (Percival Marley), Oswald Laurence (Doctor)

Milestones and Millstones: Pat Boone, Robert Lippert

Comment: Understandably not one of Fisher's favourites: the combination of a weak screenplay that lacks in both good scares and amusing comedy and a leading man unsuited to his role add up to a forgettable miss.

Reviews: "There are some engaging ideas in this burlesque, but they lie buried fathoms deep beneath an inept script and dispirited direction." *Monthly Film Bulletin*

"… a weak mixture of unfunny gags and standard horror situations that get laughs when they aren't supposed to… Pat Boone's thesping is on a high school level." *Variety*

Night Train to Paris (1964) 64 mins (b&w)

"MURDER RIDES AMONG THE MERRYMAKERS"

Lippert Films; d: Robert Douglas; p: **Robert L Lippert**, Jack Parsons; screenplay: Henry Cross (aka Harry Spalding); ph: Arthur Lavis; ed: Robert Winter; ad: George Provis; m: Kenny Graham
 Synopsis: When former OSS agent Leslie Nielsen who now lives in London agrees to help his former superior officer he ends up Paris with foreign spies trying to kill him
 Cast: Leslie Nielsen (Alan Holiday), Alizia Gur (Catherine Carrel), Dorinda Stevens (Olive Davies), Eric Portman (Krogh), Edina Ronay (Julie), André Maranne (Louis Vernay), Cyril Raymond (Inspector Fleming), Stanley Morgan (Plainclothesman), Hugh Latimer (Jules Lemoine), Jenny White (Vernay's model)
 Milestones and Millstones: Leslie Nielsen, Robert L Lippert
 Comment: Succeeds in outstaying its 64-minute welcome: very minor second feature thriller on all levels.
 Reviews: "Weak invention, mediocre playing an nondescript direction make this a very flat-footed espionage melodrama… the more lively climax, with its moderately unexpected twist, is insufficient compensation for the film's prevailing mediocrity." *Monthly Film Bulletin*

Witchcraft (1964) 79 mins (b&w)

"COULD THEY STOP THE MYSTIC CULT THAT KILLED BY THE BLOOD CURSE!
ONLY THE WITCH DETECTOR CAN SAVE YOU FROM THE EERIE WEB OF THE UNKNOWN!"

Lippert Films; d: Don Sharp: p: **Robert L Lippert**, Jack Parsons; screenplay **Harry Spalding**; ph: Arthur Lavis; ed: Robert Winter; ad: George Provis; Carlo Martelli
 Synopsis: Lon Chaney Jr and a woman burned alive as a witch in the 17th century return from the dead to seek vengeance against the descendants of their tormentors.

Cast: Lon Chaney Jr (Morgan Whitlock), Jack Hedley (Bill Lanier), Jill Dixon (Tracy Lanier), David Weston (Todd Lanier), Diane Clare (Amy Whitlock), Yvette Rees (Vanessa Whitlock), Marie Ney (Malvina Lanier), Viola Keats (Helen Lanier); Victor Brooks (Inspector Baldwin), Barry Linehan (Myles Forrester)

Milestones and Millstones: Lon Chaney Jr, Robert J Lippert, Harry Spalding

Comment: Chaney Jr serves up the requisite over-cooked performance in an under-cast but smartly directed and holding second-feature shocker.

Reviews: "Eerie music, low-key photography, competent acting and a gimmick-filled plot combine to make the horror-feature "Witchcraft" a good example of its kind... Chaney tends to overact." *Variety*

You Must Be Joking! (1964) 100 mins (b&w)

"IT'S A MAD-MAD-WHIRL OF A HUNT FOR GUYS AND GALS AND GOODIES!"

Ameran Films; d: Michael Winner; p: **Charles H Schneer**; screenplay: Alan Hackney; story by: Alan Hackney, Michael Winner; ph: Geoffrey Unsworth; ed: Bernard Gribble; sfx: Garth Inns, Curly Nelhams; ad: Maurice Carter; m: Laurie Johnson

Synopsis: A British army psychologist sends USAAF lieutenant Michael Callan and four British soldiers on a wild 48-hour initiative test involving a scavenger hunt.

Cast: Michael Callan (Lieutenant Tim Morton), Lionel Jeffries (Sergeant Major McGregor), Denholm Elliott (Captain Tabasco), Wilfrid Hyde-White (General Lockwood), Bernard Cribbins (Sergeant Clegg), Terry-Thomas (Major Foskett) James Robertson Justice (Librarian), Gabriella Licudi (Annabelle Nash)

Milestones and Millstones: Charles H Schneer

Comment: Slapstick comic capers relying on the long roster of popular British comic actors to support imported American star Callan: director Winner, before he found fame and profit in brutal action thrillers in the *Death Wish* vein delivers corny comedy in Swinging Sixties style.

Reviews: "No strain on the brain, it provides fairly consistently amusing, light entertainment… Callan (presumably introduced to boost American interest?) is pleasantly dashing." *Variety*

Catacombs/The Woman Who Wouldn't Die (1965) 84 minutes (b&w)

… a Masterpiece of Suspense! THE STORY OF THE GIRL WHO TWICE RETURNED FROM THE GRAVE!"

Jack Parsons-Neil McCallum Productions; d: **Gordon Hessler**; p: Jack Parsons; co-p: Neil McCallum; screenplay: Daniel Mainwaring; from the novel *Catacombs* by Jay Bennett; ph: Arthur Lavis; ed: Robert Winter; ad: George Provis; m: Carlo Martelli

Synopsis: Faithless husband Gary Merrill kills his businesswoman wife: but does she stay dead?

Cast: Gary Merrill (Raymond Garth), Georgina Cookson (Ellen Garth), Jane Merrow (Alice Taylor), Neil McCallum (Richard 'Dick' Corbett), Rachel Thomas (Christine), Jack Train (Solicitor), Frederick Piper (Police Inspector Merkot)

Milestones and Millstones: Gary Merrill, Gordon Hessler, Daniel Mainwaring

Comment: A smart screenplay and sufficiently taut direction raise this B movie into A movie territory. The screenplay is based on a book that was initially considered for Hitchcock's television show.

Reviews: "… comes off something better than average…taut direction by Gordon Hessler of Dan Mainwaring's spare but neat screenplay." *Variety*

City of Fear (1965) 90 mins (b&w)

"ESPIONAGE…TERROR…PASSION! Where they play the World's most deadly game… Matching wits with beauties as the pawns!"

Towers of London Productions; d: Peter Bezencenet; p: Harry Alan Towers, Arthur Steloff, Sandy Howard; screenplay: Harry Alan Towers, Max

Bourne; ph: Martin Curtis; ed: Peter Boita; ad: Peter Best; m: Johnny Douglas

Synopsis: During the Cold War, a Canadian journalist becomes caught up in espionage and romance in Eastern Europe.

Cast: Paul Maxwell (Mike Foster), **Terry Moore** (Suzan), Marisa Mell (Ilona), Albert Lieven (Dr Paul Kovak), Pincas Braun (Ferenc), Helga Lehner (Eva), Zsuzsa Bánki (Magda), Brigitte Heiberg (Zsu Zsu), Maria Rohm (Maid)

Milestones and Millstones: Terry Moore

Comment: Editor-turned-director Bezencenet does better than might be expected when faced with a script co-written by Harry Alan Towers but the film never manages to rise above its low-low budget supporting feature origins.

Reviews: "Conventional escape thriller, with a more than usually implausible plot. But it is quite crisply done in its own way." *Monthly Film Bulletin*

City Under the Sea/City in the Sea/War Gods of the Deep
(1965) 84 mins (color)

"They dared the most fantastic journey that has ever challenged imagination!"

Bruton Film Productions; d: **Jacques Tourneur**; p: **Samuel Z Arkoff**, George Willoughby, **Daniel Haller**; screenplay: Charles Bennett, **Louis M Hayward**, David Whitaker; from the story *City in the Sea* by Edgar Allan Poe; ph: Stephen Dade; ed: Gordon Hales; sfx: Les Bowie, Frank George, Eiji Tsuburaya from movie *Atragon* (1963); ad: Frank White; m: Stanley Black

Synopsis: In 1903 Cornwall American mining engineer Tab Hunter ends up in a lost undersea city populated by never-ageing smugglers, gill-equipped slaves and ruled by a tyrannical overlord.

Cast: Tab Hunter (Ben Harris), David Tomlinson (Harold Tufnell-Jones), **Vincent Price** (Captain Sir Hugh Tregathian), **Susan Hart** (Jill Tregellis), John Le Mesurier (Reverend Jonathan Ives), Derek Newark (Dan), Roy Patrick (Simon), Dennis Blake (Harry), Jim Spearman (Jack), Tom Selby (George)

Milestones and Millstones: Tab Hunter, Vincent Price, Daniel Haller, Jacques Tourneur, Susan Hart, Samuel Z Arkoff, Louis M Hayward

Comment: Impressive (for the budget) sets, some good special effects and a spectacular climax help disguise the relative dullness of the intervening exposition.

Reviews: "... a brisk and colorful sci-fi actioner...excellent direction and special effects plus good performances, provides zip for standard plot... Tourneur rates special mention for drawing good performances and framing them adroitly." *Variety*

Coast of Skeletons (1965) 90 mins (color)

> They fought for hidden diamonds...sunken gold...
> and a woman's desire!

Towers of London Films/Hallam Productions; d: Robert Lynn; p: Harry Alan Towers, Oliver A Unger: screenplay: Anthony Scott Veitch; story by: Peter Welbeck (aka Harry Alan Towers); inspired by the story *Sanders of The River* by Edgar Wallace; ph: Stephen Dade; ed: John Trumper; m: Christopher Whelen

Synopsis: British insurance investigator Harry Sanders probes diamond and gold smuggling in South Africa masterminded by villain Dale Robertson.

Cast: Richard Todd (Commissioner Harry Sanders), **Dale Robertson** (A J Magnus), Heinz Drache (Janny von Koltze), Marianne Koch (Helga), Elga Andersen (Elisabeth von Koltze), Derek Nimmo (Tom Hamilton), Gabriel Bayman (Charlie Singer), George Leech (Carlo Seton)

Milestones and Millstones: Dale Robertson

Comment: Some attractive South African locations fail to compensate for an otherwise typically underpowered Harry Alan Towers second feature. The use of the word "inspired" (by... Edgar Wallace) is unintentionally amusing since the film itself is hardly uninspiring.

Reviews: "Much of the technique is derivative of television series with a minimum of character development and a failure to establish plot continuity... Robertson has a suitably nihilistic approach..." *Films and Filming*

"It's fast, tough and thoroughly saturated with excellent African scenery, in good color." *New York Times*

The Crooked Road (1965) 92 mins (b&w)

"Bribe him, frame him...poison him...if necessary, seduce him... do what you must—BUT STOP THE AMERICAN...!"

Argo Film Productions/Nora/Triglar Films; d: Don Chaffey; p: Jack Lamont, David Henley; screenplay: J Garrison, Don Chaffey; from the novel *The Big Story* by Morris L West; ph: Stephen Dade; ed: Peter Tanner; m: Bojan Adamic

Synopsis: 10 years after Duke Stewart Granger married the woman they both loved, journalist Robert Ryan sets out for revenge and to topple the Balkan leader.

Cast: Robert Ryan (Richard Ashley), **Stewart Granger** (Duke of Orgagna), Nadia Gray (Cosima), Katherine Woodville (Elena), Marius Goring (Harlequin), Robert Rietty (Chief of Police)

Milestones and Millstones: Stewart Granger

Comment: Too much talk and unconvincing melodrama leave the stars stranded and working hard to inject some life and entertainment value into the narrative.

Reviews: "Made in 1964, this is a slow-moving, talkative and stagey story, barely convincing and seldom exciting but it has the benefit of star appeal, good performances by the two leading men...moderate supporting fare for the average audience." *CEA Film Report*

The Curse of the Fly (1965) 86 mins (b&w)

"HUMANS INVISIBLY TELEPORTED THROUGH TIME AND SPACE... Re-entering Earth as Half-Human Monsters from the 4th Dimension!"

Lippert Films; d: Don Sharp; p: **Robert J Lippert**, Jack Parsons; screenplay: **Harry Spalding**; ph: Basil Emmott; ed: Robert White; ad: Harry White; special effects makeup (sfx mu): Harold Fletcher; m: Bert Shefter

Synopsis: Monsters are created when things go badly wrong for scientists experimenting in matter transmission.

Cast: Brian Donlevy (Henri Delambre), George Baker (Martin Delambre), Carole Grey (Patricia Stanley), Jeremy Wilkins (Inspector

Ronet), Yvette Rees (Wan), Michael Graham (Albert Delambre), Charles Carson (Inspector Charas), Burt Kwouk (Tai), Mary Manson (Judith), Stan Simmons (The Creature)

Milestones and Millstones: Brian Donlevy, Robert J Lippert, Harry Spalding

Comment: When in doubt, seek a sequel: this acceptable second feature shocker followed 1958's *The Fly* and the following year's *Return of the Fly* but, unlike its predecessors, was filmed in England with Donlevy as imported box-office bait.

Reviews: "… the film attempts to make good the lack of surprise by multiplying the horror of its effects… Sharp had a deft way with interesting shock effects." *Kine Weekly*

Curse of the Voodoo/Voodoo Blood Death/Curse of Simba
(1965) 77 mins (b&w)

"JUNGLE TERROR! *NATIVE FURY!* BLOOD SACRIFICE OF THE SIMBAZI!"

Futurama Entertainment Corp/Galaworldfilm Productions-Gordon Films; d: Lindsay Shonteff; p: **Richard Gordon**, Kenneth Rive; screenplay: Tony O'Grady (aka Brian Clemens), additional scenes and dialogue: Leigh Vance; ph: Gerald Gibbs; ed: Barry Vince; ad: Tony Inglis; m: Brian Fahey

Synopsis: After white hunter Bryant Halliday shoots a lion in Africa he ends up as the victim of a voodoo curse imposed on him by a lion-worshipping tribe.

Cast: Bryant Halliday (Mike Stacey), Dennis Price (Major Lomas), Lisa Daniely (Janet Stacey), Mary Kerridge (Janet's Mother), Ronald Leigh Hunt (Doctor), Jon Witty (Police Inspector), Jean Lodge (Mrs. Lomas), Danny Daniels (Simbaza), Denis Alaba Peters (Saidi), Tony Thawnton (Radlett)

Milestones and Millstones: Bryant Halliday, Richard Gordon

Comment: For all its titles *Curse of the Voodoo, Voodoo Blood Death* and *Curse of Simba* this aspirant shocker adds up to little more than simply stale schlock that even genre completists might wish they had missed.

Reviews: "With few real horror or suspense jolts, a cliché story, and only occasional action, *"Curse of the Voodoo"* stacks up in the sub-standard programmer category... for horror-suspense patrons, this kind of mild fare has low lure." *Variety*

Die, Monster, Die! /Monster of Terror (1965) 80 mins (color)

"Can you face the ULTIMATE in DIABOLISM...
can you stand PURE TERROR?
It COULD happen! It MAY happen! It MIGHT happen! To YOU!"

Alta Vista Productions/American International Productions; d: **Daniel Haller**: ep: **Samuel Z Arkoff, James M Nicholson**; p: **Louis M Hayward**, Pat Green; screenplay: **Jerry Sohl**; from the short story *The Colour Out of Space* by H P Lovecraft; ph: Paul Beeson; ed: Alfred Cox; ad: Colin Southcott; sfx: Wally Veevers, Ernie Sullivan; m: Don Banks

Synopsis: American college student Nick Adams visits his fiancée's family and faces mounting horror when he finds her father Boris Karloff is using a radioactive meteorite to mutate plants, animals and people.

Cast: Boris Karloff (Nahum Whitley), **Nick Adams** (Stephen Reinhart), Freda Jackson (Letitia Witley), Suzan Farmer (Susan Witely), Terence De Marney (Merwyn), Patrick Magee (Dr Henderson), Paul Farrell (Jason), Gretchen Franklin (Miss Bailey), Sidney Bromley (Pierce), Billy Milton (Henry)

Milestones and Millstones: Boris Karloff, Nick Adams, Daniel Haller, Samuel Z Arkoff, James H Nicholson, Louis M Heayward, Jerry Sohl

Comment: Karloff towers effortlessly over the other players and, with Haller creating an effective atmosphere of mounting unease and terror, the film frequently rises above its second feature origins.

Reviews: "Routine sci-fi programmer... Boris Karloff in for marquee value. Very good production values, but slowly paced in scripting and direction...Karloff is appropriately menacing." *Variety*

Fanatic/US: Die! Die! My Darling! (1965) 97 mins (color)

"THE ULTIMATE IN SHEER SHOCK! ... THE ULTIMATE IN STABBING SUSPENSE! ... DON'T DARE MISS IT!"

Columbia Pictures Corporation/Hammer Films; d: Silvio Narizzano; p: Antony Hinds; screenplay: **Richard Matheson**; from the novel *Nightmare* by Anne Blaisdell; ph: Arthur Ibbetson; ed; John Dunsford; pd: Peter Proud; m: Wilfred Josephs

Synopsis: When young American Stephanie Powers comes to Britain to be married she ends up imprisoned by deranged religious maniac Tallulah Bankhead.

Cast: Tallulah Bankhead (Mrs. Trefoile), **Stefanie Powers** (Patricia Carroll), Peter Vaughan (Harry), Maurice Kaufman (Alan Glentower), Yootha Joyce (Anna), Donald Sutherland (Joseph), Gwendolyn Watts (Gloria), Robert Dorning (Ormsby), Philip Gilbert (Oscar), Winifred Dennis (Shopkeeper)

Milestones and Millstones: Tallulah Bankhead, Stefanie Powers, Richard Matheson

Comment: Not as good a shocker as it is claimed to be, although seeing a nascent Donald Sutherland is interesting: Bankhead, in one of her final screen appearances, is more ham than Hammer.

Reviews: " .. a surprisingly frightening horror thriller and a hoot-fest for lovers of over-the-top acting... Bankhead, in her last film, has never been known for her subtle acting, but in this she lets go of all restraint and gives a performance equal to that of Bette Davis in *What Ever Happened to Baby Jane?* Her maniacal intensity is comic, camp, and surprisingly effective." *The New York Times*

"... should click with fright fans. Expert thesping by Tallulah Bankhead...Powers... does a very creditable job....Narizzano's direction is imaginative." *Variety*

Five Golden Dragons (1965) 93 mins (color)

"girls! gold! intrigue!"

Blansfillm/Constantin Film Produktion/Sargon; d: Jeremy Summers; p: Harry Alan Towers; screenplay: Peter Welbeck (aka Harry Alan Towers);

from the story *Sanders* by Edgar Wallace; ph: John Von Kotze; ed: Donald J Cohen; ad: Scott MacGregor; m: Malcolm Lockyer

Synopsis: American playboy Robert Cummings falls foul of the nefarious schemes of five master criminals in Hong Kong.

Cast: Robert Cummings (Bob Mitchell), Rupert Davies (Commander Sanders), Margaret Lee (Magda), Maria Perschy (Margret), Klaus Kinski (Gert), Maria Rohm (Ingrid), **Dan Duryea** (Dragon ≠1), **George Raft** (Dragon ≠2) **Brian Donlevy** (Dragon ≠3), Christopher Lee (Dragon ≠4), Yukari Itô (Singer)

Milestones and Millstones: Robert Cummings, Dan Duryea, George Raft, Brian Donlevy

Comment: Complete hokum decorated with attractive Hong Kong locations and an overwrought screenplay by sensibly pseudonymous producer Towers: for Cummings, Duryea, Raft and Donlevy, a depressing reminder that most movie careers eventually go downhill.

Reviews: A fast-moving adventure story." *Kine Weekly*

"…unfortunately lacks anything good to make it memorable although there are a few bad things which might stick in your mind." *The Movie Scene*

Hysteria (1965) 85 mins (b&w)

TERRIFYING SUSPENSE…it will shock you out of your seat!"

Hammer Films; d: Freddie Francis; p, screenplay: Jimmy Sangster; ph: John Wilcox; ed: James Needs; ad: Edward Carrick; m: Don Banks

Synopsis: American Robert Webber wakes up in a London hospital suffering from amnesia after a car crash and then finds himself involved in a bizarre murder plan.

Cast: Robert Webber (Chris Smith), Anthony Newlands (Dr. Keller), Jennifer Jayne (Gina McConnell), Maurice Denham (Hemmings), Lelia Goldoni (Denise James), Peter Woodthorpe (Marcus Allan), Sandra Boize (English Girl), Sue Lloyd (French Girl), Marianne Stone (Marcus Allan's secretary)

Milestones and Millstones: Robert Webber

Comment: While Sangster's screenplay features familiar film noir tropes, Freddie Francis maintains a suitably fast pace and delivers an enjoyable suspenseful faux-Hitchcockian thriller.

Reviews: "… a well-made little shocker that should please audiences who catch it at the bottom of a double bill…script contains many clichés of the genre but production values are solid and Freddie Francis' direction is brisk and intelligent." *Variety*

The Murder Game (1965) 76 mins (b&w)

"Pick a victim…Choose a weapon…And go for the kill…
BECAUSE YOU'RE 'IT' IN THE MURDER GAME"

Lippert Pictures; d: **Sidney Salkow**; p: **Robert L Lippert**, Jack Parsons; screenplay: **Harry Spalding**; story by: Irving Yergin; ph: Geoffrey Faithfull; ed: Robert Winter; ad: Harry White; m: Carlo Martelli

Synopsis: A husband discovers on his honeymoon that his bigamous wife and her first husband intend to murder him.

Cast: Ken Scott (Steve Baldwin), Marla Landi (Marie Aldrich), Trader Faulkner (Chris Aldrich), Conrad Phillips (Peter Shanley), Gerald Sim (Larry Landstrom), Duncan Lamont (Inspector Telford), Peter Bathurst (Dr Knight), Ballard Berkeley (Sir Colin Chalmers), **Dyan Cannon** (no character name)

Milestones and Millstones: Sidney Salkow, Harry Spalding, Dyan Cannon, Robert L Lippert

Comment: Ordinary, efficiently directed but resolutely second feature.

Reviews: "… a slap-dash, low-budget suspense melodrama that gets better and better as it goes along, thanks to a good, snug little plot. But it finally collapses and trickles down the drain, like most fly-by-night thrillers." *New York Times*

"… a slow-paced British melodrama that is generally too wordy and lacking in punch. Languid stride melodrama as directed by Sidney Salkow plus lack of marquee names, spells little favorable commercial prospect for the film in the U.S. aside from filling bottom half of dual bill." *Variety*

Spaceflight IC-1 (1965) 65 mins (b&w)

"SEE…Life in the 21ˢᵗ Century…The brain that lives without a body… Humans "frozen" for rebirth in space…"

Lippert Films; d: Bernard Knowles; p: **Robert J Lippert**, Jack Parsons; screenplay: **Harry Spalding**; ph: Geoffrey Spalding; ed: Robert Winter; ad: Harry White; m: Elisabeth Lutyens

Synopsis: A cadet plans a mutiny against brutal captain Bill Williams, commander of a spacecraft traveling through Outer Space in 2015 seeking a suitable planet to settle on.

Cast: Bill Williams (Captain Ralston), Kathleen Breck (Kate Saunders), John Cairney (Dr Steven), Donald Churchill (Carl Wolcott), Jeremy Longhurst (Chief Engineer John Saunders), Linda Marlowe (Dr Helen Thomas), Margo Mayne (Joyce Wolcott), Norma West (Jan Ralston), Tony Doonan (Dr Griffith)

Milestones and Millstones: Bill Williams, Harry Spalding, Robert J Lippert

Comment: A patently low budget makes the movie (not released in the US until 1967) resemble a minor television series episode more than a feature film. Future child star Mark Lester makes a brief appearance.

Reviews: "Weak story… entirely a dialogue play with the entire plot unfolded on a spaceship; but it is a muddled affair, almost dull in content, with no action or excitement to help it along… it has little beyond its title to attract." *CEA Film Report*

"…thin in story, acting and direction departments, thus negating a solid original plot premise… Williams is adequate… film's length indicates more than a casual eye to eventual sale to television." *Variety*

Ten Little Indians/Agatha Christie's Ten Little Indians
(1965) 91 mins (b&w)

"FOR THE FIRST TIME IN FILM HISTORY. THE WHODUNNIT BREAK 60 SECONDS FOR YOU TO DECIDE THE KILLER'S IDENTITY!"

Tenlit In association with Harry M Popkin; d: George Pollock; p: Harry Alan Towers; screenplay: Peter Yeldham, Peter Welbeck (aka Harry Alan Towers); from the novel and the play by Agatha Christie; ph: Ernie Steward; ed: Peter Boita; ad: Frank White; m: Malcolm Lockyer
  Synopsis: Eight strangers who have been summoned to an isolated house in the Austrian Alps find they are marked for murder.
  Cast: Hugh O'Brian (Hugh Lombard), Shirley Eaton (Ann Clyde), **Fabian** (Mike Raven), **Leo Genn** (General Mandrake), Stanley Holloway (Detective William Henry Blore), Dennis Price (Dr Edward Armstrong), Wilfrid Hyde White (Judge Cannon), Daliah Lavi (Ilona Bergen), Mario Adorf (Herr Grohmann), Mr Owen (Christopher Lee) (uncredited voice)
  Milestones and Millstones: Hugh O'Brian, Fabian, Leo Genn
  Comment: The first of producer Towers' three versions of Christie's classic is tepid compared with René Clair's definitive 1945 version: moviegoers were offered a "whodunit break" to give them time to figure out the identity of the killer while watching repeat footage of the slayings. The Austrian mansion was actually in Ireland.
  Reviews: "None of the characters begins to come alive, and there are acres of dreary dialogue as they stand around waiting for the next murder... George Pollock's direction manages to record 10 deaths and pseudo-deaths without a single jolt of excitement anywhere." *Monthly Film Bulletin*

24 Hours to Kill (1965) 83 mins (color)

"run…run… before the killers catch you!"

Grixflag Films Limited/Towers of London; d: Peter Bezencenet; p: Harry Alan Towers; ap: Bernard Coote; screenplay: Peter Welbeck (aka Harry Alan Towers); from a story by Peter Yeldham; ph: Ernest Steward; ed: John Trumper; ad: Scott MacGregor; m: Wilfred Josephs

Synopsis: Passenger plane captained by Lex Barker en route to Athens has engine trouble and is diverted to Beirut for 24 hours where crooked purser Mickey Rooney falls foul of a gang of gold smugglers.

Cast: Mickey Rooney (Jones), **Lex Barker** (Jamie), **Walter Slezak** (Malouj), Michael Medwin (Tommy), Helga Sommerfeld (Louise), Hans Clarin (Elias), France Anglade (Françoise), Helga Lehner (Helga), Wolfgang Lukschy (Kurt), Maria Röhm (Claudine), Shakib Khouri (Andronicus), Nadia Gamel (Mimi)

Milestones and Millstones: Mickey Rooney, Lex Barker, Walter Slezak

Comment: Rooney and Barker follow in the B film tracks of many Hollywood counterparts and end up in yet another Towers skimped second feature which relies as usual on former star names rather than polished filmmaking or a good screenplay. Excellent cinematography puts a minor gloss on a film that holds little other interest.

Reviews: "This thriller is a little short on action and excitement, with the promise of tension and thrills never fully materializing, but it is well acted and has the advantage of unusual settings in its Beirut locale." *CEA Film Report*

Walk a Tightrope (1965) 69 mins (b&w)

"THE THIN LINE BETWEEN DISASTER AND AVENTURE"

Jack Parsons-Neil McCallum Productions; d: Frank Nesbitt; p: Jack Parsons; screenplay: Neil McCallum; story by; **Mann Rubin**; ph: Basil Emmott; ed: Robert Winter; ad: Harry White; m: Buxton Orr

Synopsis: Things go horribly wrong for a happily married woman when she hires gunman Dan Duryea to kill her former husband who is blackmailing her.

Cast: Dan Duryea (Carl Lutcher), Patricia Owens (Ellen Sheppard), Terence Cooper (Jason Sheppard), Richard Leech (Doug Randle), Neil McCallum (Counsel), Trevor Reid (Inspector MacMitchell), A J Brown (Magistrate), David Bauer (Ed)

Milestones and Millstones: Dan Duryea, Mann Rubin

Comment: Duryea's innate Hollywood charisma adds valuable impact to both his routine bad guy role and the sometimes sloppily constructed screenplay.

Reviews: "The story might not be convincing, but it is nevertheless quite gripping and certainly ingenious… weak dialogue, slow and talkative episodes and some ineffective acting. Despite its faults it makes useful second-feature fare" *CEA Film Report*

The Frozen Dead (1966) 95 mins (color)

FROZEN ALIVE FOR 20 YEARS! *NOW* they return from their icy graves to seek vengeance!

Gold Star Productions Ltd, Seven Arts Pictures; d/p/s: **Herbert J Leder**; ep: Robert Goldstein; ap: Tom Sachs; ph: Davis Boulton; ed: Tom Simpson; pd: Scott McGregor; m: Don Banks

Synopsis: Mad scientist Dana Andrews keeps the severed heads of Nazi war criminals alive intending to graft them onto suitable bodies and so revive the Third Reich.

Cast: Dana Andrews (Dr. Norberg), Anna Palk (Jean Norberg), Philip Gilbert (Dr. Ted Roberts), Kathleen Breck (Elsa Tenney), Karel Stepanek (General Lubeck), Basil Henson (Dr. Tirpitz), Alan Tilvern (Karl Essen), Anne Tirard (Mrs Schmidt), Edward Fox (Norburg's Brother/Prisoner #3), Tom Chatto (Inspector Witt).

Milestones and Millstones: Dana Andrews, Herbert J Leder

Comment: Andrews helps the lunatic narrative along with a convincing portrait of a crazy 20th century Frankenstein but Leder's dull direction encourages mounting tedium. Future star Edward Fox turns up without noticeable impact.

Reviews: "… neither thrilling nor persuasive. Staging is adequate but most of the acting does not impress, pace is rather slow and macabre moments not frequent." *CEA Film Report*

"This low-budget, English-made production is a skillfully contrived, clinically ghoulish pic that should keep the young set riveted to their seats…Andrews' talents lends a special credence to this ugly presentation." *Variety*

Our Man in Marrakesh/US: Bang! Bang! You're Dead! (1966)
92 mins (color)

"STRANGE GIRLS IN HIS ROOM...LOADED GUNS IN HIS BACK... Looks like it'll be a bang-up vacation!"

Landau/Unger, Marrakesh/Towers of London; d: Don Sharp; p: Oliver A Unger, **Louis M Hayward**, Harry Alan Towers; screenplay: Peter Yeldham; from a story by Peter Welbeck (aka Harry Alan Towers); ph: Michael Reed; ed: Teddy Darvas; ad: Frank White; m: Malcolm Lockyer

Synopsis: One of six people travelling on a bus from Casablanca airport to Marrakesh is carrying $2 million to pay a local fixer to rig United Nations votes on behalf of an unnamed country.

Cast: Tony Randall (Andrew Jessel), Senta Berger (Kyra Stanovy), Terry-Thomas (El Caid), Herbert Lom (Mr Casimir), Wilfrid Hyde-White (Arthur Fairbrother), Grégoire Aslan (Achmed), John Le Mesurier (George Lillywhite), Klaus Kinski (Jonquil), Margaret Lee (Samia Voss), Burt Kwouk (Import Manager)

Milestones and Millstones: Tony Randall, Louis M Hayward

Comment: Attractive locations easily upstage the actors, the largely uninvolving comedy-thriller screenplay and the dull direction.

Reviews: "Programmer that doesn't live up to its cast...Technical flaws and inept script hold down potential...most of Peter Yeldham's rambling script is carried by Tony Randall who, too often, appears bored with the whole thing." *Variety*

The Projected Man (1966) 77 mins (color)

"BORN A MAN... TURNED INTO A LIVING LASER BEAM BY SCIENCE'S MOST GRUESOME EXPERIMENT! A BILLION VOLTS OF DEATH IN EVERY FINGER!"

Compton Films; d: Ian Curteis, John Croydon (uncredited); ep: Michael Klinger, Tony Tenser; p: John Croydon, Maurice Foster, **Richard Gordon**; ap: Pat Green; screenplay: John C. Cooper (aka John Croydon), Peter Bryan; story by: Frank Quattrocchi; ph: Stanley Pavey; ed: Derek Holden; sfx: Flo Nordhoff, Robert Hedges, Mike Hope; ad: Peter Mullins; m: Kenneth V Jones

Synopsis: Scientist Bryant Halliday enters a matter transmission machine and comes out in a monstrous mess.

Cast: Bryant Halliday (Professor Steiner), Mary Peach (Dr Pat Hill), Norman Wooland (Dr. Blanchard), Ronald Allen (Christopher Mitchell), Derek Farr (Inspector Davis) Tracy Crisp (Sheila Anderson), Derrick de Marney (Latham), Gerard Heimz (Professor Lembach), Sam Kydd (Harry), Terry Scully (Steve)

Milestones and Millstones: Bryant Halliday, Richard Gordon

Comment: Routine mad scientist shocker with unhappy echoes of 1958's similarly matter-transmission-driven *The Fly*. John Croydon replaced original director Ian Curteis after filming fell behind schedule and the budget was overrunning.

Reviews: "…badly written, woodenly acted, and abounding in the clichés of the horror film genre." *Ottawa Citizen*

"One of a pair of British imports released without being tradeshown by Universal. "The Projected Man" is made with sufficient care and skill that it need not have been bypassed." *Variety*

Circus of Fear/US: Psycho Circus (1966) 90 mins (b&w and color)

"THE MOST HORRIFYING SYNDICATE OF EVIL IN HISTORY!"

Circus Films/Proudweeks; d: John Llewellyn Moxey (English version), Werner Jacobs (German version); p: David Henley, Harry Alan Towers; screenplay: Peter Welbeck (aka Harry Alan Towers); from the novel *The Three Just Men* by Edgar Wallace; ph: Ernest Steward; ed: John Trumper; ad: Frank White; stunts: Nosher Powell; m: Johnny Douglas

Synopsis: The hunt for the criminals who robbed a London bank and shot a guard leads Scotland Yard detective Leo Genn to a travelling circus plagued by mysterious deaths.

Cast: Christopher Lee (Gregor), **Leo Genn** (Elliott), Anthony Newlands (Barberini), Heinz Drache (Carl), Eddi Arent (Eddie), Klaus Kinski (Manfred Hart), Suzy Kendall (Natasha), Margaret Lee (Gina), Cecil Parker (Sir John) Victor Maddern (Mason), Maurice Kaufmann (Mario)

Milestones and Millstones: Leo Genn

Comment: Despite the presence of Lee (who, sadly for his fans, wears a black wool hood for much of the time in his role as a facially scarred lion-tamer) this is not a horror movie but rather a weak and often, wearisome whodunit. Ironically, it was filmed at the home of Hammer, Britain's Bray Studios.

Reviews: "… little excitement apart from a few tense moments… acting is adequate but Leo Genn tends to overplay the role of the inspector." *CEA Film Report*

"… ineptly titled for America and bogged down with a confused storyline, still carries enough weight to rate as an okay entry for the smaller program market…Genn handles his part with his usual aplomb." *Variety*

The Vulture (1966) 91 mins (color)

"Talons of terror Half-man half beast-bird swooping on his human prey… drinking blood…mutilating flesh!"

Homeric Films Ltd/Iliad Films/Film Financial Co; d/p/s: Lawrence Huntingdon; ep: Jack O Lamont; story by Lawrence Huntingdon; ph: Stephen Dade; ed: John S Smith; ad: Duncan Sutherland; m: Eric Spear

Synopsis: Mad scientist Akim Tamiroff's teleportation machine causes him to turn into a savage half-bird, half-man monster.

Cast: Robert Hutton (Dr Eric Lutens), **Akim Tamiroff** (Professor Hans Koniglich), **Broderick Crawford** (Brian Stroud), Diane Clare (Trudy Lutens), Gordon Sterne (Edward Stroud), Edward Caddick (Melcher the Sexton), Philip Friend (The Vicar), Keith McConnell (Superintendent Wendell), Annette Carell (Ellen West)

Milestones and Millstones: Robert Hutton, Broderick Crawford, Akim Tamiroff

Comment: Unconvincing monster movie—the title creature is reduced to a just pair of legs—over-talkative and more risible than scary for an apiring shocker.

Reviews: "…its thrills will chill only the simple-minded." *Kine Weekly*

"… a well-developed chiller with sufficient mounting suspense… stars Robert Hutton, Akim Tamiroff and Broderick Crawford for identification in the American market… soundly turned out with an eye for appropriate values." *Variety*

The Witches (1966) 90 mins (color)

"DOES WITCHCRAFT EXIST TODAY! "

Hammer Film Productions/Seven Arts: d: Cyril Frankel; p: Anthony Nelson Keys; screenplay: Nigel Kneale; from the novel *The Devil's Own* by Peter Curtis (aka Norah Lofts); ph: Arthur Grant; ed: Chris Barnes; pd: Bernard Robinson; ad: Don Mingaye; m: Richard Rodney Bennett

Synopsis: Schoolteacher Joan Fontaine has a nervous breakdown after an encounter with voodoo in Africa and goes to teach in an English village where she is trapped by a witch cult.

Cast: Joan Fontaine (Gwen Mayfield), Kay Walsh (Stephanie Bax), Alec McCowen (Alan Bax), Ann Bell (Sally), Ingrid Brett (Linda Rigg), John Collin (Dowsett), Michele Dotrice (Valerie Creek), Gwen Ffrangcon Davies (Granny Rigg), Duncan Lamont (Bob Curd), Leonard Rossiter (Dr Wallis)

Milestones and Millstones: Joan Fontaine

Comment: Fontaine had bought the rights to Nora Loft's book *The Devil's Own* when she pitched the movie to Hammer. Her strong performance was a major asset since neither screenplay nor direction made the most of the story's inherent horror elements.

Reviews: "… a very professional cast. Despite that, the Nigel Kneale script doesn't spark off enough horror and tension to make the picture more than routine entertainment…Fontaine looks delightful and brings a sensitive air to her thesping." *Variety*

"This import should do okay as part of the program with a fairly interesting plot, all be it on the far-fetched size, adequate performances." *Motion Picture Exhibitor*

Battle Beneath the Earth (1967) 91 mins (color)

"THE MOST EXCITING ADVENTURE ON EARTH IS <u>UNDER</u> IT!"

Reynolds-Vetter Productions Ltd; d: Montgomery Tully; ep: **Charles F Vetter**; p: Charles Reynolds; screenplay and story by: L Z Hargreaves (aka **Charles F Vetter**); ph: Kenneth Talbot; ed: Sidney Stone; sfx: Tom Howard; ad: Jim Morahan; m: Ken Jones

Synopsis: US Navy Commander Kerwin Mathews is assigned to thwart the Chinese who are tunneling under the United States prior to invasion.

Cast: Kerwin Mathews (Commander Jonathan Shaw), Viviane Ventura (Tila Yung), Robert Ayres (Admiral Hillebrand), Peter Arne (Arnold Kramer), Al Mulock (Sergeant Mulberry), Martin Benson (General Kengh Lee), Peter Elliott (Dr. Lee), Earl Cameron (Sergeant Hawkins), **Edward Bishop** (Lieutenant Commander Cassidy)

Milestones and Millstones: Kerwin Mathews, Edward Bishop, Charles F Vetter

Comment: Entertaining comic-strip hokum played and directed with commendable straight-faced enthusiasm.

Reviews: "Metro has a suspenseful entry for the sci-fi market in this British import… it's a well-made film after a slow opening…Kerwin Matthews does a good job… special effects by Tom Howard particularly impressive." *Variety*

"Sadly, the film itself is neither as naive nor as adventurous as its premise." *Time Out*

Berserk! (1967) 96 mins (color)

"THE MOTION PICTURE THAT PITS STEEL WEAPONS AGAINST STEEL NERVES!"

Herman Cohen Productions; d: Jim O'Connolly; p: **Herman Cohen**; ap: Robert Sterne; screenplay and story by: **Aben Kandel**, Herman Cohen; ph: Desmond Dickinson; color; ed: Raymond Poulton; ad: Maurice Pelling; m: Patrick John Scott

Synopsis: Joan Crawford is owner and ringmaster of a travelling circus where an outbreak of mysterious murders boosts her takings.

Cast: Joan Crawford (Monica Rivers), **Ty Hardin** (Frank Hawkins), Diana Dors (Matilda), Michael Gough (Albert Dorando), Judy Geeson (Angela Rivers) Robert Hardy (Detective Superintendent Brooks), Geoffrey Keen (Commissioner Dalby), Sydney Tafler (Harrison Liston), Philip Madoc (Laszlo)

Milestones and Millstones: Joan Crawford, Ty Hardin, Aben Kandel, Herman Cohen

Comment: Crawford deserves some praise for giving her all (and then rather too much as well) in an otherwise routine British second-feature that she appears to have mistaken for a major Hollywood production.

Reviews: "…the capable Mr. O'Connolly is no Hitchcock. And what drains the picture of merit and real persuasiveness is the round-up of bloodless characterizations, a petty and conniving gang of meanies." *New York Times*

"Story is full of holes, but is makes no difference. All the elements of the thrill picture are present. Promotion will bring them in." *Variety*

Danger Route (1967) 92 mins

"HE IS A WEAPON! Government Issue! He Kills on Assignment!

Amicus Productions; d: Seth Holt: p: **Max J Rosenberg, Milton Subotsky**, ap: Ted Wallis; screenplay: Meade Roberts, Robert Banks Stewart; based on the novel *The Eliminator* by Andrew Yorke; ph: Harry Waxman; ed: Oswald Hafenrichter; pd: Bill Constable; ad: Don Mingaye; m: John Mayer

Synopsis: When a leading British secret agent with a licence to kill returns from a mission in the Caribbean he fears his nerve has gone but is persuaded by his superiors to embark on a final exercise in assassination.

Cast: Richard Johnson (Jonas Wilde), **Carol Lynley** (Jocelyn), Barbara Bouchet (Marita), Sylvia Syms (Barbara Canning), Gordon Jackson (Brian Stern), Diana Dors (Rhoda Gooderich), Maurice Denham (Peter Ravenspur), **Sam Wanamaker** (Lucina), David Bauer (Bennett), Harry Andrews (Canning)

Milestones and Millstones: Carol Lynley, Sam Wanamaker, Max J Rosenberg, Milton Subosky

Comment: Artistically inept and financially devastating attempt by Amicus to latch onto the secret agent-in-blazing-action James Bond-style bandwagon: my score—002.

Reviews: "For the less discriminating action market, this may be a suitable entry on lower half of dual bill…overly confused in unfoldment and winds on a rather indefinite note…Lynley is pretty but distaff interest rests primarily on Barbara Bouchet." *Variety*

"Pretty familiar, yes, but still pretty good." *New York Times*

Follow That Camel/Carry On, Follow That Camel/US: Follow That Camel/Carry On in the Legion (1967) 95 mins (color)

"BILKO' JOINS THE 'CARRY ON' LEGION!"

Peter Rogers Productions; d Gerald Thomas; p: Peter Rogers; screenplay: Talbot Rothwell; ph: Alan Hume; ed: Alfred Roome; ad: Arthur Vetchinsky; m: Eric Rogers

Synopsis: A falsely accused of cheating Englishman joins the French Foreign Legion and faces the leadership and training of sergeant Phil Silvers.

Cast: Phil Silvers (Sergeant Ernie Knocker), Jim Dale (Bertram Oliphant "Bo" West), Kenneth Williams (Commandant Burger), Peter Butterworth (Simpson), Charles Hawtrey (Captain Le Pice), Joan Sims (Zig-Zig), Angela Douglas (Lady Jane Ponsonby), Bernard Bresslaw (Sheikh Abdul Abulbul)

Milestones and Millstones: Phil Silvers

Comment: Silvers' vaudevillian comic shtick is uncomfortably out of key with the *Carry On* comedy style (he was cast optimistically to give the movie uniquely US appeal after *Carry On* regular Sidney James suffered a heart attack). The British beach Camber Sands in East Sussex plays the Sahara Desert, but not very convincingly.

Reviews: "Coming from the tried-and-true stable still turning out the "Carry On" features, this one has all the same ingredients…(Silvers)…though he doesn't happily fit this peculiarly British idiom, he adds some relish." *Variety*

"The result must be the oddest Carry On of them all, and a big failure at the box office." *Empire Magazine* (verdict arrived at years after the event, needless to say!)

It! (1967) 96 mins; (color)

"BULLETS CANT KILL IT! FIRE CAN'T BURN *IT* WATER CAN'T DROWN *IT*. HOW CAN WE DESTROY *IT* BEFORE *IT* DESTROYS US?"

Gold Star Films Ltd; Seven Arts Pictures: d/p/s: **Herbert J Leder**; ep: Robert Goldstein; ap: Tom Sachs; ph: Davis Boulton; ed: Tom Simpson; ad: Scott McGregor; m: Carlo Martelli

Synopsis: Crazy museum curator Roddy McDowall brings an ancient Golem back to life and uses it for his own nefarious ends.

Cast: Roddy McDowall (Arthur Pimm), Jill Haworth (Ellen Grove), Paul Maxwell (Jim Perkins), Aubrey Richards (Professor Weal), Ernest Clark (Harold Grove), Oliver Johnston (Curator Trimingham), Noel Trevarthen (Inspector White), Richard Goolden (Old Rabbi), Alan Seller (The Golem)

Milestones and Millstones: Roddy McDowall, Herbert J Leder

Comment: Psychiatrists might appreciate McDowall's character since he keeps the mummified body of his dead mother above ground (homage to Hitchcock?). McDowall overacts enthusiastically and the daft scene of the destruction of London's Hammersmith Bridge by the Golem is a masterpiece of cheap filmmaking.

Reviews: "However, a Golem story is at any rate a novelty these days and the really mobile sculpture together with title and certificate should pull them in." *CEA Film Report*

"Production values on this color suspense thriller are excellent and Roddy McDowall has a grand time going mad…there are some unintended funny lines but for the most part producer-director Herbert J Leder has kept the proceedings under stiff-lip control." *Variety*

Frankenstein Created Woman (1967) 92 mins (color)

FROM FLESH AND INNOCENCE… FRANKENSTEIN HAS CREATED THE ULTIMATE IN EVIL… A BEAUTIFUL WOMAN WITH THE SOUL of the DEVIL!

Hammer Films; d: Terence Fisher; p: Anthony-Nelson Keys; screenplay: John Elder (aka Anthony Hinds); ph: Arthur Grant; ed: Spencer Reeve; pd: Bernard Robinson; ad: Don Mingaye; sfx: Les Bowie; m: James Bernard

Synopsis: Frankenstein revives a grief-stricken girl who killed herself because of the death of her lover by placing the dead boy's soul in her body—with gruesome results.

Cast: Peter Cushing (Baron Frankenstein), **Susan Denberg** (Christina), Thorley Walters (Doctor Hertz), Robert Morris (Hans), Duncan Lamont (The Prisoner), Peter Blythe (Anton), Barry Warren (Karl), Derek Fowlds (Johann), Alan MacNaughton (Kleve) Peter Madden (Police Chief), Philip Ray (Mayor)

Milestones and Millstones: Susan Denberg

Comment: The Baron does not actually create Woman, but instead fills Denberg's body with malevolent evil. After making movie history with 1957's *The Curse of Frankenstein*, Fisher's third slice off the Creature organizes sex, scares and gory gusto, featuring content that pushed genre limits as far as the British censor would then permit.

Reviews: "...excellent programmer...considering the result is a beautiful blond Susan Denberg (who did a well-remembered walkon as the maid in Warners' "An American Dream"), most film fans would like to see the doctor get a grant form the Ford Foundation, or even the C.I.A." *Variety*

"An original and subversive Hammer movie starring Peter Cushing. Cleverly scripted by Anthony Hinds as a complex variation—well suited to the late 60s freer notions of sexuality and horror—on the Frankenstein story." *Film 4*

Submarine X-1 (1967) 89 mins (color)

"OUTSIDE THE LAW HE WAS A TARGET IN A KILLING GAME!"
"CAT AND MOUSE AT 60 FATHOMS!"

Mirisch Films/Oakmont Productions; d: **William A Graham**; ep: **Irving Temaner**; p: **John C Champion**; ap: Ted Lloyd; screenplay: **Donald S Sanford**, Guy Elmes; story by: John C Champion, **Edmund H North**; ph: Paul Beeson; ed: John D Smith; sfx: Les Bowie; ad: William C Andrews; m: Ron Goodwin

Synopsis: Royal Navy Commander James Caan loses a submarine and crew battling a German ship during WW2 but gets a second chance to lead a daring raid in midget subs.

Cast: James Caan (Commander. Richard Bolton, RNVR), David Sumner (Lt. Davies R.N.V.R), Norman Bowler (Sub-Lt. Pennington, RN), Brian Grellis (CPO Barquist X 3), Paul Young (Leading Seaman Quentin), William Dysart (Lt. Robert Talbot Gogan R.N.R.), John Kelland (Sub-Lt. Keith Willis, RNVR)

Milestones and Millstones: James Caan, William A Graham, Irving Temaner, John C Champion, Donald S Sanford, Edmund H North

Comment: Routine and ultimately clichéd (despite being based on fact) and lacking exciting action or much dramatic interest: not released in the United States until two years after its production in 1967.

Reviews: "... excitement seldom rises above a modest level and much of the acting is indifferent. But it is just about an acceptable supporting offering for general audiences." *CEA Film Report*

"A bit quiet on the action side, compared with today's product, it moves quickly enough for family entertainment...Caan... stolid and almost as underplayed as the British members of the cast." *Variety*

The Man Outside (1967) 97 mins (color)

"OUTSIDE THE LAW HE WAS A TARGET IN A KILLING GAME!"

London Independent Films/Trio Films/Group W; d: **Samuel Gallu**; p: William J Gell; screenplay; Samuel Gallu, Roger Marshall, Julian Bond; from the novel *Double Agent* by Gene Stackleborg; ph: Gilbert Taylor; ed: Thom Noble; ad: Peter Mullins; m: Richard Arnell

Synopsis: Former CIA agent Van Heflin, living in London after dismissal, joins another ex-agent to deliver a top Russian secret police official—for a price.

Cast: Van Heflin (Bill MacLean), Heidelinde Weis (Kay Sebastian), Pinkas Braun (Rafe Machek), Peter Vaughan (Nikolai Volkov), Charles Gray (Charles Griddon), Paul Maxwell (Judson Murphy), Ronnie Barker (George Venaxas), Linda Marlowe (Dorothy), **Gary Cockrell** (Brune Parry), Bill Nagy (Morehouse)

Milestones and Millstones: Gary Cockrell, Samuel L Gallu

Comment: Firm second-feature thriller directed with pace and tension and solidly acted.

Reviews: "Spy story with atmosphere and a kick and Van Heflin leading a sharp British cast...Heflin...gives an excellent chunky performance...paired with a suitable duellar, this modest but well-conceived thriller will be a good bet." *Variety*

Maroc 7 (1967) 91 mins (color)

"MOROCCO—The double crossroads of the world!"

Cyclone; d: Gerry O'Hara; p: Martin C Schute, John Gale, Leslie Phillips; screenplay; David D Osborn; ph: Kenneth Talbot; ed: John Jympson; ad: Seamus Flannery, Terry Pritchard; m: Kenneth V Jones

Synopsis: Secret agent Gene Barry poses as a safecracker to infiltrate a gang of thieves whose crimes are masterminded by fashion magazine editor Cyd Charisse.

Cast: Gene Barry (Simon Grant), Elsa Martinelli (Claudia), Leslie Phillips (Raymond Lowe), **Cyd Charisse** (Louise Henderson), Denholm Elliott (Inspector Barrada), Alexandra Stewart (Michelle Craig), Angela Douglas (Freddie), Eric Barker (Professor Bannen), Tracy Reed (Vivienne)

Milestones and Millstones: Gene Barry, Cyd Charisse

Comment: Watchable star-driven thriller but otherwise hardly noteworthy: the only film produced by British comedy actor Leslie Phillips.

Reviews: "… the final phases are entertaining with surprise developments and concluding twists, compensating well enough for previous occasions when the tale tends to get bogged down." *CEA Film Report*

"…so uneven: one gets the impression that nobody connected with it has really made up his mind in what direction it should go…the acing is efficient." *Films and Filming*

The Million Eyes of Su-Muru (1967) 95 mins (color)

"The most DIABOLICAL…BIZARRE…SADISTIC WOMAN WHO EVER LIVED!"

Sumuru Films; d: Lindsay Shonteff; p: Harry Alan Towers; screenplay: Peter Welbeck (aka Harry Alan Towers), Kevin Kavanagh; based on a character created by Sax Rohmer; ph: John Von Kötze; ed: Allan Morrison; ad: Scott MacGregor; m: John Scott, Daniel White

Synopsis: Secret agents George Nader and Frankie Avalon take on an evil woman planning to employ her all-female army to achieve world domination.

Cast: Frankie Avalon (Agent Tommy Carter), **George Nader** (Agent Nick West), Shirley Eaton (Sumuru), Wilfrid Hyde-White (Colonel Sir Anthony Baisbrook), Klaus Kinski (President Boong), Maria Rohm (Helga Martin), Patti Chandler (Louise), Paul Chang Chung (Inspector Koo), Ursula Rank (Emo)

Milestones and Millstones: Frankie Avalon, George Nader

Comment: Drivel: with a screenplay infected with witless wisecracks and a ludicrous plot the action sequences, when they arrive, are really welcome.

Reviews: "This is a preposterous but lively thriller which has a good measure of action but is largely presented in comedy style which engagingly "guys" the melodramatic situations… a colourful and acceptable popular offering." *CEA Film Report*

"Although Frankie Avalon top-lines (obviously just for name) he still doesn't know how to handle a gun and most action and story movement falls to George Nader… Avalon poses, moves and talks like a nightclub entertainer." *Variety*

Submarine X-1 (1967) 89 mins (color)

"CAT AND MOUSE AT 60 FATHOMS!"

Mirisch Films/Oakmont Productions; d: **William A Graham**; ep: **Irving Temaner**; p: **John C Champion**; ap: Ted Lloyd; screenplay: **Donald S Sanford**, Guy Elmes; story: John C Champion, **Edmund H North**; ph: Paul Beeson; ed: John D Smith; sfx: Les Bowie; ad: William C Andrews; m: Ron Goodwin

Synopsis: Royal Navy Commander James Caan loses a submarine and crew battling a German ship during WW2 but gets a second chance to lead a daring raid in midget subs.

Cast: James Caan (Commander. Richard Bolton, RNVR), David Sumner (Lt. Davies R.N.V.R), Norman Bowler (Sub-Lt. Pennington, RN), Brian Grellis (CPO Barquist X 3), Paul Young (Leading Seaman Quentin), William Dysart (Lt. Robert Talbot Gogan R.N.R.), John Kelland (Sub-Lt. Keith Willis, RNVR)

Milestones and Millstones: James Caan, William A Graham, Irving Temaner, John C Champion, Donald S Sanford, Edmund H North

Comment: Routine and ultimately clichéd (despite being based on fact) and lacking exciting action or much dramatic interest: not released in the United States until two years after its production in 1967.

Reviews: "... excitement seldom rises above a modest level and much of the acting is indifferent. But it is just about an acceptable supporting offering for general audiences." *CEA Film Report*

"A bit quiet on the action side, compared with today's product, it moves quickly enough for family entertainment...Caan... stolid and almost as underplayed as the British members of the cast." *Variety*

Some May Live (1967) 89 mins (color)

Foundation Pictures/Krasne Entertainments; d: Vernon Sewell; ep: Philip N Krasne; p: Clive Sharp, Peter Snell; screenplay: David T Chantler; ph: Ray Parslow; ed: Gordon Pilkington; ad: George Lack; m: Cyril Ornadel

Synopsis: A communist agent in Saigon forces military secrets from his wife Martha Hyer and US Army intelligence officer Joseph Cotton sets out to find the spy.

Cast: Joseph Cotten (Colonel Woodward), **Martha Hyer** (Kate Meredith), Peter Cushing (John Meredith), John Ronane (Captain Elliott Thomas), David Spenser (Inspector Sung), Alec Mango (Ducrai), Walter Brown (Major Matthews), Kim Smith (Alan Meredith), Burnell Tucker (Lawrence)

Milestones and Millstones: Joseph Cotten, Martha Hyer

Comment: Forgettable, apart from the Viet Nam setting: the stars deserve considerably better than the banal material they have to work with.

Reviews: "... story... engages the interest as melodrama, though it is slow going until the concluding episodes which to manage to engender some tension." *CEA Film Report*

The Sorcerers (1967) 86 mins (color)

HE TURNS THEM ON...HE TURNS THEM OFF... *to live... love...die or KILL!*

Curtwell Productions/Global/Tigon; d: Michael Reeves; ep: Arnold L Miller; p: Tony Tenser, Patrick Curtis and Michael Reeves (uncredited); screenplay; Michael Reeves, Tom Baker; from an idea by John Burke; ph: Stanley A Long; ed: David Woodward, Susan Michie and Ralph Sheldon (uncredited); ad: Tony Curtis; m: Paul Ferris

Synopsis: When professor Boris Karloff creates a machine that controls other people's minds he and his wife pick a sullen youth as their victim.

Cast: Boris Karloff (Professor Marcus Monserrat), Ian Ogilvy (Mike Roscoe), Catherine Lacey (Estelle Monserrat), Elizabeth Ercy (Nicole), Victor Henry (Alan), Sally Sheridan (Laura Ladd), Alf Joint (Ron, the mechanic), Meier Tzelniker (Jewish baker), Susan George (Audrey Woods), Ivor Dean (Inspector Matalon)

Milestones and Millstones: Boris Karloff

Comment: Karloff's charisma adds valuable dramatic weight to Reeves quite stylish storytelling that holds your attention even as the plot becomes increasingly implausible.

Reviews: "One of a pair of British imports released without being trade shown by Universal. "The Projected Man" is made with sufficient care and skill that it need not have been bypassed." *Variety*

After a slow start, this picture works up to satisfactory horror hokum. Useful double bill for the uncritical." *Kine Weekly*

They Came From Beyond Space (1967) 85 mins (color)

"CONQUERORS FROM A DYING WORLD INVADE EARTH!"

Amicus Productions; d: Freddie Francis; p: **Max J Rosenberg, Milton Subotsky**; screenplay: Milton Subotsky; from the novel *The Gods Hate Kansas* by Joseph Millard; ph: Norman Warwick; ed: Peter Musgrave; pd: Bill Constable; ad: Don Mingaye, Scott Simon; sfx: Les Bowie; m: James Stevens

Synopsis: When scientists led by Robert Hutton investigate a mysterious meteor shower over rural Cornwall, aliens possess them to use them as slaves—but a metal plate in Hutton's head makes him immunes to the extraterrestrials' powers.

Cast: Robert Hutton (Dr Curtis Temple), Jennifer Jayne (Lee Mason), Zia Mohyeddin (Farge) Bernard Kay (Richard Arden), Michael Gough (Master of the Moon), Geoffrey Wallace (Alan Mullane), Maurice Good (Agent Stilwell), Luanshya Greer (Petrol station attendant), John Harvey (Bill Trethowan)

Milestones and Millstones: Robert Hutton, Max J Rosenberg, Milton Subosky

Comment: Former Oscar-winning cinematographer Francis does his best with Subotsky's underpowered screenplay that suffers, among other aspects, from switching locale from Kansas to Cornwall. Amicus trimmed their budget by reusing props and sets from their previous picture *Daleks—Invasion Earth: 2150 AD* (1966).

Reviews: "Even Freddie Francis, who gives routine sci-fi scripts considerably more than they deserve, isn't able to help this tired tale…" *Variety*

"…the acting is uninspired, and the same must be said for other production values." *Motion Picture Exhibitor*

Torture Garden (1967) 93 mins (color)

"DO YOU DARE SEEWHAT DR DIABO SEES? From the shock-author of "PSYCHO""

Amicus Productions/Columbia; d: Freddie Francis; p: **Max J Rosenberg**, **Milton Subotsky**; screenplay; **Robert Bloch**; ph: Norman Warwick; ed: Peter Elliott; pd: Bill Constable; ad: Don Mingaye, Scott Simon; m: James Bernard, Don Banks

Synopsis: Weird fairground showman Burgess Meredith shows four visitors the appalling futures that lie ahead of them.

Cast: Jack Palance (Ronald Wyatt), **Burgess Meredith** (Dr Diabolo), **Beverly Adams** (Carla Hayes), Peter Cushing (Lancelot Canning), Michael Bryant (Colin Williams), Barbara Ewing (Dorothy Endicott), John Standing (Leo), John Phillps (Storm), Michael Ripper (Gordon Roberts), Bernard Kay (Dr Heim)

Milestones and Millstones: Jack Palance, Burgess Meredith, Beverly Adams, Max J Rosenberg, Milton Subotsky, Robert Bloch

Comment: Bloch's smart screenplay ensures Amicus compendium of a four short shock stories delivers the requisite shivers. Columbia's insistence on Hollywood leads led to Christopher Lee's non-appearance as a double act with Cushing. Francis' background as a two-time Oscar-winning cinematographer adds eerie atmosphere while Meredith gives it his all—and then much more.

Reviews: "Good horror programmer for duals…situations are developed economically and inventively, both by script and Francis' very good direction…cast is competent." *Variety*

"Something of a connoisseur's piece, in its class" *Western Daily Press*

"… a simple-minded forthright horror movie, made without condescension." *The New York Times*

The Viking Queen (1967) 91 mins (color)

"NO MAN COULD TAME HER SAVAGE PASSIONS!"

Hammer Films/Seven Arts; d: Don Chaffey; John Temple-Smith: screenplay; Clarke Reynolds; from an original story by John Temple-Smith; ph: Stephen Dade; ed: Peter Boita; sfx: Allan Bryce; pd: George Provis; m: Gary Hughes

Synopsis: Bloody warfare erupts in first century AD Britain when Roman Don Murray and the local Queen anger the Druids and hardline Romans by joining forces to rule Icena.

Cast: Don Murray (Justinian), Carita (Salina), Donald Houston (Maelgan), Andrew Keir (Octavian), Adrienne Corri (Maelgan), Niall MacGinnis (Tiberian), Wilfred Lawson (King Priam), Nicola Paget (Talia), Percy Herbert (Catus), Patrick Troughton (Tristram), Denis Shaw (Osiris), Sean Caffrey (Fergus)

Milestones and Millstones: Don Murray

Comment: Juvenile sword and sandal-style action drivel filmed in Ireland with a silly screenplay: justifiably a box-office failure for Hammer Films for attempting to duplicate the success of *One Million Years B.C.*(1966) on a malnourished budget.

Reviews: "Murray acquits himself vigorously…Chaffey's direction is sufficiently rugged to sustain the intended spirit of spectacle...editing by Peter Boita is fast." *Variety*

"...interesting, well-photographed attempt to depict the land of the blue-painted troglodytes...The costumes reveal more flesh than might have been wise in the cold, damp climate of the Irish mountains where location scenes were shot." *TV Guide*

Assignment K (1968) 97 mins (color)

"A Mission That Follows Its Rules to the Letter K For Kill!"

Gildor Productions/Mazurka Productions Ltd; d: Val Guest: p: Ben Arbeid, Morris Foster; screenplay: Val Guest, Maurice Foster; Bill Strutton; based on the novel by Hartley Howard (aka Leopold Horace Ognall); ph: Ken Hodges; ed: Jack Slade; ad: John Blezard; m: Basil Kirchin

Synopsis: Toy Company chief Stephen Boyd blazes into action in his real-life role as a spy when enemy agents seeking information kidnap his girlfriend.

Cast: Stephen Boyd (Philip Scott), Camilla Sparv (Toni Peters), Michael Redgrave (Harris), Leo McKern (Smith), Robert Hoffman (Paul Spiegler), Jane Merrow (Martine), Catherine Schell (Maggi), Carl Möhner (Inspector), John Alderton (George), Ursula Howells (Estelle), Basil Dignam (Howlett)

Milestones and Millstones: Stephen Boyd

Comment: Director Chaffey makes the most of attractive German and Austrian locations in a failed attempt to decorate dullness with a good-looking wrapping.

Reviews: "...an earnest and totally confusing little spy melodrama starring Stephen Boyd." *New York Times*

"a boring spy meller...Poorly written, routinely acted, but on occasion, well directed by Val Guest...strictly lowercase material." *Variety*

Attack on the Iron Coast (1968) 89 mins (b&w and color)

"THEY TURNED A DEAD SHIP INTO A LIVE BOMB AND SAILED IT DOWN THE THROAT OF THE ENEMY!"

Mirisch Films/Oakmont Productions; d: **Paul Wendkos**; ep: **Irving Temaner**; p: **John C Champion**; ap: Ted Lloyd; screenplay: **Herman Hoffman**; from a story by John C Champion; ph: Paul Beeson; sfx: Les Bowie; ed: Ernest Hosler; production design (pd), ad: William C Andrews; m: Gerard Schurmann

Synopsis: WW2 commando Lloyd Bridges leads a squad on a suicide mission to destroy a Nazi naval base on the coast of France.

Cast: Lloyd Bridges (Major James Wilson), Andrew Keir (Captain Owen Franklin), Sue Lloyd (Sue Wilson), Mark Eden (Lieutenant Commander Kimberly), Maurice Denham (Rear Admiral Sir Frederick Grafton), Glyn Owen (Forrester), Howard Pays (Lieutenant Graham), Walter Gotell (Colonel von Horst)

Milestones and Millstones: Lloyd Bridges, Paul Wendkos, John C Champion, Irving Temaner, Herman Hoffman

Comment: A standard low-budget war movie with not entirely achieves aspirations gains interest from Bridges' performance which gives depth to his essentially by-numbers role.

Reviews: "Filmed entirely on location in Britain and with name of Lloyd Bridges as an added plus… builds after a slow opening… Wendkos' direction is somewhat handicapped by episodic action…Bridges is okay." *Variety*

'British crispness enhances a new United Artists double bill, … first and better of these imports—is down-right old-fashioned in essence. "Attack on the Iron Coast," … cuts straight ahead, with little sideline nonsense, to a slambang finale, excellently piloted by Paul Wendkos" *New York Times*

The Blood of Fu Manchu (1968) 92 mins (color)

"LUSCIOUS LIPS—LETHAL In their biting sting of death!"

Ada Films/Commonwealth United Entertainment/Constantin Film Produktion/ Terra-Filmkunst/Towers of London Productions/Udastex Films; d: Jess Franco; screenplay and story by: Jess Franco, Manfred R

Köhler, Peter Welbeck (aka Harry Alan Towers); from novels by Sax Rohmer; ph: Manuel Merino; ed: Allan Morrison (original version), Waltraut Lindenau; Angel Serrano, Stanley Frazen (uncredited); pd: Peter Gasper; m: Daniel White

Synopsis: Fu Manchu and his daughter infect women with deadly venom, the women are not harmed but kill men with a kiss—but Lee's would-be nemesis Nayland Smith survives and comes after him.

Cast: Christopher Lee (Fu Manchu), **Richard Greene** (Nayland Smoth), Shirley Eaton (The Black Widow), Tsai Chin (Lin Tang), Maria Rohm (Ursula), Howard Marion Crawford (Dr Petrie), Götz George (Carl Jansen), Richard Palacios (Sancho Villa), Loni Von Friedl (Celeste), Frances Khan (Carmen)

Milestones and Millstones: Richard Greene

Comment: A truly dire screenplay is well matched by Franco's dismal storytelling, rendering Lee's fourth time out as Rohmer's legendary villain almost unwatchable. Filmed in Brazil.

Reviews: "Lurid but exceptionally scrappy melodrama... both the tale and the dialogue are corny but the succession of violence and sudden death may entertain uncritical fans." *CEA Film Report*

"Christopher Lee, in the type of role to which he has become accustomed, is good..." *Kine Weekly*

Curse of the Crimson Altar/US: The Crimson Cult (1968) 87 mins (color)

THE HIGH PRIESTESS OF EVIL... A MONSTROUS FIEND
WITH AN OVERPOWERING LUST FOR BLOOD...

Tigon British Film Productions Limited; d: Vernon Sewell; ep: Tony Tenser; p: **Louis M Heyward**; ap: Gerry Levy; screenplay: Mervyn Halsman, Henry Lincoln, **Louis M Heyward** (uncredited), Gerry Levy (uncredited); story by: **Jerry Sohl**; from the story *Dreams in the Witch House* by H P Lovecraft; ph: John Coquillon; ed: Howard Lanning; ad: Derek Barrington; m; Peter Knight

Synopsis: Professor Boris Karloff saves a young man from being sacrificed when he and his girlfriend are invited to visit evil wizard Christopher Lee's mansion.

Cast: Boris Karloff (Professor Marshe), Christopher Lee (Morley), Mark Eden (Robert Manning), Barbara Steele (Lavinia Morley), Michael Gough (Elder), Virginia Wetherell (Elder), Rosemary Reede (Esther), Derek Tansley (Judge), Michael Warren (Chauffeur), Ron Pember (Gas Attendant), Rupert Davies (Vicar)

Milestones and Millstones: Boris Karloff, Louis M Heyward, Jerry Sohl

Comment: 80-year-old Karloff, in the last film he made in England, in a wheelchair and virtually unable to walk, still dominated and adds valuable dramatic weight to a largely predicable shocker.

Reviews: "Boris Karloff, Christopher Lee, and things that go bump in the night should make a fast but average buck in multiples on the teen-scare circuit." *Variety*

"Getting Boris Karloff and Christopher Lee together in a story about witchcraft is about as sound insurance against failure as anything could be." *Kine Weekly*

"Karloff himself, cadaverous and almost wholly crippled, acts with a quiet lucidity of such great beauty that it is a refreshment merely to hear him speak old claptrap...I should be hard pressed to defend 'The Crimson Cult' on any grounds other than affection for the subject and some of the cast." *New York Times*

The Face of Eve/Eve/Diana, Daughter of the Wilderness
(1968) 97 mins (color)

> "*Everybody's Talking About EVE!* "LOVES TO LOVE,
> HATES TO MATE!"

Ada Films/Harold Goodman Associates/Hispamer Films/Sargon Etablishment/Towers of London Productions/Udastex Films; d: Robert Lynn, Jeremy Summers; screenplay/story: Harry Alan Towers; ph: Manuel Merino; ed: Allan Morrison; ad: Santiago Ontañón; m: Malcolm Lockyer

Synopsis: While searching for missing Inca treasure in the Amazon jungle, Robert Walker Jr saves a lost woman worshipped as a goddess from showman Fred Clark who wants her for his freak show.

Cast: Celeste Yarnall (Eve), **Robert Walker Jr** (Mike Yates), Herbert Lom (Diego), **Fred Clark** (John Burke), Christopher Lee (Colonel Stuart), Rosenda Monteros (Conchita), Maria Rohm (Anna), José Maria

Caffarel (José), Ricardo Diaz (Bruno),
> **Milestones and Millstones:** Robert Walker Jr, Fred Clark
> **Comment:** Colourful hokum, even by the usual cut-price standards of Towers B features: reportedly (and sensibly) unbilled Towers regular Jess Franco completed the film when credited director Lynn quit.
> **Reviews:** "A thin and routine story…this is a weak presentation… for popular audiences it rates only as a poor supporting entertainment but it might better entertain the uncritical and unsophisticated." *CEA Film Report*
> "… amiable nonsense suitable for children and the undemanding." *Today's Cinema*

The Last Shot You Hear (1968) 90 mins (color/b&w)

"Sex becomes a murder weapon…"

Lippert Pictures; d: **Gordon Hessler**; ep: **Robert L Lippert**; p: Jack Parsons; screenplay: Tim Shields; based on the play *The Sound of Murder* by William Fairchild; ph: David Holmes; ed: Robert Winter; ad: Kenneth Ryan; m: **Bert Shefter**

Synopsis: A woman and her lover devise an amateurish scheme to murder her husband who refuses to give her a divorce but it miscarries.

Cast: Hugh Marlowe (Charles Nordeck), Zena Walker (Eileen Forbes), Patricia Haines (Anne Nordeck), William Dysart (Peter Marriott), Thorley Walters (General Jowett), Lionel Murton (Rubens), Joan Young (Mrs Jowett), Helen Horton (Dodie Rubens), John Nettleton (Detective Inspector Nash)

Milestones and Millstones: Gordon Hessler, Robert L Lippert, Bert Shefter

Comment: Under-cast and saddled with an undernourished screenplay, Hessler cooks up a boring B.

Reviews: "A dreary suspense item… turned up yesterday at the bottom of a double bill. The only surprising thing is that this British film managed to squeak past customs." *New York Times*

"Produced in England for an obvious price that was both too low for what was intended and too high for what was obtained… a dull, lower-case suspenser…flat writing, direction and production." *Variety*

The Limbo Line (1968) 99 mins

London Independent Producers/ Trio Films/Group W Films; d: Samuel Gallu; ep: William J Gell, Edward G Barnes; p: Frank Bevis: screenplay: Donald James; based on the novel by Victor Canning; ph: John Wilcox; ed: Peter Weatherley; pd: Scott MacGregor; m: Johnnie Spence

Synopsis: Intelligence agent Craig Stevens sets out to stop Soviet spies who kidnap defectors to the West and send them back to Russia via "the Limbo Line."

Cast: Craig Stevens (Manston), Kate O'Mara (Irina), Moira Redmond (Ludmilla), Vladek Sheybal (Oleg), Robert Urquhart (Hardwick), Norman Bird (Chivers), Yolande Turner (Pauline), Frederick Jaeger (Alex), Alan Barry (Williams), Eugene Deckers (Cadillet), Jean Marsh (Dilys), Eric Mason (Castle)

Milestones and Millstones: Craig Stevens, Samuel Gallu

Comment: Standard second feature spy-action thriller, with the obligatory American lead.

Reviews: "Crammed with gunplay scrapping and doublecrossing, this is one of those spy actioners that gets a bit complicated plotwise but are useful entertainment as blenders with a contrasting film in easy-going situations...Stevens gives a strong solid performance." *Variety*

The Lost Continent (1968) 97 mins (color)

"A Living Hell That Time Forgot!"

Hammer Films/Seven Arts Pictures; d/p: Michael Carreras, Leslie Norman (uncredited); ep: Anthony Hinds; ap: Peter Manley; screenplay: Michael Nash (aka Michael Carreras); from novel *Uncharted Seas* by Dennis Wheatley; ph: Paul Beeson; ed: Chris Barnes; sfx: Arthur Hayward, Robert A Mattey, Cliff Richardson; Peter Hutchinson; m: Gerard Schürmann

Synopsis: Passengers on a tramp steamer stranded in the Sargasso Sea end up shipwrecked on a remote island inhabited by a bizarre inbred colony—and worse...

Cast: Eric Porter (Captain Lansen), **Hildegard Knef** (Eva Peters), Suzanna Leigh (Unity Webster), Tony Beckley (Harry Tyler), Nigel Stock:

(Dr Webster), Neil McCallum (First Officer Hemmings), Ben Carruthers (Ricaldi), Jimmy Hanley, (Bartender), James Cossins (Chief engineer), Dana Gillespie (Sarah)
Milestones and Millstones: Hildegard Knef
Comment: Hammer hokum at its least impressive, saddled with a broken-backed screenplay, tacky monsters and killer seaweed created by patently cheap special effects. Partially compensated for by climactic action sequences.
Reviews: "Action-laden to an extreme, film may do okay in suburbun situations and in drive-ins, where audience "discrimination" is no problem... special effects are second-rate." *Variety*
"...marvelously absurd, straight-faced anthology of comic-strip plots, dialogue, devices and special effects... consumes stock characters and situations with all the appetite of one of its own oversized plastic snails." *New York Times*

Mosquito Squadron (1968) 90 mins (color/b&w)

"THE NAZIS DARED THEM, THE ALLIES DAMNED THEM! THEY FLEW IN WITHOUT A CHANCE AND CAME OUT COVERED IN GLORY!"

Oakmont Productions; d: **Boris Sagal**; p: **Lewis J Rachmil**; screenplay: Donald S Sandford, Joyce Perry; ph: Paul Beeson; ed: John S Smith; sfx: Les Bowie; ad: William C Andrews; m: Frank Cordell
Synopsis: WW2 Mosquito pilot David McCallum loses his oldest friend to the war and rekindles a romance with his widow but, sent on a mission to destroy a German rocket factory, finds his friend alive and imprisoned at the target.
Cast: David McCallum (Squadron Leader Quint Munroe), Suzanne Neve (Beth Scott) Donald Gray (RAF Air Commodore Hufford), David Buck (Squadron Leader David ("Scotty") Scott), David Dundas (Flight Lieutenant Douglas Shelton), Dinsdale Landen (Wing Commander Clyde Penrose)
Milestones and Millstones: Boris Sagal, Lewis J Rachmil
Comment: A bombardment of war movie clichés decorated with matching wooden performances, re-using the title sequence from *Opera-*

tion *Crossbow* (1965) and footage from 1964's *633 Squadron* to boost its B feature impact. Not released in US until 1970.

Reviews: "Other than an excellent rescue mission sequence at the end of the film, it generates little excitement." *Variety*

Subterfuge (1968) 89 mins (color)

BLACKMAIL, BULLETS AND SEDUCTIVE WOMEN MAY BE DANGEROUS TO YOUR HEALTH!"

Commonwealth United Entertainment/Intertel; d: Peter Graham Scott; ep: Trevor Wallace; p: Peter Snell; ph: Roy Garner; ed: Bill Lewthwaite; pd: Ronald Fouracre; ad: Roy Fouracre; m: Cyril Ornadel

Synopsis: American agent Gene Barry comes to London on vacation and lands in danger when he joins the British intelligence to help break up a spy ring.

Cast: Gene Barry (Donovan), **Joan Collins** (Anne Langley), Richard Todd (Colonel Victor Redmayne), Tom Adams (Peter Langley), Suzanna Leigh (Donetta), Michael Rennie (Goldsmith), Marius Goring (Shevik), Scott Forbes (Pannell), Colin Gordon (Kitteridge), Guy Deghy (Dr. Lundgren)

Milestones and Millstones: Gene Barry, Joan Collins

Comment: Old-fashioned TV movie-style spy thriller with an over-complex storyline: Collins does rather more posing than actual acting.

Reviews: "...a not-too-adept action programmer, slow script, bland plotline and generally pale thesping add up to lower half slot in general release double-bill program." *Variety*

"... a fairly routine secret agent story, but it is confusing, with many loose ends and assorted characters, so that it is hard to keep pace with who are the enemy and who are secret agents... has good star appeal..." *CEA Film Report*

Witchfinder General/US: The Conqueror Worm (1968) 87 mins (color)

"LEAVE THE CHILDREN HOME... AND IF YOU ARE SQUEAMISH STAY HOME WITH THEM!!!!!!!"

Tigon British Film Productions/American International Productions; d: Michael Reeves; ep: **Samuel Z Arkoff**, Tony Tenser; p: **Louis M Heyward**; Arnold L Miller, Philip Waddilove: screenplay: Michael Reeves, Tom Baker; from the novel by Robert Basett; ph: John Coquillon; ed: Howard Lanning; sfx: Roger Dicken; ad: Jim Morahan; m: Paul Ferris

Synopsis: A vengeful soldier hunts sadistic 17th century English witch-finder Vincent Price who travels the country exploiting local superstitions and killing people for cash.

Cast: Vincent Price (Matthew Hopkins), Ian Ogilvy (Richard Marshall), Rupert Davies (John Lowes), Hilary Dwyer (Sara), Robert Russell (John Stearne), Patrick Wymark (Oliver Cromwell), Wilfrid Brambell (Horse dealer), Michael Beint (Captain Gordon), Nicky Henson (Trooper Swallow), Godfrey James (Webb)

Milestones and Millstones: Vincent Price, Samuel Z Arkoff, Louis M Heyward

Comment: Initially castigated for its bloody violence and sadism (justified by storyline), Price's vivid portrayal and strong direction confirm its superiority. US release title *The Conqueror Worm* has nothing to do with Poe's poem: presumably used simply to cash in on Price's Poe shockers.

Reviews: "...attractive young aspiring stars who seem to have been cast ...mainly for their ability to scream. Scream as though they were being slowly burned to death, or kicked, or poked, or stabbed—mainly about the eyes—with sticks, or shot through, or otherwise tortured, which, in fact, they are. Vincent Price has a good time..." *New York Times*

"Is of a genre that 20 years ago would pack the small fry into the nabe bijou on a Saturday afternoon. But this 1968 edition substitutes gore for suspense and action, and inclusion of too-explicit sex scenes makes the film unsuitable for kids." *Variety*

Doppelganger/US: Journey to the Far Side of the Sun
(1969) (color)

"MAN HAS CONQUERED THE MOON WITH THE EPIC APOLLO 11 FLIGHT! NOW TAKE ANOTHER MOMENTOUS JOURNEY!"

Century 21 Television; d: **Robert Parrish**; p: Gerry Anderson, Sylvia Anderson; ap: Ernest Holding; screenplay: Gerry Anderson, Sylvia Anderson, Donald James; story by: Gerry Anderson, Sylvia Anderson; ph: John Read; ed: Len Walter; sfx: Derek Meddings, Norman Foster; ad: Bob Bell; music: Barry Gray

Synopsis: American Roy Thinnes and a British astronaut are sent into space in 2089 to investigate a new planet discovered on the other side of the sun but their craft crashes on landing—and their troubles double up...

Cast: Roy Thinnes (Colonel Glenn Ross), Patrick Wymark (Jason Wobb), Ian Hendry (John Kane), **Lynn Loring** (Sharon Ross), Loni Von Friedl (Lisa Hertman), Herbert Lom (Dr Hassler), Franco Derosa (Paulo Landi), George Sewell (Mark Neuman), **Edward Bishop** (David Poulson), Philip Madoc (Dr Pontini)

Milestones and Millstones: Robert Parrish, Roy Thinnes, Lynn Loring, Edward Bishop

Comment: Gerry and Sylvia Anderson's first feature with human actors rather the puppets from their TV series, among them *Stingray* (1964-1965) and *Thunderbirds* (1965-1966): film's concept—a human's alien double returns to Earth—is good but dramatically underdeveloped.

Reviews: "Interesting sci-fi premise falls apart... despite some of the finest and most imaginative special effects, sharp production values... so burdened with confusing elements that it frequently fails to make sense." *Variety*

"The basic story is an intriguing and intelligent science fiction idea but on the screen it emerges as confusing and intricate.... overall popular appeal is unlikely to be great." *CEA Film Report*

"Modest-sized and unspectacular, it snugly cuts corners with some crisp dialogue and an adroit blend of sleekly futuristic sets and miniature settings in nice color... Parrish's direction rather deftly integrates the whole setup." *New York Times*

Moon Zero Two (1969) 100 mins (color)

"SEE THE MOON COMMUNITY IN THE YEAR 2021 SEE THE
FIRST SPACE GUN BATTLE ON THE MOON SEE THE
FABULOUS GO JOS DANCING ON THE MOON
SEE THE TRAVEL VEHICLE OF THE FUTURE"

Warner Brothers/Seven Arts/Hammer Films; d: Roy Ward Baker; p/screenplay: Michael Carreras; from an original story by Gavin Lyall, Frank Hardman, Martin Davison; ph: Paul Beeson; special effects photography (sfx ph): Nick Allder; sfx: Les Bowie; ed: Spencer Reeve; ad: Scot MacGregor; m: Don Ellis

Synopsis: In 2021 a multimillionaire hires astronaut James Olson to blast an oncoming asteroid out of its orbit—but Olson goes up against the millionaire when he finds his 'sponsor' is a crook.

Cast: James Olson (Bill Kemp), Catherine Schell (Clementine Taplin), Warren Mitchell (J. J. Hubbard), Adrienne Corri (Elizabeth Murphy), Ori Levy (Korminski), Dudley Foster (Whitsun), Bernard Bresslaw (Harry), Sam Kydd (Barman), Neil McCallum (Space Captain), Carol Cleveland (Hostess)

Milestones and Millstones: James Olson

Comment: Marketed as a "Space Western" and featuring shootouts and saloon brawls in Moon City, Hammer's attempt to cash in on the success of *2001: A Space Odyssey* (1968) features effective special effects seriously adulterated by a poor screenplay.

"As silly a piece of pseudo-science fiction as you could loathe to find." *The Observer*

"…never makes up its mind whether it is a spoof or a straightforward space-adventure yarn and the uneasy combo comes adrift…Olson is a melancholy hero." *Variety*

The Oblong Box (1969) 91 mins (color)

"Edgar Allan Poe's classic tale of the restless dead and their
subterranean world of horror and the unspeakable!"

American International Productions; d: **Gordon Hessler**; ep: **Louis M Heyward**; p: Gordon Hessler; ap: Pat Green; screenplay: Lawrence

Huntingdon; add dial: Christopher Wicking, Michael Reeves; from a story by Edgar Allan Poe; ph: John Coquillon; ed: Max Benedict; ad: George Provis; m: Harry Robinson

Synopsis: An insane disfigured 19th century Englishman imprisoned by his brother Vincent Price is accidentally buried alive but embarks on a revenge-killing spree when grave robbers unearth him.

Cast: Vincent Price (Julian), Christopher Lee (Dr. Neuhartt), Alastair Williamson (Sir Edward Markham), Rupert Davies (Kemp), Uta Levka (Heidi), Sally Geeson (Sally Baxter), Peter Arne (Samuel Trench), Hilary Dwyer (Elizabeth Markham), Maxwell Shaw (Tom Hackett), Carl Rigg (Mark Norton)

Milestones and Millstones: Vincent Price, Gordon Hessler, Louis M Heyward

Comment: Price and Lee's first picture together was sold as AIP's eleventh Edgar Allan Poe-based movie. Hessler replaced original director Michael Reeves. Obvious but effective period shocker with Price in fine form but Lee largely wasted.

Reviews: "… a sort of a chiller, if the audience isn't too demanding … Price as usual overacts, but it is an art here to fit the mood and piece and as usual Price is good in his part." *Variety*

"The British and American producers, who have been mining Edgar Allan Poe's seemingly inexhaustible literary lode like mad, now have unearthed "The Oblong Box" to illustrate once again that horror can be made to be quaint, laughable and unconvincing at modest prices." *The New York Times*

When Dinosaurs Ruled The Earth (1969) 96 mins (color)

Enter an age of unknown terrors, pagan worship and virgin sacrifice…

Hammer Films; d: Val Guest; p: Aida Young; screenplay: Val Guest; treatment: J G Ballard; ph: Dick Bush; ed: Peter Curran; special visual effects/sfx: **Jim Danforth**, Allan Bryce, Roger Dicken, Brian Johnson; ad: John Blezard; m: Mario Nascimbene

Synopsis: In prehistoric time a cave girl who escapes from being sacrificed to the gods has to survive dinosaurs and rival tribes people.

Cast: Victoria Vetri (Sanna), Robin Hawdon (Tara), Patrick Allen (Kingsor/narrator), Drewe Henley (Khaku), Magda Konopka (Ulido), Imogen Hassell (Ayak), Patrick Holt (Ammon), Jan Rossini (Rock Girl), Carol Hawkins (Yani), Mara O'Brien (Omah), Connie Tilton (Land Mother)

Milestones and Millstones: Victoria Vetri, Jim Danforth

Comment: Hammer's follow-up to 1966's *One Million Years B.C.* is eminently enjoyable despite being simply a seriously silly prehistoric saga smartly decorated with Jim Danforth's impressive, Academy Award-nominated special effects.

Reviews: "The story is no great shakes but makes a passable peg on which to hang the trick work and special effects… good entertainment of its kind for unsophisticated and juvenile audiences." *CEA Film Report*

"Alas, the budget was too small for the facts to convince, but the film still includes a few of the strangest shots in British cinema." *Time Out*

The 1970s 4

> "Horror movies are the best date movies. There's no wondering, 'When do I put my arm around her?'"
>
> – Eli Roth

Crescendo (1970) 83 mins (color)

"The night the loving ended and the kiling began!"

Hammer Films; d: Alan Gibson; p: Michael Carreras; screenplay: Jimmy Sangster, Alfred Shaughnessy; from an original screenplay by Alfred Shaughnessy and Michael Reeves; ph: Paul Beeson; ed: Chris Barnes; ad: Scott McGregor; m: Malcolm Williamson

Synopsis: Stephanie Powers faces mounting terror when she goes to the South of France to write a thesis on a recently dead composer and meets his drug-addicted son James Olson.

Cast: Stefanie Powers (Susan Roberts), **James Olson** (Georges / Jacques), Margaretta Scott (Danielle Ryman), Jane Lapotaire (Lillianne), Joss Ackland (Carter), Kirsten Lindholm (Catherine)

Milestones and Millstones: Stefanie Powers, James Olson

Comment: Shaughnessy wrote the original script in the mid-1960s, Reeves brought Hammer a screenplay in 1966, James Carreras spent two years in the mid-1960s trying to produce *Crescendo* with Joan Crawford but could not raise the budget. Finally filmed with Sangster's predictable screenplay featuring too many *Psycho*-influenced chiller tropes. Overdirected and ultimately unremarkable.

Reviews: "It is soundly acted ... maybe its quota of suspense and shock will be sufficient to put is across with less sophisticated popular audiences." *CEA Film Report*

"For keen followers of Hammer's efforts, it makes a new departure. To the usual blood, some sex is added—mainly underwater nudity and a few bare bottoms. Everyone acts with conviction beyond the call of duty..." *Films and Filming*

Cry of the Banshee (1970) 91 mins (color)

"EDGAR ALLAN POE probes new depths of TERROR!"

American International Pictures; d: **Gordon Hessler**; ep: **Louis M Heyward**, Gordon Hessler; p **Samuel Z Arkoff**; ap: Clifford Parkes; screenplay: Christopher Wicking; story by: Tim Kelly; ph: John Coquillon; ed: Oswald Hafenrichter; pd: George Provis; m: **Les Baxter**

Synopsis: Evil Lord Vincent Price pays horribly for murdering the members of a witches' coven when a murderous 'banshee' is summoned to avenge his victims.

Cast: Vincent Price (Lord Edward Whitman), Hilary Heath (Maureen Whitman), Carl Rigg (Harry Whitman), Patrick Mower (Roderick), Essy Persson (Lady Patricia Whitman), Elisabeth Bergner (Oona), Stephan Chase (Sean Whitman), Sally Geeson (Sarah) Hugh Griffith (Mickey)

Milestones and Millstones: Vincent Price, Gordon Hessler, Samuel Z Arkoff, Les Baxter

Comment: Routine shocker mildly redeemed by Price at full throttle and interesting opening credits by *Monty Python's Flying Circus* animator/star Terry Gilliam.

Reviews: "...slickly produced and photographed programmer about gillies and ghosties and things that go bump in the night...Price is again the medieval evil...Hessler evokes a heavy brooding sense of evil, getting thoroughly good performances." *Variety*

"Mr. Price, a veteran of a score of these hapless horror items, plays it all with proper pseudo gusto. "Where does she get all that power?" he asks, eyes glaring and nostrils flaring. Unfortunately there's no power here, just nice bogey men and women." *New York Times*

Every Home Should Have One (1970) 94 mins (color)

Example/British Lion Film Corporation; d: Jim Clark; p: Ned Sherrin; ap: Terry Ginwood; screenplay: Marty Feldman, Denis Nordern, Barry Took; story by: Herbert Krelzmer, Milton Shulman; ph: Ken Hodges; ed: Ralph Sheldon; ad: Roy Stannard; m: John Cameron

Synopsis: An adman runs into trouble when he tries to promote porridge as something sexy.

Cast: Marty Feldman (Teddy Brown), Judy Cornwell (Liz Brown), **Shelley Berman** (Nat Kaplan), Julie Ege (Inga Guteborg), Dinsdale Landen (Reverend Geoffrey Mellish), Harry Miller (Richard Brown), Moray Watson (Frank Chandler), Penelope Keith (Lotta van Gelstein), Patrick Cargill (Truffitt)

Milestones and Millstones: Shelley Berman

Comment: Slipshod comedy with fewer laughs than a botched post mortem and sex sequences that do nothing to improve it. Berman wasted in non-role; Feldman was incredibly fortunate to work in Hollywood after this misfire.

Reviews: "Too many cooks have spoiled the Feldman broth in his first feature film. He's mixed up in plenty cockeyed and funny situations, but not enough…scrappy and flabby…Berman registers strongly." *Variety*

"… covers a wide range of humour ranging from brash and vulgar farce to wit, thereby providing something for most tastes. For some, Marty Feldman might be an acquired taste…" *CEA film Report*

Hell Boats (1970) 95 mins (color)

"THEIR TARGET; HELL-ON-EARTH! THEIR JOB: HIT IT HEAD-ON!"

Oakmont Productions/Mirisch Films; d: **Paul Wendkos**: p: **Lewis J Rachmil**; screenplay: **Anthony Spinner**, Donald Ford, Derek Ford; story by: S.S. Schweitzer; ph: Paul Beeson; ed: John S Smith; sfx: Ron Ballanger; ad: Anthony Pratt; m: Frank Cordell

Synopsis: Serving with the Royal Navy American commander James Franciscus is assigned in 1941 to command a flotilla of motor torpedo boats on a top-secret mission against the Nazis.

Cast: James Franciscus (Lieutenant Commander Jeffords, RNVR) Elizabeth Shepherd (Alison), Ronald Allen (Commander Ashurst, RN), Reuven Bar-Yotam (Chief Petty Officer Yacov), Mark Hawkins (Lieutenant Barlow, RN), Drewe Henley (Sun Lieutenant Johnson RN), Philip Madoc ('E' Boat Captain)

Milestones and Millstones: James Franciscus, Paul Wendkos, Lewis J Rachmil

Comment: Passable World War Two action/adventure: although some action sequences are staged rather too obviously by employing models.

Reviews: "...a straightforward story which is some respects is rather stereotyped and is not very impressively played, but it has enough action plus a moderately and spectacular support to make it an acceptable support." *CEA Film Report*

"...feeble Second World War drama..." *Radio Times*

Scream and Scream Again (1970) 95 mins (color)

"TRIPLE DISTILLED HORROR ...as powerful as a vat of boiling ACID!"

American International Pictures/Tigon; d: **Gordon Hessler**; ep: **Louis M Heyward**; p: **Max Rosenberg, Milton Subotsky**; screenplay: Christopher Wicking; from the novel *The Disorientated Man* by Peter Saxon; ph: John Coquillon; ed: Peter Elliott; ad: Don Mingaye; m: David Whitaker

Synopsis: The police hunt for a grisly serial killer in London who drains his victims' blood to use to create a super-race.

Cast: Vincent Price (Dr Browning), Christopher Lee (Fremont), Peter Cushing (Benedek), Alfred Marks (Superintendent Bellaver), Christopher Matthews (David Sorel), Judy Huxtable (Sylvia), Yutte Stensgaard (Erika), Anthony Newlands (Ludwig), Julian Holloway (Griffin), Peter Sallis (Schweitz)

Milestones and Millstones: Vincent Price, Gordon Hessler; Louis M Heyward, Max Rosenberg, Milton Subotsky

Comment: The three Horror Greats—together on screen for the first and sadly only time and, with Price enjoying the lion's share of screen time—give this gaudy horror show a welcome boost despite Wicking's unsure screenplay.

Reviews: "Very effective, suspensefully developed and gory horror story with spy and sci-fi overtones...Price is once again effective as the rock generation's Boris Karloff." *Variety*

"A lively mixture of melodrama, police routine and investigation, espionage, foreign totalitarian power and traditional horror hokum of the clinical and severed-hand school...Price plays a characteristic role in his own inimitable way." *CEA Film Report*

"Familiar territory is explored yet again... will make you scream—either with terror or laughter, depending on your temperament." *Jewish Chronicle*

Toomorrow (1970) 95 mins (color)

Lowndes Productions Limited; d/screenplay: Val Guest; p: **Harry Saltzman, Don Kirshner**; ap: John Palmer; ph: Dick Bush; ed: Julien Caunter, Alan Osbiston; pd: Michael Stringer; sfx: John Stears; visual fx: Ray Caple, Cliff Culley; ad: Ernest Archer, Bert Davy; m: Hugo Montenegro

Synopsis: Extraterrestrials abduct the British pop group *Toomorrow* in order to use their unique 'vibrations' to save their sterile race.

Cast: Olivia Newton-John (Olivia), Roy Marsden (Alpha), Imogen Hassall (Amy), Roy Dotrice (John Williams), Karl Chambers (Karl), Vic Cooper: (Vic), Benny Thomas (Benny), Tracy Crisp (Suzanne Gilmore), Shakira Caine (Karl's Friend), Robert Raglan (Principal), Diane Keen (Music Student)

Milestones and Millstones: Harry Saltzman, Don Kirshner

Comment: Pop music maven Kirshner (creator of The Monkees) joined forces with James Bond producer Saltzman in 1965 intending to manufacture another hit band: they failed. The film took two years to make and ran for just a week in London. The sound-track record flopped and the movie was withdrawn from circulation.

Reviews: "Despite the talent involved, the project was a misfire, with the songs and production sounding saccharine and gimmicky, and the movie more silly than anything else." *Billboard*

"This is an entertainingly ridiculous lark which is an uncommon blend of pop music, science-fiction and high-spirited youthful hi-jinks... bright and lively, is decidedly unsophisticated and should appeal well to young audiences..." *CEA Film Report*

Trog (1970) 93 mins (color)

"From the boiling rage of a world hurled back one million years comes... TROG"

Herman Cohen Productions; d: Freddie Francis; p: **Herman Cohen**, Harry Wolveridge; screenplay: **Aben Kandel**; story by: Peter Bryan, John Gilling; ph: Desmond Dickinson; ed: Oswald Hafenrichter; ad: Geoffrey Tozer; designer *Trog*: Charles Parker; m: John Scott

Synopsis: Anthropologist Joan Crawford captures a killer troglodyte and sets out to domesticate the part man-part ape with ultimate unfortunate results when a villain releases him.

Cast: Joan Crawford (Dr Brockton), Michael Gough (Sam Murdock), Bernard Kay (Inspector Greenham), Kim Braden (Anne Brockton), David Griffin (Malcolm Travers), John Hammill (Cliff), Thorley Walters (Minister), Jack May (Dr Selbourne), Geoffrey Case (Bill), Simon Lack (Colonel Vickers)

Milestones and Millstones: Joan Crawford, Herman Cohen, Aben Kandel

Comment: Crawford's final feature film in a career spanning almost 50 years was easily her worst with little going for it apart from her bravery in the face of an execrable screenplay. Director (and two time Oscar winner for cinematography) Francis makes *Trog* look good which, sadly, simply serves to underline its awfulness.

Reviews: "There is, however, a rudimentary virtue in *Trog*...in that it proves that Joan Crawford is grimly working at her craft. Unfortunately, the determined lady, who is fetching in a variety of chic pants suits and dresses, has little else going for her." *New York Times*

"However, Joan Crawford's authority is such that she turns the melodramatics of the plot into a plea for tolerance..." *Films and Filming*

The Firechasers (1971) 101 mins (color)

Incorporated Television Company (ITC); d: Sidney Hayers; p: Julian Wintle; ap: Philip Levene, Barry Delmaine; screenplay: Philip Levene; ph: Alan Hume; ed: Lionel Selwyn; sfx: Cliff Culley; ad: Harry Pottle; m: Laurie Johnson

Synopsis: When Insurance investigator Chad Everett goes on the trail of an arsonist in London he meets reporter Anjanette Comer and falls for her.

Cast: Chad Everett (Quentin Barnaby), **Anjanette Comer** (Toby Collins), Keith Barron (Jim Maxwell), Joanne Dainton (Valerie Chrane), Rupert Davies (Prentice), James Hayter (Inspector Herman), Robert Flemyng (Carlton), Roy Kinnear (Roscoe), Allan Cuthbertson (Jarvis), John Loder (Routledge)

Milestones and Millstones: Chad Everett, Anjanette Comer

Comment: British independent TV producers ITC hoped to follow the success in the US of British-made TV series like *Robin Hood* and *The Persuaders* with American-aimed B features decorated with Hollywood stars. This average offering deservedly went straight to TV in the US without a cinema release.

Reviews: "... a fairly routine mystery plot...Some of the fires are fairly spectacular but the script and acting are the film's let down." *CEA Film Report*

Death Line/US: Raw Meat (1972) 87 mins (color)

"BENEATH MODERN LONDON buried alive in its plague-ridden tunnels lives a tribe of once-humans. Neither men nor women, they are less than animals...they are the raw meat of the human race"

Harbor Ventures/K-L Productions; d: **Gary Sherman**; p: **Paul Maslansky**; screenplay: Ceri Jones; story by: **Gary Sherman**; ph: Alex Thompson; ed: Geoffrey Foot; sfx: John Horton; ad: Dennis Gordon-Orr; m: Will Malone, Jeremy Rose

Synopsis: A prominent politician vanishes in London and, after questioning eyewitnesses Alan Ladd Jr and his girlfriend, the investigating police inspector discovers a tribe of cannibals living underground in the subway system.

Cast: Donald Pleasence (Inspector Calhoun), **David Ladd** (Alex Campbell) Sharon Gurney (Patricia Wilson) Norman Rossington (Detective Sergeant Rogers), Christopher Lee (Stratton-Villiers, MI5), Clive Swift (Inspector Richardson), Hugh Armstrong (The 'Man'), June Turner (The 'Woman')

Milestones and Millstones: David Ladd, Gary Sherman, Paul Maslansky

Comment: Re-edited for the US as *Raw Meat* this rocky horror show attained something of cult status despite its not that effective blending of grisly horror, black comedy and deliberate larger-than-life acting, notably by Pleasence. (Lee has major billing but worked for only one morning). Shooting in the London Underground adds valuable atmosphere. Sherman, who reportedly helped finance the film with money from Coke ads, stated: *"Death Line* was the first of its kind…there had never been anything like it before. I'm very proud of it! … just a really fun film to make."

Reviews: "… it's undermined by several vast improbabilities in the script and by the painfully inept performance of one of its leads, David Ladd" *Roger Ebert*

"… we spend an inordinate amount of time in the madman's dark, dark and bloody lair…peering through the murk at the most revolting sights imaginable and wondering how such a sick and sick-making film ever came to be made." *Daily Mail*

Horror Express/Panico en el Transiberiano (1972) 88 mins (color)

"A NIGHTMARE OF TERROR TRAVELLING ABOARD
THE HORROR EXPRESS!"

Benmar Productions/Granada Films; d: Gene Martin (aka Eugenio Martin); p: **Bernard Gordon**; Gregorio Sacristán; screenplay: Arnaud d'Usseau, Julian Halevy (aka Julian Zimet); based on *Who Goes There?* (1938) by John W. Campbell, Jr.; ph: Alejandro Ulloa; ed: Robert C Dearberg; sfx: Pablo Pérez; visual fx: Brian Stevens; pd: Ramiro Gómez; m: John Cacavas

Synopsis: A strange frozen fossil brought aboard the Trans-Siberian Express in 1905 defrosts and the killer creature runs rampant causing terror and chaos—and worse happens when Cossack policeman Telly Savalas boards the train…

Cast: Christopher Lee (Professor Alexander Saxton), Peter Cushing (Dr Wells), Alberto de Mendoza (Inspector), Silvia Tortosa (Irina), **Telly Savalas** (Captain Kazak), Julio Peña (Mirov), Ángel del Pozo (Yevtuchenko), Helga Liné (Natasha), Georges Rigaud (Count Petrovski),

Alice Reinheart (Miss Jones)

Milestones and Millstones: Telly Savalas, Bernard Gordon

Comment: Cushing and Lee at their horror-film double-act best, plentiful suspense and action and an unusual setting add up to an entertaining second-feature shocker with unfamiliar Spanish actors adding atmosphere.

Reviews: "A good, gory giggle." *Jewish Chronicle*

"…the supernatural and medical horrors are enjoyably absurd…and it is always a pleasure to see Peter Cushing and Christopher Lee together." *The Sunday Times*

The Legend of Hell House (1973) 95 mins (color)

"FOR THE SAKE OF YOUR SANITY, PRAY IT ISN'T TRUE!"

Academy Pictures Corporation; d: John Hough; ep: **James H Nicholson, Susan Hart**; p: Albert Fennell, **Norman T Herman**; screenplay: **Richard Matheson**, from his novel *Hell House*; ph: Alan Hume, Tony White; ed: Geoffrey Foot; sfx; Tom Howard, Roy Whybrow; ad: Robert Jones; m: Della Derbyshire, Brian Hodgson, Dudley Simpson

Synopsis: When Roddy McDowall and three other people spend time in a haunted house they are subjected to a series of supernatural events.

Cast: Roddy McDowall (Benjamin Fischer), Pamela Franklin (Florence Tanner). **Gayle Hunnicutt** (Ann Barrett), Clive Revill (Dr. Lionel Barrett), Roland Culver (Mr. Rudolph Deutsch), Peter Bowles (Hanley). Michael Gough (Emeric Belasco)

Milestones and Millstones: Roddy McDowall, Richard Matheson, James H Nicholson, Susan Hart, Gayle Hunnicutt, Norman T Herman

Comment: Efficient if ultimately unexceptional haunted house shocker, one of two films produced by Nicholson after quitting AIP. Matheson's screenplay tones down his original novel.

Reviews: "It comes as some kind of a relief to discover a horror film which strives for more than the happy hokum which has saturated the cinema screens over the past few years." *Films and Filming*

"… labours when it begin to explore the psychic phenomena in layman's terms. Until then it's quite chilling." *Photoplay*

The Beast Must Die (1974) 93 mins (color)

"ONE OF THESE EIGHT PEOPLE WILL TURN INTO A WEREWOLF CAN YOU GUESS WHO IT IS WHEN WE STOP THE FILM FOR THE WEREWOLF BREAK?
SEE IT…SOLVE IT…BUT DON'T TELL!"

Amicus Productions/British Lion Film Corporation; d/s: Paul Annett; ep: Robert H. Greenberg; p: **Max Rosenberg, Milton Subotsky**; ap: John Dark; screenplay: Michael Winder, Paul Annett, Scott Finch; based on the story *There Shall Be No Darkness* by James Blish; ph: Jack Hildyard; ed: Peter Tanner; sfx: Ted Samuels; ad: John Stoll; m: Douglas Gamley

Synopsis: Millionaire hunter Calvin Lockhart invites eight guests to his home, intending to expose one of them as a werewolf.

Cast: Calvin Lockhart (Tom Newcliffe), Peter Cushing (Dr Christopher Lundgren), Marlene Clark (Caroline Newcliffe), Anton Diffring (Pavel), Charles Gray (Arthur Bennington), Ciaran Madden (Davina Gilmore), Tom Chadbon (Paul Foote), Michael Gambon (Jan Jarmokowski), Sam Mansary (Butler)

Milestones and Millstones: Max Rosenberg, Milton Subotsky,

Comment: Amicus dropped their familiar format of portmanteau shockers for this sluggish blend of lycanthropy and whodunit, hoping to spice it up with a William Castle-style gimmick—a 30-second "werewolf break" for filmgoers to identify the werewolf. (It hardly helps either that the wolf is patently played by a dog).

Reviews: "It may not be the beast, but someone deserves to die for this lacklustre horror tale." *Film4*

"The story of an outbreak of animalist among the fatally flawed rich, with its parallel theme of the hunter who is fated to turn hunter … is surely capable of supporting a much more serious atmospheric treatment." *Monthly Film Bulletin*

Craze (1974) 96 mins (color)

"where BLACK MAGIC explodes into HORROR!"

Harbour Productions Limited; d: Freddie Francis; ep: Gustave Berne; p: **Herman Cohen**; screenplay: **Aben Kandel**, Herman Cohen; based on the novel *Infernal Idol* by Henry Seymour; ph: John Wilcox; ed: Henry Richardson; ad: George Provis; m: John Scott

Synopsis: Psychotic antiques dealer Jack Palance sacrifices women to the statue of an African god hoping for wealth and power in exchange.

Cast: Jack Palance (Neal Mottram), Diana Dors (Dolly Newman), Julie Ege (Helena), Edith Evans (Aunt Louise), Hugh Griffith (Solicitor), Trevor Howard (Inspector Bellamy), Suzy Kendall (Sally), Michael Jayston (Wall), Martin Potter (Ronnie), Percy Herbert (Detective Russet), Kathleen Byron (Muriel Sharp)

Milestones and Millstones: Jack Palance, Herman Cohen, Aben Kandel

Comment: Pitiable Herman Cohen production with wasted stylish direction failing to save it from its dire screenplay: it probably would not even have received an American release without Palance.

Reviews: "The film is a waste of everybody's time—including yours if you are misguided enough to see it." *Daily Express*

"… a poor and perfunctory script which quickly establishes Palance as nutty as they come and reduces him to uttering every line as though it had been dragged out of him only after half-an-hour's torture." *Time Out*

Madhouse/The Revenge of Dr Death (1974) 89 mins (color)

"IF STARK TERROR WERE ECSTACY… living here would be sheer bliss!" 'RECOMMENDED AS ADULT ENTERTAINMENT'

AIP/Amicus; d: Jim Clark; ep: **Samuel Z Arkoff; p: Max J Rosenberg**, **Milton Subotsky**; ap: John Dark; screenplay; Greg Morrison; adapted by: Ken Levison, **Robert Quarry** (uncredited); from the novel *Devilday* by Angus Hall; ph: Ray Parslow, Ken Coles; ed: Clive Smith; sfx: Kerss and Spencer; ad: Tony Curtis; m: Douglas Gamley

Synopsis: Murders bearing the Dr Death trademark erupt when horror film star Vincent Price, who found fame as Dr Death, comes to Britain to make a TV series.

Cast: Vincent Price (Paul Toombes), Peter Cushing (Herbert Flay), **Robert Quarry** (Oliver Quayle), Adrienne Corri (Faye Carstairs Flay), Natasha Pyne (Julia Wilson), Michael Parkinson (TV Interviewer), Linda Hayden (Elizabeth Peters), Barry Dennen (Gerry Blount), Jennie Lee Wright (Carol)

Milestones and Millstones: Vincent Price, Robert Quarry, Samuel Z Arkoff, Max J Rosenberg, Milton Subotsky

Comment: More comic than scary with Price gleefully over the top: clips from his AIP shockers, including *The Haunted Palace*, *The Pit and the Pendulum*, *House of Usher*, Karloff in *The Raven* and Rathbone in *Tales of Terror* stand in for *Dr Death* movies. British audiences were amused seeing real-life television chat show host Michael Parkinson embarrassing himself playing a TV chat show host.

Reviews: "Though it at times aspires to the level of Price's classic of macabre humor *Theater of Blood*, this film tends to stumble due to a middling script that dodges the opportunity to generate energy from the interaction of its two superb leads." *New York Times*

"A partially successful mixing of squeal-worthy shocks and in-jokes for film buffs." *Cinema TV Today*

The Mutations/The Freakmaker (1974) 92 mins (color)

"It's not nice to fool with Mother Nature...
... it can be HORRIFYING!"

Getty Picture Corporation; d: Jack Cardiff; ep: J Ronald Getty; p: **Robert D Weinback**; ap: Brad Harris, **Herbert G Luft**; screenplay: Robert D Weinback, Edward Mann; ph: Paul Beeson; ed: John Trumper; sfx: Mike Hope; special makeup: Charles C Parker; ad: Herbert Smith; m: Basil Kirchin, Jack Nathan

Synopsis: A mad scientist uses humans supplied by a freak show to try and create a new being by combining elements of both plants and animals.

Cast: Donald Pleasence (Professor Nolte), Tom Baker (Lynch), **Brad Harris** (Brian Redford), Julie Ege (Hedi), Michael Dunn (Burns), Scot

Antony (Tony), Jill Haworth (Lauren), Olga Anthony (Bridget), Lisa Collings (Prostitute), Tony Mayne (Tony), Kathy Kitchen (Kathy), Fran Fullenwider (Fat Lady)

Milestones and Millstones: Brad Harris, Robert D Weinback, Herbert G Luft

Comment: The grotesque creations are mildly memorable, unlike the film which soon evaporates from the viewer's memory. The most bizarre aspect is that famed cinematographer and director Jack Cardiff helmed it.

Reviews: "If these British-made science-fiction capers appear to be as up-to-date as genetic research, the end results are as basically familiar—or convincing—as a Boris Karloff going berserk in an underground laboratory." *New York Times*

"You've seen it all before but not, perhaps, Miss Ege stretched out on the operating table, the sprouting…not, surely, fig leaves!" *Daily Telegraph*

Persecution/The Graveyard/Sheba/The Terror of Sheba
(1974) 95 mins (color)

"LANA TURNER IN HER MOST DRAMATIC ROLE
SINCE "MADAME X"
SHEBA THE ULTIMATE MACACBRE"

Tyburn Film Productions/Fanfare Film Productions; d: Don Chaffey; p: Kevin Francis; screenplay: Robert B Hutton; Rosemary Wootten, Frederick Warner; ph: Kenneth Talbot; ed: Mike Campbell; ad: Jack Shampan; m: Paul Ferris

Synopsis: Crippled after her husband pushed her downstairs because of her infidelity, Lana Turner persecutes her son by exploiting his terror of cats—and he grows up seeking vengeance.

Cast: Lana Turner (Carrie Masters), Ralph Bates (David Masters), Trevor Howard (Paul Bellamy), Olga Georges-Picot (Monique Kalfon), Suzan Farmer (Janie Masters), Craig Weavers (Young David), Patrick Allen (Robert Masters), Ronald Howard (Dr Ross), Shelagh Fraser (Mrs Banks)

Milestones and Millstones: Lana Turner

Comment: Kevin Francis (son of cinematographer/director Freddie Francis) created Tyburn Films in the 1970s, presumably hoping to follow in the bloody footsteps of Hammer but stumbled and made little impact. This lusterless *homage* (so cheesy it would be better described as fromage) to *Baby Jane* is brain-dead from the start.

Reviews: "It's all heavy with Freud-laden symbols…The old-fashioned meller is riddled with ho-hum and sometimes laughably trite scripting. Also, very tame in the shock-horror department." *Variety*

… a very bad film; its plot is a horror story that lurches into farce, its dialogue moves on stilts; it even makes cats unlikeable. … Chaffey … Lana Turner … and Trevor Howard have all wasted their time and talents in this ludicrous picture." *The Tablet*

Phase IV (1974) 84 mins (color)

"THE DAY THE EARTH WAS TURNED INTO A CEMETERY!"

Alced Productions/Paramount; d: **Saul Bass**; p: **Paul B Radin**; screenplay: Mayo Simon; ph: Dick Bush; ed: Willy Kemplen; sfx: John Richardson, Rex Neville; ad: John Barry; m: Brian Gascoigne

Synopsis: Scientists investigate structures constructed in the Arizona desert by intelligent killer ants that have developed after a strange cosmic event.

Cast: Michael Murphy (James Lesko), Nigel Davenport (Dr Ernest Hubbs), Lynne Frederick (Kendra Eldridge), Helen Horton (Mildred Eldridge), Robert Henderson (Clete), David Healey (Voice: contact on radio)

Milestones and Millstones: Saul Bass

Comment: *Them!* (1954) revisited: yet another giant creature shocker largely notable for being the only film directed by Saul Bass, renowned for iconographic title sequences for such films as Preminger's *The Man With the Golden Arm* (1955) and Hitchcock's *North By Northwest* (1959) and *Psycho* (1960). While the ant sequences work well enough, the film as a whole does not. It has minor cult status, possibly because of having been shown on *Mystery Science Theater 3000*. Kenya, standing in for Arizona, gives the best performance.

Reviews: " … a concept and a script that is initially spellbinding but then quickly turns into mystifying vacillations between fact and largely unconvincing fiction … For all of its good, scientific and human intentions, "Phase IV" cries for a Phase V of fuller explanations." *New York Times*

"Despite endless conversation and dial twirling, Davenport and Murphy never focus the story in any dramatic direction. Joining them as an ant attack refugee, Lynne Frederick only adds to the confusion." *Variety*

I Don't Want to Be Born/US: The Devil Within Her/ Sharon's Baby (1975) 95 min (color)

"NOT SINCE ROSEMARY'S BABY! CONCEIVED BY THE DEVIL"

The Rank Organisation/Unicapital; d: Peter Sasdy; ep: Nato de Angeles; p: Norma Corney; screenplay: Stanley Price; story by: Nato de Angeles. ph: Kenneth Talbot; ed: Keith Palmer; sfx: Bert Luxford; ad: Roy Stannard; m: Ron Grainer; choreo: Mia Nada

Synopsis: After spurning a dwarf former stripper Joan Collins she gives birth to a murderous demonically possessed baby.

Cast: Joan Collins (Lucy Carlesi), Ralph Bates (Gino Carlesi), Eileen Atkins (Sister Albana), Donald Pleasence (Dr Finch), Hilary Mason (Mrs Hyde), Caroline Munro (Mandy Gregory), John Steiner (Tommy Morris), Janet Key (Jill Fletcher), George Clayden (Hercules), Derek Benfield (Police Inspector)

Milestones and Millstones: Joan Collins

Comment: Overwrought and underpowered attempt to meld elements from *Rosemary's Baby* (1968), *The Exorcist* (1973) and *It's Alive* (1974) and flavour them with tourist-friendly locations in Venice which fails to be much more than risible much of the time.

Reviews: "Although the suspense is weakened by the paternity subplot…the horrific scenes are numerous enough and busy enough to keep the averagely undemanding horror fan more than happy." *CinemaTV Today*

"This is an exceedingly stylish thriller … pacing is near flawless." *Variety*

"… both derivative and disastrous in every respect: a poor idea… an abominable screenplay, ludicrous acting and worst of all, Sasdy's direction." *Time Out*

The Land that Time Forgot (1975) 90 mins (color)

"THE ADVENTURE YOU WILL NEVER FORGET EDGAR RICE BURROUGHS' THE LAND THAT TIME FORGOT"

Amicus Productions/Lion International/Edgar Rice Burroughs Inc./Land Associates; d: Kevin Connor: ep: Robert H Greenberg; p: John Dark; **Max J Rosenberg; Milton Subotsky, Samuel Z Arkoff**; ap: John Peverall; screenplay: Michael Moorcock, James Cawthorn; from the novel by Edgar Rice Burroughs; ph: Alan Hume; ed: John Ireland; sfx: Derek Meddings, Roger Dickens (dinosaur sequences), production design: Maurice Carter; ad: Bert Davey; m: Douglas Gamley

Synopsis: Survivors from a British ship sunk by a German U-Boat are taken on board a submarine and end up in a world of prehistoric creatures and primitive people.

Cast: Doug McClure (Bowen Tyler), John McEnery (Captain Von Schoenvorts), Susan Penhaligon (Lisa Clayton), Keith Barron (Bradley), Anthony Ainley (Dietz), Godfrey James (Borg), Bobby Parr (Ahm), Declan Mulholland (Olson), Colin Farrell (Whiteley), Ben Howard (Benson)

Milestones and Millstones: Doug McClure, Max J Rosenberg, Milton Subotsky, Samuel Z Arkoff

Comment: Sometimes-rickety special effects (the submarine and ships were models while the prehistoric creatures were puppets) (since using stop-motion animation was unaffordable by Amicus), failed to prevent the film from becoming a hit and spawning sequels.

Reviews: "Despite arthritic dinosaurs and puffy pink smoke from volcanoes, this British adaptation of Edgar Rice Burroughs…should do okay in the juve market where thrills count more than technique." *Variety*

"This is rather fun… at least the action is unremitting… (the model work is excellent)…the monsters, too, are especially interesting." *Films and Filming*

"Despite arthritic dinosaurs and puffy pink smoke from volcanoes, this British adaptation of Edgar Rice Burroughs…should do okay in the juve market where thrills count more than technique." *Variety*

The Spiral Staircase (1975) 89 mins (color)

"There's always another twist to… THE SPIRAL STAIRCASE."

Raven Films; d: Peter Collinson; ep: Josef Shaftel; p: Peter Shaw; ap: Tom Sachs, David Munro; screenplay: Allan Scott, Chris Bryant; based on the 1946 screenplay *The Spiral Staircase* by Mel Dinelli, from the novel *Some Must Watch* by Ethel Lina White; ph: Ken Hodges; ed: Raymond Poulton; ad: Disley Jones; m: David Lindup

Synopsis: A woman unable to speak due to psychological shock over the death of her husband and daughter is trapped in a house and believes the serial killer who is stalking and murdering women with handicaps is also there.

Cast: Jacqueline Bisset (Helen Mallory), **Christopher Plummer** (Joe Sherman), **John Philip Law** (Steven Sherman), **Mildred Dunnock** (Mrs Sherman), **Gayle Hunnicutt** (Blanche), **Elaine Stritch** (Nurse), **Sam Wanamaker** (Lieutenant Fields), John Ronane (Dr Rawley), Ronald Radd (Oates)

Milestones and Millstones: Christopher Plummer, John Philip Law, Mildred Dunnock, Gayle Hunnicutt, Elaine Stritch, Sam Wanamaker

Comment: Redundant second feature (posing as an A feature by packing in American actors) remake of 1946 classic largely lacking in atmosphere and suspense and featuring an all-too-obvious, too soon revealed perpetrator. The 2000 TV movie remake was even worse.

Reviews: "Siodmak's 1946 version …was a classic thriller of its day… Collinson has undertaken a remake, of which one can say that it provides an object less in comparisons between today's casting and the equivalents of the 'forties." *Films and Filming*

Milestones & Millstones

A

Beverly Adams
Born: Edmonton, Canada 1940
Movie Milestone: *The Silencers* (1966)
Movie Millstones: *Birds Do It* (1966), *Kiss the Girls and Make Them Die* (1966)

Nick Adams
Born: (Nicholas Aloysius Adamschock) Nanicoke Pennsylvania 1931, died Los Angeles California 1968
Movie Milestones: *No Time For Sergeants* (1958), AA Nomination Best Supporting Actor: *Twilight of Honor* (1963)
Movie Millstones: *Invasion of the Astro-Monster* (1965) *Mission Mars* (1968)

Mari Aldon
Born: Taurage Lithuania 1925, died Las Vegas, Nevada 2004
Movie Milestone: *Distant Drums* (1951)
Movie Millstone: *Tangier Incident* (1953)

Robert Aldrich
Director, producer
Born: Cranston, Rhode Island 1918, died Los Angeles, California 1983
Milestones: Director/producer: *Kiss Me Deadly* (1955), director/producer: *The Big Knife* (1955), *Whatever Happened to Baby Jane?* (1962), *The Dirty Dozen* (1966)
Millstones: *Sodom and Gomorrah* (1963)

Irving Allen
Producer
Born: Austria-Hungary 1905, died Encino, California 1987
Milestones: Director Oscar Best Short Subject: *Climbing the Matterhorn* (1948), producer: *The Trials of Oscar Wilde* (1960)
Millstone: Producer: *Slaughter Trail* (1951)

Lewis Allen
Director
Born: Shropshire, England 1905, died Santa Monica, California 2000
Milestones: *The Uninvited* (1944), *Suddenly* (1954)

Keith Andes
Born: Ocean City New Jersey 1920, died Santa Clarita California 2005
Milestones: *Clash By Night* (1952), *Blackbeard the Pirate* (1952)
Millstones: *Project X* (1949), *Hell's Bloody Devils* (1970)

Dana Andrews
Born: Collins, Mississippi 1909, died Los Alamitos, California (1992)
Milestones: *Laura* 1944), *The Best Years of Our Lives* (1946), *Boomerang* (1947), *My Foolish Heart* (1950)
Millstones: *The Frozen Dead* (1967), *Hot Rods to Hell* (1967)

Samuel Z Arkoff
Producer, co-founder, with **James H Nicholson**, American International Pictures

Born: Fort Dodge, Iowa 1918, died Burbank, California 2001
Milestones: *The Pit and the Pendulum* (1961), *Premature Burial* (1962), *Tales of Terror* (1962), *The Raven* (1963), *X: The Man With the X-Ray Eyes* (1963), *The Comedy of Terrors* (1963), *The Tomb of Ligeia* (1964), *Die, Monster, Die* (1965), *The Abominable Dr Phibes* (1971), *Dr Phibes Rises Again* (1972), *The Island of Dr Moreau* (1977)
Millstones: *She Creature* (1956), *Voodoo Women* (1957) *The Saga of the Viking Women and their Voyage to the Waters of the Great Sea Serpent* (1957), *Earth Versus the Spider* (1958), *How to Stuff a Wild Bikini* (1965), *Blacula* (1972)

Richard Arlen
Actor
Born: Cornelius Richard Van Mattemore in Charlottesville, Virginia 1900, died Los Angeles, California 1976
Milestones: *Wings* (1927), *The Four Feathers* (1928) *The Virginian* (1929)
Millstones: *The Lady and the Monster* (1944), *The Crawling Hand* (1963)

Frankie Avalon
Singer, Actor
Born: Francis Thomas Avallone in Philadelphia, Pennsylvania 1939
Milestones: *Beach Party* (1963), *Grease* (1978)
Millstones: *Operation Bikini* (1963), *The Haunted House of Horror/Horror House* (1969)

B

Carroll Baker
Actress
Born: Karolina Piekarski in Johnstown Pennsylvania in 1931
Milestones: *Giant* (1956), AA nomination Best Actress: *Baby Doll* (1956), *How The West Was Won* (1962), *Harlow* (1965)
Millstones: *Sylvia* (1965), *Paranoia* (1969), *The Private Lesson* (1975)

Burt Balaban
Producer, director
Born: Chicago, Illinois 1922), died 1965
Milestones: Co-director: *Murder, Inc* (1960)
Millstones: Director: *Lady of Vengeance* (1957)

Tallulah Bankhead
Actress
Born: Huntsville, Alabama 1902, died New York 1968
Milestone: *Lifeboat* (1943),
Millstones: *Main Street to Broadway* (1953)

Lex Barker
Actor
Born: Alexander Crichlow Barker Jr. Rye New York 1919, died New York 1973
Milestones: *Tarzan's Magic Fountain* (1948), *La Dolce Vita* (1960), *Winnetou* (1963)
Millstones: *Dick Tracy Meets Gruesome* (1947), *Robin Hood and the Pirates* (1960)

Gene Barry
Actor
Born: Eugene Klass New York 1919, died Los Angeles, California 2009
Milestones: *The Atomic City* (1952), *The War of the Worlds* (1953), *Burke's Law* (TV) (1963-1966),
Millstones: *The Second Coming of Suzanne* (1974), *Burke's Law* (TV) (1994-1995)

Richard Basehart
Actor
Born: Zanesville, Ohio 1914, died Los Angeles, California 1984
Milestones: *He Walked by Night* (1948), *Fourteen Hours* (1951), *La Strada* (1954), *The Brothers Karamazov* (1958), *Hitler* (1963)
Millstones: *Visa to Canton* (1961), *Mansion of the Doomed* (1976)

Saul Bass
Graphic artist, titles creator, director
Born: New York 1920, died Los Angeles 1996
Milestones: Oscar Best Documentary, Short Subjects: *Why Man Creates* (1969), titles designer: *The Man With the Golden Arm* (1955), *Around the World in 80 Days* (1956), *Vertigo* (1958), *North by Northwest* (1958), *Psycho* (1960)
Millstones: *Phase IV* (1974)

Barbara Bates
Actress
Born: Denver, Colorado 1925, died (suicide) Denver 1969
Milestones: *The Inspector General* (1949)
Millstones: *Salome Where She Danced* (1945), *All Ashore* (1953)

George Baxt
Screenwriter, novelist, playwright
Born: Brooklyn, New York 1923, died New York 2003
Milestones: *The City of the Dead* (1960), Hugo Award nomination Best Dramatic Presentation: *Night of the Eagle* (1963)
Millstones: *Horror on Snape Island* (1972)

Alan Baxter
Actor
Born: East Cleveland, Ohio 1908, died Los Angeles, California 1976
Milestones: *Saboteur* (1942)
Millstones: *Wild Weed* (1949), *Willard* (1971)

Les Baxter
Musician, composer
Born: Maxia, Texas 1922, died Newport Beach, California 1996
Milestones: *House of Usher* (1960), *The Pit and the Pendulum* (1961), *The Comedy of Terrors* (1963), *X: The Man With X-Ray Eyes* (1963)
Millstones: *Voodoo Island* (1957), *Untamed Youth* (1957)

Charles Beaumont
Writer
Born: Charles Leroy Nutt Chicago, Illinois 1929, died Woodlands, California 1967
Milestones: *Premature Burial* (1962), *The Intruder* (1962), *The Haunted Palace* (1963), *The Masque of the Red Death* (1964)
Millstones: *Queen of Outer Space* (1958), *Brain Dead* (1990)

William Bendix
Actor
Born: New York 1906, died Los Angeles, California 1964
Milestones: Oscar nomination Best Supporting Actor: *Wake Island* (1942), *The Glass Key* (1942), *Lifeboat* (1943), *The Blue Dahlia* (1946), *The Babe Ruth Story* (1948),
Millstones: *A Girl in Every Port* (1952), *The Phony American* (1961)

Lazlo Benedek
Director
Born: Budapest, Hungary1905, died the Bronx, New York 1992
Milestones: *Port of New York* (1949), won Golden Globe for Best Director: *Death of a Salesman* (1952), *The Wild One* (1954)
Millstones: *The Kissing Bandit* (1948)

Shelley Berman
Actor
Born: Sheldon Leonard Berman Chicago, Illinois 1925
Milestones: *The Best Man* (1964), *Meet the Fockers* (2004)
Millstones: *Every Home Should Have One* (1970), *Beware! The Blob!* (1972)

Edward Bishop
Actor
Born: George Bishop Brooklyn, New York 1932, died Kingston upon Thames, England 2005
Milestones: *The War Lover* (1962), *2001: A Space Odyssey* (1968)
Millstones: *The Cool Mikado* (1963), *The Lonely Lady* (1983)

Betsy Blair
Actress
Born: Elizabeth Winifred Boger in Cliffside Park, New Jersey 1923, died London, England 2009
Milestones: *Another Part of the Forest* (1948), AA nominated for Best Supporting Actress: *Marty* (1955)
Millstones: *Meeting in Paris* (1956)

Robert Bloch
Writer
Born: Chicago, Illinois 1917, died Los Angeles, California 1994
Milestones: *Psycho* (novel, filmed by Hitchcock), *Strait Jacket* (1964), *The Night Walker* (1964), *The House that Dripped Blood* (1971)
Millstones: *The Deadly Bees* (1967)

John Boles
Actor
Born: Greenville, Texas 1895, died San Angelo, Texas 1969
Milestones: *The Desert Song* (1929), *Rio Rita* (1929), *Only Yesterday* (1933)
Millstones: *Babes in Bagdad* (1952)

Pat Boone
Singer, actor
Born: Charles Eugene Patrick Boone in Jacksonville, Florida in 1934
Milestones: *Bernardine* (1957), *Journey to the Center of the Earth* (1959)
Millstones: *All Hands on Deck* (1961), *The Horror of it All* (1964)

Karin Booth
Actress
Born: June Hoffman in Minneapolis, Minnesota 1916, died Jupiter, Florida 2003
Milestones: *Tobor the Great* (1954), *Beloved Infidel* (1959)
Millstones: *African Manhunt* (1955)

Stephen Boyd
Actor
Born: William Millar in Glengormley, County Antrim, Northern Ireland, died Northridge, California 1977
Milestones: *The Man Who Never Was* (1956), *Ben-Hur* (1959), *The Fall of the Roman Empire* (1964), *Fantastic Voyage* (1966)
Millstones: *The Devil with Seven Faces* (1971), *One Billion for a Blonde* (1972), *Lady Dracula* (1977)

Scott Brady
Actor
Born: Gerard Kenneth Tierney in Brooklyn, New York 1924, died Los Angeles, California 1985
Milestones: *He Walked by Night* (1948), *The Model and the Marriage Broker* (1951), *Johnny Guitar* (1954), *The China Syndrome* (1979)
Millstones: *A Perilous Journey* (1953), *Operation Bikini* (1963), *Journey to the Center of Time* (1967)

Keefe Brasselle
Actor
Born: Elyria, Ohio 1923, died Downey, California 1981
Milestones: *The Eddie Cantor Story* (1953)
Millstones: *If You Don't Stop It...You'll Go Blind!!!* (1975)

Robert Bray
Actor
Born: Kalispell, Montana 1917, died Bishop, California 1983
Milestones: *Bus Stop* (1956), *My Gun is Quick* (1957) *Lassie* (TV 1964-1968)
Millstones: *The Fiend of Dope Island* (1961), *The Traitor* (1957)

George Brent

Born George Patrick Nolan in Shannonbridge, Ireland 1904, died Solana Beach, California 1979

Milestones: *42ⁿᵈ Street (1933), The Painted Veil (1934), The Rains Came (1939), The Spiral Staircase (1945)*

Millstones: *Slave Girl (1947), Tangier Incident (1953), Born Again (1978)*

Lloyd Bridges
Actor
Born: San Leandro, California 1913, died Los Angeles, California 1998
Milestones: *Home of the Brave (1949), High Noon (1952), Sea Hunt (TV 1957-1960), The Goddess (1958), Airplane (1980)*
Millstones: *Rocketship X-M (1950), Weekend Warriors (1986)*

Albert R Broccoli
Producer
Born: Queens, New York 1909, died Beverly Hills, Los Angeles 1996
Milestones: *Dr No (1962), From Russia With Love (1963), Goldfinger (1964), Thunderball (1965), You Only Live Twice (1967), Diamonds Are Forever (1971), Live and Let Die (1973), The Man With the Golden Gun (1974), The Spy Who Loved Me (1977), Moonraker (1979), For Your Eyes Only (1981), Octopussy (1983), A View to a Kill (1985), The Living Daylights (1987), Licence To Kill (1989), Goldeneye (1995)*
Millstones: *In the Nick (1960), On Her Majesty's Secret Service (1969)*

Steve Brodie
B feature actor
Born: John Stephens in Eldorado, Kansas 1919, died Los Angeles, California 1992
Milestones: *Crossfire (1947), M (1951)*
Millstones: *Donovan's Brain (1953), Frankenstein Island (1981)*

Hillary Brooke
Actress
Born: Beatrice Sofia Mathilda Peterson in Astoria, New York 1914, died Bonsall, California 1999

Milestones: *The Philadelphia Story* (1940), *Lady in the Dark* (1944), *Ministry of Fear* (1944), *The Man Who Knew Too Much* (1956)
Millstones: *Africa Screams* (1949), *Lost Continent* (1951), *Abbott and Costello Meet Captain Kidd* (1952)

Phil Brown
Actor
Born: Cambridge, Massachusetts 1916, died Los Angeles, California 2006
Milestones: *State Fair* (1945), *The Killers* (1946), *Obsession* (1949), *Star Wars: Episode IV—A New Hope* (1977)
Millstones: *Blacklisted 1952, The Jungle Captive* (1945), *Bomb at 10:10* (1967)

Virginia Bruce
Actress
Born: Helen Virginia Briggs Minneapolis, Minnesota 1910, died Los Angeles, California 1982
Milestones: *Jane Eyre* (1934), *The Great Ziegfeld* (1936), *Night Has A Thousand Eyes* (1948)
Millstones: *Here Comes the Band* (1935), *The Invisible Woman* (1940)

C

James Caan
Actor
Born: The Bronx, New York 1940
Milestones: *The Rain People* (1969), AA nomination for Best Actor in a Supporting Role: *The Godfather* (1972), *Misery* (1990)
Millstones: *Gone With the West* (1973), *Dick Tracy* (1990), *Mickey Blue Eyes* (1999)

Rory Calhoun
Actor
Born: Francis Timothy McCown Los Angeles, California 1922, died Bur-

bank, California 1999
Milestones: *The Great John L* (1945), *The Red House* (1947), *How To Marry a Millionaire* (1953)
Millstones: *Face in the Rain* (1963), *Night of the Lepus* (1972), *Hell Comes to Frogtown* (1988)

Joseph Calleia
Actor
Born: Giuseppe Maria Spurrin-Calleja St. Julians, Malta 1897, died Valletta, Malta 1975
Milestones: *For Whom the Bell Tolls* (1943), *Touch of Evil* (1956)
Millstones: *The Gorilla* (1939), *Serenade* (1956)

Corrine Calvet
Born: Corinne Dibos Paris, France 1925, died Los Angeles, California 2001
Milestones: *Rope of Sand* (1949), *Sailor Beware* (1952)
Millstones: *Bluebeard's 10 Honeymoons* (1960), *Pound* (1970), *Dr Heckyl and Mr Hype* (1980)

Rod Cameron
Actor
Born: Nathan Roderick Cox Calgary, Alberta 1910, died Gainesville, Georgia 1983
Milestones: *G-Men vs. The Black Dragon* (1943 serial), *Panhandle* (1948), *The Gun Hawk* (1963)
Millstones: *Escapement* (1958), *Psychic Killer* (1975)

Dyan Cannon
Actress
Born: Samille Diane Friesen Tacoma Washington 1937
Milestones: AA nomination Best Actress in a Supporting Role: *Heaven Can Wait* (1971), AA nomination Best Actress in a Supporting Role: *Bob & Carol & Ted & Alice* (1970)
Millstones: Nomination for Golden Raspberry Award for Worst Supporting Actress: *Deathtrap* (1982), *The Pickle* (1993)

Macdonald Carey
Actor
Born: Edward Macdonald Carey Sioux City, Iowa 1913, died Los Angeles California 1994
Milestones: *Shadow of a Doubt* (1943), *The Lawless* (1950), *The Damned* (1963)
Millstones: *Stranglehold* (1962), *End of the World* (1977)

Philip Carey
Actor
Born: Eugene Joseph Carey, Hackensack, New Jersey 1925, died Manhattan, New York 2009
Milestones: *I Was a Communist for the FBI* (1951*)*, *Springfield Rifle* (1952), *Calamity Jane* (1953), *The Long Gray Line* (1955), *Mister Roberts* (1955)
Millstones: *The Rebel Rousers* (1970), *Monster* (1980)

Richard Carlson
Actor
Born: Albert Lea, Minnesota 1912, died Encino, California 1977
Milestones: *The Little Foxes* (1941), *King Solomon's Mines* (1950), *It Came From Outer Space* (1953), *The Creature from The Black Lagoon* (1954)
Millstones: *Bengazi* (1955), *Tormented* (1960), *Change of Habit* (1969)

John Carroll
Actor, Singer
Born: Julian Lafaye in New Orleans, Louisiana 1906, died Hollywood, California 1979
Milestones: *Zorro Rides Again* (1936), *Only Angels Have Wings* (1939), *Go West* (1940)
Millstones: *Ride in a Pink Car* (1974)

Madeleine Carroll
Actress
Born: Edith Madeleine Carroll West Bromwich, Staffordshire, England 1906, died Marbella, Spain 1987

Milestones: *Young Woodley* (1930), *The 39 Steps* (1935), *The General Died at Dawn* (1936), *The Prisoner of Zenda* (1937), *My Favorite Blonde* (1942)
Millstones: *The W Plan* (1930)

Mary Castle
Actress
Born: Mary Ann Noblett Pampa, Texas 1931, died Palm Springs, California 1998
Milestones: *The Lawless Breed* (1953)
Millstones: *The Tougher They Come* (1950)

Peggie Castle
Actress
Born: Appalachia, Virginia 1927, died Hollywood, California 1973
Milestones: *I, The Jury* (1953), *Tall Man Riding* (1955)
Millstones: *Invasion USA* (1952)

William Castle
Director, producer
Born: William Schloss, New York 1914, died Los Angeles, California 1977
Milestones: *The Tingler* (1959), *Homicidal* (1960), *Strait-Jacket* (1964), *Rosemary's Baby* (producer)
Millstones: *Serpent of the Nile* (1953)

Paul Cavanagh
Actor
Born: Chiselhust, Kent, England 1888, died London, England 1964
Milestones: *The Notorious Sophie Lang* (1934), *House of Wax* (1953)
Millstones: *Bride of the Gorilla* (1951), *Port Sinister* (1953)

John C Champion
Producer, writer, director
Born: Denver, Colorado 1923, died Tarzana, California 1994

Milestones: TV series producer: *Laramie* (1959-1963), *Zero Hour* (1957)
Millstones: Producer: *Submarine X-1* (1968)

Lon Chaney Jr
Actor
Born: Creighton Tull Chaney 1906, Oklahoma City, Oklahoma, died San Clemente, California 1973
Milestones: *Of Mice and Men (1939)*, *The Wolf Man* (1941), *The Ghost of Frankenstein* (1942), *Abbott and Costello Meet Frankenstein* (1948), *High Noon* (1952)
Millstones: *Bride of the Gorilla* (1951), *Indestructible Man* (1956), *The Cyclops* (1957), *Gallery of Horror* (1967), *Dracula vs. Frankenstein* (1971)

Sydney Chaplin
Actor
Born: Beverly Hills, California 1926, died Rancho Mirage, California 2009
Milestones: Son of Charlie Chaplin, *Limelight* (1952)
Millstones: *Abdullah The Great* (1955), *Satan's Cheerleaders* (1977)

Marguerite Chapman
Born Chatham, New York 1918, died Burbank, California 1999
Milestones: *Destroyer* (1943), *Appointment in Berlin* (1943), *The Seven Year Itch* (1955)
Millstones: *Flight to Mars* (1951), *The Amazing Transparent Man* (1960)

Cyd Charisse
Dancer, actress
Born: Tula Ellice Finklea Amarillo, Texas 1921, died Los Angeles 2008
Milestones: *The Unfinished Dance* (1947), *Singin' in The Rain* (1952), *The Band Wagon* (1953), *Brigadoon* (1954), *It's Always Fair Weather* (1955), *Invitation to the Dance* (1957)
Millstones: *Warlords of Atlantis* (1978)

Hal E Chester
Producer, actor, writer
Born: Harold Ribotsky Brooklyn, New York 1921, died London, England 2012
Milestones: Producer 11 *Joe Palooka* movies (1946-1951), *The Beast from 20,000 Fathoms* (1953), *Curse of the Demon* (1957), *The Two Headed Spy* (1958)
Millstones: Writer: *Joe Palooka, Champ* (1943)

Dane Clark
Actor
Born: Bernard Elliot Zanville Brooklyn, New York 1912, died Santa Monica, California 1998
Milestones: *Action in the North Atlantic* (1943), *A Stolen Life* (1946), *Whiplash* (1948), *Port of Hell* (1954)
Millstones: *Murder by Proxy* (1954), *Last Rites* (1988)

Fred Clark
Actor
Born: Lincoln, California 1914, died Santa Monica, California 1968
Milestones: *Sunset Boulevard* (1950), *How to Marry a Millionaire* (1953), *Auntie Mame* (1958)
Millstones: *The Younger Brothers* (1949), *The Curse of the Mummy's Tomb* (1964) *Sergeant Dead Head* (1965), *Skidoo* (1968)

June Clyde
Actress
Born: June Tetrazini St Joseph, Missouri, died Fort Lauderdale, Florida 1987
Milestones: *A Study in Scarlet* (1933)
Millstones: *24 Hours of a Woman's Life* (1952)

Steve Cochran
Actor
Born: Robert Alexander Cochran Eureka, California, died 1965 Pacific Ocean off coast of Guatemala

Milestones: *White Heat* (1949), *The Damned Don't Cry* (1950), *Private Hell 6* (1954), *Come Next Spring* (1956) *Il Grido* (1957)
Millstones: *The Gay Senorita* (1945), *Mozambique* (1964), *Tell Me in the Sunlight* (1965)

Gary Cockrell
Actor
Born: St Louis, Missouri 1932
Milestones: *Lolita* (1962), *The War Lover* (1962),
Millstones: *Gonks go Beat* (1965)

Herman Cohen
Producer, writer
Born: Detroit, Michigan 1925, died Los Angeles, California 2002
Milestones: Producer/writer: *I Was a Teenage Werewolf* (1957), producer/writer: *I Was a Teenage Frankenstein* (1957)
Millstones: Producer: *Bela Lugosi Meets a Brooklyn Gorilla* (1952), producer/writer: *The Headless Ghost* (1959), producer: *Berserk* (1967), producer: *Trog* (1970), producer: *Craze* (1974)

Joan Collins
Actress
Born: 1933 London, England
Milestones: *The Road to Hong Kong* (1962), *Dynasty* (TV series 1981-1989)
Millstones: *Empire of the Ants* (1977), *The Stud* (1978), *The Bitch* (1979), *Game for Vultures* (1979)

Anjanette Comer
Actress
Born: 1939 Dawson, Texas
Milestones: *Lepke* (1975)
Millstones: *The Firechasers* (1971), *Netherworld* (1992)

Milestones & Millstones • 223

Richard Conte
Actor
Born: Nicholas Conte Jersey City, New Jersey 1910, died Los Angeles, California 1975
Milestones: *Call Northside 777* (1948), *Thieves Highway* (1949), *Whirlpool* (1949), *Oceans 11* (1960), *Tony Rome* (1967), *The Godfather* (1972)
Millstones: *Bengazi* (1955), *Little Red Monkey* (1956), *Explosion* (1969), *The Return of the Exorcist* (1975)

Tom Conway
Actor
Born: Thomas Sanders (brother of George Sanders) St Petersburg, Russia 1904, died Los Angeles, California 1967
Milestones: Played The Falcon (taking over from brother George) in 10 films from 1942 to 1946, *Cat People* (1942), *I Walked With a Zombie* (1943), *The Seventh Victim* (1943)
Millstones: *I Cheated the Law* (1949), *Bride of the Gorilla* (1951), *The She-Creature* (1956), *12 to the Moon* (1960)

Glenn Corbett
Actor
Born: Glenn Edwin Rothenburg, El Monte, California 1933, died San Antonio, Texas 1993
Milestones: *Homicidal* (1961), *Route 66* (TV series 1963-1964)
Millstones: *The Young and the Restless* (TV series 1963), *Ride in Pink Car* (1974)

Joseph Cotton
Actor
Born: Petersburg, Virginia 1905, died Los Angeles California 1994
Milestones: *Citizen Kane* (1941), *The Magnificent Ambersons* (1942), *Journey Into Fear* (1943), *Shadow of a Doubt* (1943), *Gaslight* (1944), *Duel in the Sun* (194), *The Third Man* (1949), *The Abominable Dr Phibes* (1971)
Millstones: *White Comanche* (1968), *Lady Frankenstein* (1971), *Journey to Murder* (1971), *Doomsday Voyage* (1972), *The Hearse* (1980)

Broderick Crawford
Actor

Born: Philadelphia, Pennsylvania 1911, died Rancho Mirage 1986

Milestones: *The Runaround* (1946), AA for Best Actor in a Leading Role: *All the King's Men* (1950), *Born Yesterday* (1951), *Highway Patrol* (TV series 1955-1959) *The Private Files of J Edgar Hoover* (1978)

Millstones: *The Vulture* (1957), *Goliath and the Dragon* (1960), *Hell's Bloody Devils* (1977), *The Yin and Yang of Mr Go* (1970)

Joan Crawford
Actress

Born: Lucille Fay LeSueur San Antonio, Texas 1905, died New York 1977

Milestones: *Our Dancing Daughters* (1928), *Grand Hotel* (1932), *The Gorgeous Hussy* (1936), *The Women* (1939), AA Best Actress in a Leading Role: *Mildred Pierce* (1954) AA nomination Best Actress in a Leading Role: *Possessed* (1947), AA nomination Best Actress in a Leading role: *Sudden Fear* (1952), *Johnny Guitar* (1954), *Whatever Happened to Baby Jane* (1962), *Strait-Jacket* (1964)

Millstones: *Berserk* (1967), *Trog* (1970),

Robert Cummings
Actor

Born: Charles Clarence Robert Orville Cummings Joplin, Missouri 1910, died Los Angeles, California 1990

Milestones: *It Started With Eve* (1941), *Kings Row* (1941), *Saboteur* (1942), *Dial M For Murder* (1954), *The Carpetbaggers* (1964)

Millstones: *Touchdown Army* (1938), *Beach Party* (1963), *Five Golden Dragons* (1967)

D

Arlene Dahl
Actress
Born: Minneapolis, Minnesota 1928
Milestones: *My Wild Irish Rose* (1947), *Three Little Words* (1950), *Woman's World* (1954), *Slightly Scarlet* (1956), *Journey to the Center of the Earth* (1959)
Millstones: *The Diamond Queen* (1953), *Les Ponyettes* (1967), *Night of the Warrior* (1991)

Jim Danforth
Special/Visual Effects
Born: James Danforth, Illinois, USA
Milestones: AA nominated Best Effects, Special Visual Effects: *7 Faces of Dr Lao* (1964), AA nominated Best Effects, Special Visual Effects: *When Dinosaurs Ruled the Earth* (1970), *Day of the Dead* (1985)
Millstones: *Flesh Gordon* (1974), *The Crater Lake Monster* (1977),

Helmut Dantine
Actor
Born: Helmut Guttman Vienna, Austria 1918, died Los Angeles, California 1982
Milestones: *Mrs Miniver* (1942), *Casablanca* (1942), *To Be Or Not to Be* (1942), *Passage to Marseilles* (1944)
Millstones: *Guerilla Girl* (1953), *Stranger from Venus* (1954), *Hell on Devil's Island* (1957), *The Fifth Musketeer* (1979)

Edward J Danziger, Harry Lee Danziger
Producers of hundred of British B films and filmed TV shows
Edward J **Born:** New York City 1909, died New York City 1999
Harry Lee **Born:** New York City 1913, died Palm Springs, California 2005

Milestones: *Jigsaw* (US 1949), *The Spider's Web* (1960)
Millstones: *Babes in Baghdad* (1952), *Devil Girl from Mars* (1954), *Operation Murder* (1957), *Top Floor Girl* (1959), *An Honorable Murder* (1960) etc, etc, etc

Jim Davis
Actor
Born: Marlin Davis Edgerton, Missouri 1909, died Northridge, California 1981
Milestones: *The Big Sky* (1952), *Monte Walsh* (1970), *Dallas* (TV series 1978-1981)
Millstones: *Monster from Green Hell* (1957), *Wolf Dog* (1958), *Iron Angel* (1964), *Jesse James Meets Frankenstein's Daughter* (1966), *Dracula vs. Frankenstein* (1971), *The Day Time Ended* (1979)

Margia Dean
Actress
Born: Marguerite Louise Skliris in Chicago, Illinois 1922
Milestones: *I Shot Jesse James* (1949), *The Quatermass Xperiment* (1955),
Millstones: Actress *Mesa of the Lost Women* (1953), actress *Moro Witch Doctor* (1964), producer *The Horror of it All* (1964)

Arlene DeMarco
Actress
Born: 1933 Rome, New York, USA, died 2013 Clark, New Jersey, USA
Milestones: *Skirts Ahoy!* (1953)
Millstones: *Death Over My Shoulder* (1954)

Susan Denberg
Born Dietlinde Zechner Bad Polzin, Pomerania, Germany 1944
Milestones: *Frankenstein Created Woman* (1967)
Millstones: *The Wackiest Ship in the Army* (TV series 1966)

Richard Denning
Actor
Born: Louis Albert Heindrich Denninger Jr Poughkeepsie, New York 1914, died Escondido, California 1998
Milestones: *The Glass Web* (1953), *The Creature from the Black Lagoon* (1954), *The Day the World Ended* (1955), *Hawaii Five-O* (TV series 1968-1980)
Millstones: *Target Hong Kong* (1953), *The Creature with the Atom Brain* (1955)

John Derek
Actor, director
Born: Derek Delevan Harris Hollywood, Los Angeles 1926, died Santa Maria, California 1998
Milestones: *Knock on Any Door* (1949), *All the King's Men* (1949), *The Ten Commandments* (1956), *Exodus* (1960)
Millstones: *Fantasies* (Director 1981), *Tarzan, The Ape Man* (Director 1981), *Bolero* (Director 1984), *Ghosts Can't Do It* (1989)

Anthony Dexter
Actor
Born: Walter Reinhold Alfred Fleischmann Talmadge, Nebraska 1913, died Greeley, Colorado 2001
Milestones: *Valentino* (1951), *Thoroughly Modern Millie* (1967)
Millstones: *Fire Maidens from Outer Space* (1956), *12 to the Moon* (1960), *The Phantom Planet* (1961)

Faith Domergue
Actress
Born: New Orleans, Louisiana 1924, died Santa Barbara 1999
Milestones: *This Island Earth* (1955)
Millstones: *Vendetta* (1950), *The House of Seven Corpses* (1974)

Yolande Donlan
Actress
Born: Jersey City, New Jersey 1920, died London, England 2014

Milestones: *Mr Drake's Duck* (1951), *Expresso Bongo* (1959), *80,000 Suspects* (1963)
Millstones: *The Devil Bat* (1940)

Brian Donlevy
Actor
Born: Waldo Brian Donlevy Portadown, County Armagh, Ireland 1901, died Los Angeles, California 1972
Milestones: AA nomination Best Actor in a Supporting Role: *Beau Geste* (1940), *The Glass Key* (1942), *Wake Island* (1942), *An American Romance* (1944), *The Quatermass Experiment* (1955)
Millstones: *The Fat Spy* (1966), *Five Golden Dragons* (1965)

Jeff Donnell
Actress
Born: Jean Marie Donnell South Windham, Maine 1921, died Hollywood, California 1988
Milestones: *In a Lonely Place* (1950)
Millstones: *The Iron Maiden* (1962) *Stand Up and Be Counted* (1972)

Paul Douglas
Actor
Born: Paul Douglas Fleischer Philadelphia, Pennsylvania 1907, died Hollywood, California 1959
Milestones: *A Letter to Three Wives* (1948), *The Maggie* (1954), *Joe Macbeth* (1955), *The Solid Gold Cadillac* (1956)
Millstones: *The Gamma People* (1956)

Tom Drake
Actor
Born: Alfred Sinclair Alderdice Brooklyn, New York 1918, died Torrance, California 1982
Milestones: *Meet Me in St Louis* (1944), *The Green Years* (1946), *Words and Music* (1948)

Millstones: *Date with Disaster* (1957) *House of the Black Death* (1965), *The Spectre of Edgar Allan Poe* (1974)

Mildred Dunnock
Actress
Born: Baltimore, Maryland 1901, died Oak Bluffs, Massachusetts 1991
Milestones: AA nomination Best Actress in a Supporting Role: *Death of a Salesman* (1951), *Viva Zapata!* (1952), AA nomination Best Actress in a Supporting Role: *Baby Doll* (1956), The *Trouble With Harry* (1955), *Peyton Place* 1957)
Millstones: *Butterfield 8* (1960), *The Spiral Staircase* (1975), *Dragonfly* (1976)

Dan Duryea
Actor
Born: White Plains, New York 1907, died Hollywood, California 1968
Milestones: *The Little Foxes* (1941), *The Woman in Scarlet* (1944), *The Woman in the Window* (1944), *Black Angel* (1946), *Another Part of the Forest* (1948), *The Flight of the Phoenix* (1965)
Millstones: *36 Hours* (1952)

E

Cy Endfield
Director
Born: Cyril Raker Endfield Scranton, Pennsylvania 1914, died Shipton on Stour, Warwickshire, England 1995
Milestones: *The Sound of Fury* (1951), *Hell Drivers* (1957), *Mysterious Island* (1961), *Zulu* (1963)
Millstones: *Stork Bites Man* (screenplay, director 1947), *De Sade* (1969)

Gene Evans
Actor
Born: Holbrook, Arizona 1922, died Jackson, Tennessee 1998
Milestones: *Ace in the Hole* (1951), *Shock Corridor* (1963), *The War Wagon* (1967), *The Ballad of Cable Hogue* (1970), *Pat Garrett and Billy the Kid* (1973)
Millstones: *Devil Times Five* (1974)

Chad Everett
Actor
Born: Raymon Lee Cramton South Bend, Indiana 1937, died Los Angeles, California 2012
Milestones: *Airplane II; The Sequel* (1982), *Medical Center* TV series 1969-1975), *Mulholland Drive* (2001)
Millstones: *Get Yourself a College Girl* (1964), *Psycho* (1988), *Free Fall* (1999), *Tiptoes* (2003), *The Pink Conspiracy* (2007)

William Eythe
Actor
Born: Mars, Pennsylvania 1918, died Los Angeles, California 1957
Milestones: *The Eve of St Mark* (1944), *The House on 92nd Street* (1945)
Millstones: *The Gay Duellist* (1947)

F

Fabian
Singer
Born: Fabiano Anthony Forte Philadelphia, Pennsylvania 1943
Milestones: *Hound Dog Man* (1959), *North To Alaska* (1960), *Mr Hobbs Takes a Vacation* (1962)
Millstones: *Agatha Christie's Ten Little Indians* (1965), *Dr Goldfoot and the Girl Bombs* (1966), *Little Laura and Big John* (1973)

Douglas Fairbanks Jr
Actor. Producer
Born: New York 1909, died New York 2000
Milestones: *Stella Dallas* (1925), *The Dawn Patrol* (1930), *The Prisoner of Zenda* (1937), *Sinbad the Sailor* (1947)
Millstones: *Iz Zat So?* (1927), *The Last Moment* (1954)

Geraldine Fitzgerald
Actress
Born: Greystones, County Wicklow, Ireland 1913, died New York 2005
Milestones: *Turn of the Tide* (1935), AA nomination Best Actress in a Supporting Role *Wuthering Heights* (1939), *Wilson* (1944)
Millstones: *Easy Money* (1983), *Bye Bye Monkey* (1978)

Joan Fontaine
Actress
Born: Joan de Beauvoir de Havilland (sister of Olivia) 1917 Tokyo, Japan, died Carmel, California 2013
Milestones: AA nomination Best Actress in a Leading Role: *Rebecca* (1940), AA Best Actress in a Leading Role: *Suspicion* (1941), AA nomination Best Actress in a Leading Role: *The Constant Nymph* (1944), *Letter from an Unknown Woman* (1948)
Millstones: *Flight to Tangier* (1953)

James Franciscus
Actor
Born: Clayton, Missouri 1934, died Los Angeles, California 1991
Milestones: *Naked City* (TV series 1958-1959), *I Passed For White* (1960), *The Outsider* (1961), *Youngblood Hawke* (1964)), *Beneath the Planet of the Apes* (1970)
Millstones: *City on Fire* (1979), *Killer Fish* (1979)

Mike Frankovich
Producer, writer
Born: Bisbee, Arizona 1909, died Los Angeles, California 1992

Milestones: *Joe MacBeth* (1955), *The Looking Glass War* (1969), *Bob & Carol & Ted & Alice* (1969), *Cactus Flower* (1969), *The Shootist* (1976)
Millstones: *Malaga* (1960), *There's a Girl in My Soup* (1970)

Thornton Freeland
Director, cinematographer
Born: Hope, North Dakota 1898, died Ford Lauderdale, Florida 1987
Milestones: *Flying Down to Rio* (1933)
Millstones: *Skylarks* (1936), *Brass Monkey* (1948)

Mona Freeman
Actress
Born: Monica Elizabeth Freeman Baltimore, Maryland 1926, died Beverly Hills, Los Angeles 2014
Milestones: *Dear Ruth* (1947)
Millstones: *The Way Out* (1956)

Fred Freiberger
Producer/screenwriter
Born: The Bronx, New York 1915, died Bel-Air California 2003
Milestones: Co-writer: *The Beast from 20, 000 Fathoms* (1953), producer: *Star Trek* (TV, series 1968-1969)
Millstones: Co-writer: *Egypt by Three* (1953)

Seymour Friedman
Director
Born: Detroit, Michigan 1917, died Los Angeles, California 2003
Milestones: Low budget 1940s Hollywood B features
Millstones: *The Saint's Return/The Saint's Girl Friday* (1953)

G

Samuel 'Sam' Gallu
Producer, director, writer
Born: Woodbine, New Jersey 1918, died Doylestown, Pennsylvania 1991
Milestones: Screenwriter: *Give 'em Hell, Harry!* (1975)
Millstones: *The Limbo Line* (1968)

Leo Genn
Actor
Born: London, England 109, died London, England 1978
Milestones: *The Way Ahead* (1944), *The Snake Pit* (1948), AA nomination Best Actor in a Supporting Role *Quo Vadis* (1951), *Moby Dick* (1956)
Millstones: *Too Hot To Handle* (1960), *The Bloody Judge* (1970), *Die Screaming, Marianne* (1971)

Paulette Goddard
Actress
Born: Paulette Marion Goddard Levy Long Island, New York 1910, died Ronco, Switzerland 1990
Milestones: *Modern Times* (1936), *The Cat and the Canary* (1938), *The Great Dictator* (1940), AA nomination Best Actress in a Supporting Role: *So Proudly We Hail* (1943), *The Diary of a Chambermaid* (1946)
Millstones: *Babes in Bagdad* (1952), *Paris Model* (1953)

Willis Goldbeck
Director, screenwriter
Born: New York City, New York 1898, died Sag Harbor, New York 1979
Milestones: Producer/screenwriter: *The Man Who Shot Liberty Valance* (1962)
Millstones: Co-writer: *Tiger By The Tail* (1955)

David Zelig Goodman
Screenwriter
Born: Manhattan, New York 1930, died Oakland, California 2011
Milestones: AA Best Writing, Screenplay Based on Material from Another Medium (co-writer): *Lovers and Other Strangers* (1971), co-writer: *Straw Dogs* (1971), *Farewell My Lovely* (1975)
Millstones: *The Eyes of Laura Mars* (1978)

Bernard Gordon
Screenwriter, producer
Born: New Britain, Connecticut 1918, died Hollywood Hills, California 2007
Milestones: Producer: *Horror Express* (1972)
Millstones: Screenwriter *Earth vs. The Flying Saucers* (1956)

Richard Gordon
Producer
Born: London, England 1925, died Manhattan, New York 2011
Milestones: *Grip of the Strangler* (1958), *Corridors of Blood* (1958)
Millstones: *Curse of the Voodoo* (1965), *Tower of Evil* (1972),

William A Graham
Director
Born: New York 1921, died Malibu, California 2013
Milestones: Primetime Emmy nomination Outstanding Directing in a Limited Series or a Special for: *Guyana Tragedy: The True Story of Jim Jones* (TVM1980)
Millstones: Razzies nominations Worst Picture and Worst Director for: *The Blue Lagoon* (1991)

Stewart Granger
Actor
Born: James Leblanche Stewart London, England, died Santa Monica, California 1993
Milestones: *The Man in Gray* (1943), *Waterloo Road* (1944), *King Solomon's Mines* (1950), *Scaramouche* (1952), *Beau Brummell* (1954),

Millstones: Refused lead role in: *A Star is Born* (1954), *Sodom and Gomorrah* (1962), *Hell Hunters* (1986),

Coleen Gray
Actress
Born: Doris Bernice Jensen Staplehurst, Nebraska 1922, died Bel Air, Los Angeles, California 2015
Milestones: *Kiss of Death* (1947), *Nightmare Alley* (1947), *The Killing* (1956)
Millstones: *The Leech Woman* (1960), *The Phantom Planet* (1961)

Richard Greene
Actor
Born: Plymouth, Devon, England 1918, died Norfolk, England 1985
Milestones: *The Hound of the Baskervilles* (1939), *Little Old New York* (1940), *The Adventures of Robin Hood* (TV series 1955-1960)
Millstones: *Bandits of Corsica* (1953), *Captain Scarlett* (1953), *Island of the Lost* (1967), *The Blood of Fu Manchu* (1968)

H

Alan Hale Jr
Actor
Born: 1921 Los Angeles, California, died Los Angeles 1990
Milestones: *Gilligan's Island* (TV series 1964-1992)
Millstones: *The Giant Spider Invasion* (1975), *Terror Night* (1987)

Daniel Haller
Director, production designer, art director
Born: Glendale, California 1926
Milestones: Director: *Monster of Terror* (1965), *The Dunwich Horror* (1970) Production designer: *House of Usher* (1960), *Tales of Terror* (1962), *The Raven* (1963), *X: The Man with X-Ray Eyes* (1963), *The Comedy of Terrors* (1963), *The Masque of the Red Death* (1964) Art

director: *I, Mobster* (1958), *A Bucket of Blood* (1959), *The Little Shop of Horrors* (1960), *The Tomb of Ligeia* (1964)
Millstones: *Paddy* (1970)

Bryant Halliday
Actor, film distributor
Born: Albany, New York 1928, died Paris, France 1996
Milestones: Janus Films: film distributors founded New York 1968
Millstones: *Devil Doll* (1964), *Curse of the Voodoo* (1965)

Orville H Hampton
Screenwriter
Born: Rockford, Illinois 1917, died Los Angeles, California 1997
Milestones: *Outlaw Women* (1952), *Jack the Giant Killer* (1962)
Millstones: *Fingerprints Don't Lie* (1951), *Lady in the Fog* (1953)

Ty Hardin
Actor
Born: Orison Whipple Hungerford, Jr., New York 1930
Milestones: *The Chapman Report* (1962), *PT 109* (1963), *Battle of the Bulge* (1965)
Millstones: *I Married a Monster from Outer Space* (1958), *Man of the Cursed Valley* (1964), *Berserk!* (1967), *Image of the Beast* (1980)

Brad Harris
Actor
Born: Bradford Jan Harris St Anthony, Idaho 1933
Millstones: *King of Kong Island* (1968), *The Mutations* (1974)

Rex Harrison
Actor
Born: Reginald Carey Harrison Huyton, Lancashire, England 1908, died New York 1990
Milestones: *Storm in a Teacup* (1937), *Major Barbara* (1940), *Blithe Spirit* (1945), *The Rake's Progress* (1946) AA nomination Best Actor in a

Leading Role *Cleopatra* (1964), AA winner Best Actor in a Leading Role *My Fair Lady* (1965)
Millstones: *Ashanti* (1979), *A Time to Die* (1982)

Susan Hart
Actress
Born: Susan Neidhart Wenatchee, Washington 1941
Milestones: *Dr Goldfoot and the Bikini Machine* (1965)
Millstones: *The Slime People* (1963), Pajama Party (1964)

Paul Henreid
Born Paul Georg Julius Freiherr von Hernreid Ritter von Wasel-Waldingau in Trieste, Austro-Hungary 1908, died Santa Monica, California 1992
Milestones: *Now, Voyager* (1942), *Casablanca* (1943), *The Spanish Main* (1945)
Millstones: *Stolen Face* (1952), *Siren of Baghdad* (1954), *Exorcist II: The Heretic* (1977)

Louis M Heyward
Producer, screenwriter
Born: New York City, New York 1921, died Los Angeles, California 2002
Milestones: Producer: *Witchfinder General* (1968), *Curse of the Crimson Altar* (1968), *The Oblong Box* (1969), *Scream and Scream Again* (1970), *The Abominable Dr Phibes* (1971), *Dr Phibes Rises Again* (1972)
Millstones: Writer: *Sergeant Deadhead* (1965), Co-writer: *The Glass Sphinx* (1967), Producer: *The Haunted House of Horror* (1969), Co-writer: *Dagmar's Hot Pants, Inc.* (1971)

Stuart Heisler
Director
Born: Los Angeles, California 1896, died San Diego, California 1979
Milestones: *The Glass Key* (1942) *Storm Warning* (1951), *The Star* (1952), *I Died a Thousand Times* (1955)
Millstones: *The Monster and the Girl* (1941),

Ann Helm
Actress
Born: Toronto, Ontario, Canada 1938
Milestones: *The Interns* (1962), *Follow that Dream* (1962),
Millstones: *Unkissed* Bride (1966), *Nightmare in Wax* (1969)

Norman T Herman
Producer
Born: Newark, New Jersey 1924
Milestones: *Bloody Mama* (1970)
Millstones: *Frogs* (1972)

Gordon Hessler
Director
Born: Berlin, Germany 1925, died London, England 2014
Milestones: *Catacombs* (1965) *The Oblong Box* (1969), *Scream and Scream Again* (1970), *Cry of the Banshee* (1970), *The Golden Voyage of Sinbad* (1974)
Millstones: *Medusa* (1973), *Atraco en la Jungla* (1976), *(California Cowboys* (1984)

Herman Hoffman
Screenwriter
Born: Montgomery, Alabama 1909, died Laguna Hills, California 1989
Milestones: *The Invisible Boy* (1957), *Guns of the Magnificent Seven* (1969)
Millstones: *Attack on the Iron Coast* (1968)

Skip Homeier
Actor
Born: George Vincent Homeier Chicago, Illinois 1939
Milestones: *Tomorrow the World* (1944), *Halls of Montezuma* (1950), *The Gunfighter* (1950), *Cry Vengeance* (1954), *Stranger at My Door* (1956)
Millstones: *No Road Back* (1957), *Plunderers of Painted Flats* (1959)

Oskar Homolka
Actor
Born: Vienna, Austria 1898, died Tunbridge Wells, Kent, England 1978
Milestones: *Rhodes of Africa* (1936), *Sabotage* (1936), *The Shop at Sly Corner* (1947),
AA nomination Best Actor in a Supporting Role *I Remember Mama* (1948), *War and Peace* (1956)
Millstones: *Song of Norway* (1970)

Ann Howard
Actress
Born: Chicago, Illinois 1925, died Los Angeles, California 1991
Milestones: *The Prince and the Pauper* (1937), *Little Men* (1940)
Millstones: *The Ghost of Rashmon Hall* (1948)

Gayle Hunnicutt
Actress
Born: Virginia Gayle Hunnicutt Fort Worth, Texas 1943
Milestones: *The Legend of Hell House* (1973)
Millstones: *Fragment of Fear* (1970), *The Spiral Staircase* (1975)

Marsha Hunt
Actress
Born: Marcia Virginia Hunt 1917
Milestones: *Pride and Prejudice* (1940), *Blossoms in the Dust* (1947), *Johnny Got His Gun* (1971)
Millstones: *Diplomatic Passport* (1954)

Tab Hunter
Actor
Born: Arthur Andrew Kelm, New York 1931
Milestones: *Saturday Island* (1952), *Damn Yankees!* (1958), *Polyester* (1981), *Lust in the Dust* (1985)
Millstones: *The Golden Arrow* (1962), *Birds Do It!* (1962), *Cameron's Closet* (1982)

Robert Hutton
Actor
Born: Robert Bruce Winne Kingston, New York 1920, died Kingston, New York 1994
Milestones: *The Steel Helmet* (1951)
Millstones: *The Man Without a Body* (1957), *Man From Tangier* (1957), *The Slime People* (1963), *They Came From Beyond Space* (1967), *Can Heironymus Merkin Ever Forget Mercy Humppe and Find True Happiness?*(1969), *Trog* (1970)

Martha Hyer
Actress
Born: Fort Worth, Texas 1924, died Santa Fe, Mexico 2014
Milestones: *Sabrina* (1954), AA nomination Best Actress in a Supporting Role: *Some Came Running* (1958), *The Carpetbaggers* (1964), *The Sons of Katie Elder* (1965)
Millstones: *Bikini Beach* (1964), *Picture Mommy Dead* (1966), *House of 1,000 Dolls* (1967)

I

John Ireland
Actor
Born: Vancouver, Canada 1914, died Santa Barbara, California 1992
Milestones: *A Walk in the Sun* (1945), *Red River* (1948), AA nomination Best Actor in a Supporting Role: *All the King's Men* (1949) *I Shot Jesse James* (1949), *The Good Die Young* (1954), *Gunfight at the OK Corral* (1957), *Farewell My Lovely* (1975)
Millstones: *Stormy Crossing* (1958), *Day of the Nightmare* (1965), *Northeast of Seoul* (1972), *The House of Seven Corpses* (1974), *The Shape of Things to Come* (1979), *Miami Golem* (1985), *Hammer Down* (1992)

J

Dean Jagger
Actor
Born: Ira Dean Jagger Columbus Grove, Ohio 1903, died Santa Momica, California 1991
Milestones: *Western Union* (1941), *The North Star* (1943), *Sister Kenny* (1946), AA winner Best Actor in a Supporting Role: *Twelve O'Clock High* (1949), *The Robe* (1953), *Executive Suite* (1954), *Bad Day at Black Rock* (1955), *X the Unknown* (1956), *Elmer Gantry* (1960)
Millstones: *Revolt of the Zombies* (1936), *The Great Lester Boggs* (1974), *Evil Town* (1977), *End of the World* (1977)

Rick Jason
Actor
Born: Richard Jacobson New York 1923, died Moorpark, California 2000
Milestones: *The Lieutenant Wore Skirts* (1956), *The Wayward Bus* (1957), *Combat!* (TV series 1962-1967),
Millstones: *Illegally Yours* (1988)

Nunnally Johnson
Screenwriter, producer, director
Born: Columbus, Georgia 1897, died Hollywood, Los Angeles, California 1977
Milestones: Screenplay: *The House of Rothschild* (1934), screenplay/producer: *The Prisoner of Shark Island* (1935), screenplay/producer: *Rose of Washington Square* (1939), producer and AA nomination Best Writing, Screenplay: *The Grapes of Wrath* (1940), screenplay/producer: *Roxie Hart* (1942), producer and AA nomination Best Writing, Screenplay: *Holy Matrimony* (1943), producer/screenplay: *Woman in the Window* (1944), producer/screenplay: *The Dark Mirror* (1946), producer/screenplay: *The Mudlark* (1950), screenplay/producer/director: *The Three Faces of Eve* (1957)
Millstones: Producer/director/co-writer: *Oh Men! Oh Women!* (1957)

Nathan Juran
Director, art director
Born: Naftuli Hertz Juran Gura Humorului, Bukovina, Romania 1907, died Palos Verdes Estates, California 2002
Milestones: AA winner Best Art Direction-Interior Decoration, Black-and-White (with Richard Day, Thomas Little) *How Green Was My Valley* (1942), AA nomination Best Art Direction-Interior Decoration, Black-and-White (with Richard Day, Thomas Little, Paul S Fox) *The Razor's Edge* (1946), director: *The 7th Voyage of Sinbad* (1958), *First Men in the Moon* (1964)
Millstones: Director: *The Deadly Mantis* (1967)

K

Aben Kandel
Writer
Born: Romania 1897, died Los Angeles, California 1993
Milestones: *Kid Monk Baroni* (1952), *I Was a Teenage Werewolf* (1957), *I Was a Teenage Frankenstein* (1957)
Millstones: *Beserk* (1967), *Trog* (1970), *Craze* (1974)

Boris Karloff
Actor
Born: William Henry Pratt Camberwell, London, England 1887, died Midhurst, Sussex, England 1969
Milestones: *Frankenstein* (1931), *The Old Dark House* (1932), *The Mask of Fu Manchu* (1932), *The Mummy* (1932), *The Bride of Frankenstein* (1935), *The Raven* (1935), *Charlie Chan at the Opera* (1937), *Son of Frankenstein* (1939), *House of Frankenstein* (1944), *The Body Snatcher* (1945), *The Secret Life of Walter Mitty* (1947), *Grip of the Strangler* (1958), *Targets* (1968)
Millstones: *The Phantom Buster* (1927), *Gift of Gab* (1934), *The Island Monster* (1954), *Sabaka* (1954), *Voodoo Island* (1957), *Frankenstein 1970* (1958), *The Ghost in the Invisible Bikini* (1966), *House of Evil* (1968), *Island of the Snake People* (1971), *Alien Terror* (1971)

Stubby Kaye
Actor
Born: Bernard Katzin, New York 1918, died Los Angeles, California 1997
Milestones: *Guys and Dolls* (1955), *Who Framed Roger Rabbit?* (1988)
Millstones: *The Cool Mikado* (1963), *Can Heironymus Merkin Ever Forget Mercy Humppe and Find True Happiness?* (1969), *Sixpack Annie* (1975)

Howard Keel
Actor, singer
Born: Harold Clifford Keel Gillespie, Illinois 1919, died Palm Desert, California 2004
Milestones: *Annie Get Your Gun* (1950), *Show Boat* (1951), *Kiss Me Kate* (1953), *Seven Brides For Seven Brothers* (1954), *Floods of Fear* (1958), *Dallas* (TV series 1981-1991)
Millstones: *The Day of the Triffids* (1963)

Arthur Kennedy
Actor
Born: John Arthur Kennedy Worcester, Massachusetts 1914, died Branford, Connecticut 1990
Milestones: AA nomination Best Actor in a Supporting Role: *Champion* (1949), AA nomination Best Actor in a Leading Role: *Bright Victory* (1951), AA nomination Best Actor in a Supporting Role: *Trial* (1955), AA Best Actor in a Supporting Role: *Peyton Place* (1957), AA nomination Best Actor in a Supporting Role: *Some Came Running* (1958)
Millstones: *Shark!* (1969), *As of Tomorrow* (1976), *Emmanuelle on Taboo Island* (1976), *Cave of the Sharks* (1978), *The Humanoid* (1979)

King Brothers—Frank, Herman, Maurice
Producers
Frank King: born Frank Kozinski New York 1913, died Beverly Hills, California 1989
Herman King: born Herman Kozinski Chicago, Illinois 1916, died Inglewood, California 1992

Maurice King: born Maurice Kozinski New York 1914, died Los Angeles, California 1977
Milestones: *Dillinger* (1945), *Gorgo* (1961)
Millstones: *Rodan* (US version 1956)

Phyllis Kirk
Actress
Born: Phyllis Kirkegaard Plainfield, New Jersey 1927, died Los Angeles, California 2006
Milestones: *Two Weeks with Love* (1950), *House of Wax* (1953), *Crime Wave* (1954)
Millstones: *Canyon Crossroads* (1955)

Don Kirshner
Producer, music department
Born: The Bronx, New York 1934, died Boca Raton, Florida 2011
Milestones: Music supervisor: *The Monkees* (TV series 1966-1967)
Millstones: Producer: *Toomorrow* (1970)

Hildegard Kneff/Neff
Actress
Born: Ulm, Baden-Württemberg, Germany 1925, died Berlin, Germany 2002
Milestones: *Film Without a Title* (1947), *Decision Before Dawn* (1951), *The Snows of Kilimanjaro* (1952)
Millstones: *Mozambique* (1964), *The Lost Continent* (1968), *Witchery* (1988)

Howard Koch
Screenwriter
Born: New York 1901, died Kingston, New York 1995
Milestones: Cowriter: *The Letter* (1940), *The Sea Hawk* (1940), AA nomination Best Writing, Original Screenplay (with John Huston, Abem Finkel, Harry Chandlee): *Sergeant York* (1941), AA nomination Best Writing, Screenplay (with Julius J Epstein, Philip G Epstein): *Casablanca* (1942), *Letter from an Unknown Woman* (1947)

Millstones: Backlisted by the House Un-American Activities Committee (1950)

L

Jack LaRue
Actor
Born: Gaspere Biondolillo New York 1902, died Santa Monica, California 1984
Milestones: *Road to Utopia* (1945)
Millstones: *No Orchids for Miss Blandish* (1948)

David Ladd
Actor, producer
Born: Los Angeles, California 1947 (son of Alan Ladd)
Milestones: Actor: *Shane* (1952)
Millstones: Actor: *Death Line* (1972), *The Klansman* (1974), *Beyond the Universe* (1981)

Richard H Landau
Screenwriter
Born: New York, 1940, died Century City, California 1993
Milestones: *Stolen Face* (1952), *The Quatermass Xperiment* (1955),
Millstones: *Lost Continent* (1951), *Sins of Jezebel* (1953), *Voodoo Island* (1957), *Frankenstein* (1970)

Carole Landis
Actress
Born: Frances Lillian Mary Ridste Fairchild, Wisconsin 1919, died Pacific Palisades, California 1948
Milestones: *One Million B.C* (1940), *Topper Returns* (1941), *I Wake Up Screaming* (1941)
Millstones: *Brass Monkey* (1948)

Harry Lauter

Actor

Born: Herman Arthur Lauter White Plains, New York 1914, died Ojai, California 1990

Milestones: *Tales of the Texas Rangers* (TV series 1955-1958)

Millstones: *Women Without Men* (1956), *Superbeast* (1972)

John Philip Law

Actor

Born: Los Angeles, California 1937, died Los Angeles, California 2008

Milestones: Nomination Golden Globe Most Promising Newcomer—Male: *The Russians Are Coming, The Russians Are Coming* (1966), *Barbarella* (1967)

Millstones: *The Spiral Staircase* (1975), *Skidoo* (1968), *Doctor Justice* (1975), *American Commandos* (1986), *Space Mutiny* (1988), *Alienator* (1990), *The Three Faces of Terror* (2004)

Marc Lawrence

Actor

Born: Max Goldsmith New York 1910, died Palm Springs, California 2005

Milestones: *Shepherd of the Hills* (1941), *This Gun For Hire* (1942), *The Ox-Bow Incident* (1943), *Dillinger* (1945) *Cloak and Dagger* (1947), *Key Largo* (1949), *The Asphalt Jungle* (1950)

Millstones: Blacklisted by House Un-American Activities Committee (1950), *Kill Her Gently* (1957), *King of Kong Island* (1968), *Dream No Evil* (1970), director/writer/actor: *Pigs* (1972), *Blood Red* (1989)

Reginald Le Borg

Director, writer

Born: Reginald Grobel, Vienna, Austria 1902, died Los Angeles, California 1989

Milestones: Co-wrote screenplay AA winning Best Short Subject, Two-reel: *Heavenly Music* (1943), Director: *San Diego, I Love You* (1944), *Diary of a Madman* (1963)

Millstones: *Voodoo Island* (1947), *The Eyes of Annie Jones* (1964)

Anton Leader
Director
Born: Boston, Massachusetts 1913, died Los Angeles, California 1988
Milestones: *Children of the Damned* (1963)

Gypsy Rose Lee
Actress, screenwriter, novelist, ecdysiast
Born: Rose Louise Hovick Seattle, Washington 1911, died Los Angeles, California 1970
Milestones: *The Stripper* (1963)
Millstones: *Babes in Bagdad* (1952)

Herbert J Leder
Director, producer, screenwriter
Born: New York 1922, died 1983
Milestones: Screenplay: *Fiend Without a Face* (1958), screenplay: *It!* (1967)
Millstones: Director/producer/screenwriter: *The Frozen Dead* (1966), co-director: *Doomsday Machine* (1972)

Bela Lugosi
Born: Béla Ferenc Dezső Blaskó in Lugos, Kingdom of Hungary (now Luggi, Romania) 1882, died Los Angeles, California 1956
Milestones: *Dracula* (1931), *White Zombie* (1932), *Island of Lost Souls* (1932), *The Black Cat* (1934), *Son of Frankenstein* (1939)
Millstones: *Ghosts on the Loose (1943), Bela Lugosi Meets a Brooklyn Gorilla* (1952), *Old Mother Riley Meets the Vampire/Vampire Over London* (1952) *Glen or Glenda* (1953)

Julian Lesser
Producer
Born: San Francisco, California 1915, died Ranch Mirage, California 2005
Milestones:
Son of producer Sol Lesser, *Whispering Smith Hits London* (1951)

Robert L Lippert
Producer, director
Born: Alameda, California 1909, died Alameda, California 1976
Milestones: Producer: *I Shot Jesse James* (1949), *The Steel Helmet* (1951), *The Quatermass Xperiment* (1955), *The Fly* (1958), *The Last Man on Earth* (1964), *The Earth Dies Screaming* (1964),
Millstones: Co-director: *Last of the Wild Horses* (1948), Producer: *Square Dance Jubilee* (1949), *Hollywood Varieties* (1950), *Radar Secret Service* (1950), *Lost Continent* (1951), *The Horror of It All* (1964), *Spaceflight IC-1* (1965), *The Last Shot You Hear* (1968)

Harold Lloyd Jr
Actor
Born: Los Angeles, California 1931, died North Hollywood, California 1971
Milestones: *Married Too Young* (1962)
Millstones: *A Yank in Ermine* (1955), *Frankenstein's Daughter* (1958), *Girls Town* (1959), *Mutiny in Outer Space* (1965)

Julie London
Actress, singer
Born: Julie Peck Santa Rosa, California 1926, died Encino, California 2000
Milestones: *The Great Man* (1956),
Millstones: *A Question of Adultery* (1958)

Lynn Loring
Actress
Born: Lynn Zimring New York 1944
Milestones: *Search for Tomorrow* (TV series 1951-1961),
Millstones: *Doppelganger* (1969)

Peter Lorre
Actor
Born: Laszlo (Ladislav) Löwenstein in Rózsahegy, Hungary 1904, died Los Angeles, California 1964

Milestones: *M* (1930), *The Man Who Knew Too Much* (1934), *Mad Love* (1935), *Crime and Punishment* (1935), *The Face Behind the Mask* (1941), *The Maltese Falcon* (1941), *The Mask of Dimitrios* (1944), *The Beast With Five Fingers* (1946), *Tales of Terror* (1962)
Millstones: *Double Confession* (1950), *Scent of Mystery* (1960)

Joseph Losey
Director
Born: Las Crosse, Wisconsin 1909, London, England 1984
Milestones: *The Prowler* (1950), 1951 left USA after pressure from House Un-American Activities Committee; 1956 replaced by British director Leslie Norman when Dean Jagger refused to work with him on *The Quatermass Experiment*, *The Damned* (1961), *The Servant* (1961), *Accident* (1971)
Millstones: *Modesty Blaise* (1966), *Boom* (1968), *Steaming* (1985)

Eugène Lourié,
Director, production designer, art director
Born: Kharkiv, Ukraine 1903, died Woodland Hills, Los Angeles, California 1991
Milestones: Art Director *La Grande Illusion* (1937), *The Southerner* (1944); Director: *The Beast from 20,000 Fathoms* (1953), Production Designer/co-director *The Giant Behemoth* (1959), AA nomination (with Alex Weldon) Best Effects, Special Visual Effects *Krakatoa: East of Java* (1968), Art Director *The Royal Hunt of the Sun* (1969)
Millstones: Art Director *Bikini Paradise* (1967)

Bessie Love
Actress
Born: Juanita Horton Midland, Texas 1898, died London, England 1986
Milestones: *The Birth of a Nation* (1915), *Intolerance* (1916), AA nomination Best Actress in a Leading Role: *The Broadway Melody* (1929), *Nowhere to Go* (1957)
Millstones: *The Weak and the Wicked* (1954), *Too Young to Love* (1959), *Touch and Go* (1955), *Promise Her Anything* (1965)

Herbert G Luft
Producer
Born: Essen, Germany 1907, died Beverly Hills, Los Angeles, California 1992
Milestones: Two-term president Hollywood Foreign Press Association
Millstones: Co-writer: *Hong Kong Affair* (1958), associate producer: *The Mutations* (1974), associate producer: *The Devil's Men* (1976)

William Lundigan
Actor
Born: Syracuse, New York 1914, died Duarte, California 1975
Milestones: *I'd Climb the Highest Mountain* (1951)
Millstones: *Serpent of the Nile* (1953), *The White Orchid* (1954)

Carol Lynley
Actress
Born: Carole Ann Jones, New York City, New York 1942
Milestones: *Blue Denim* (1959), *Bunny Lake is Missing* (1965), *Harlow* (1965), *The Poseidon Adventure* (1972)
Millstones: *Danger Route* (1967), *The Maltese Bippy* (1969), *Beware! The Blob!* (1972), *Spirits* (1990)

Leni Lynn
Actress, singer
Born: Angelina Ciofani Waterbury, Connecticut 1923, died Croton-on-Hudson, New York 2010
Milestones: *Babes in Arms* (1939)
Millstones: *Give Me the Stars* (1945)

M

David MacDonald
Director
Born: Helensburgh, Scotland 1904, London, England 1983

Milestones: Assistant Director *Cleopatra* (1934), Assistant Director *The Crusades* (1935)
Millstones: Director *Christopher Columbus* (1949), *Devil Girl From Mars* (1954), *Alias John Preston* (1955)

Richard Maibaum
Writer, producer
Born: New York 1908, died Santa Monica, California 1991
Milestones: *Dr No* (1962), *From Russia With Love* (1963), *Goldfinger* (1964), *Thunderball* (1965), *The Spy Who Loved me* (1977), *Octopussy* (1983), 007 etc, etc
Millstones: *Zarak* (1956), *The Bandit of Zhobe* (1959)

Jayne Mansfield
Actress
Born: Vera Jayne Palmer Bryn Mawr, Pennsylvania 1933, died Slidell, Louisiana 1967
Milestones: Winner Golden Globe Most Promising Newcomer—Female: *The Girl Can't Help It* (1956), *The Burglar* (1957), *Will Success Spoil Rock Hunter?* (1957)
Millstones: *Too Hot To Handle* (1960), *The Challenge* (1960), *The Fat Spy* (1966)

Herbert Marshall
Actor
Born: London, England 1890, died Beverly Hills, Los Angeles, California 1966
Milestones: *Murder!* (1930), *Trouble in Paradise* (1932), *Foreign Correspondent* (1940), *The Letter* (1940), *The Little Foxes* (1941), *The Razor's Edge* (1946), *The Fly* (1958)
Millstones: *Andy Hardy's Blonde Trouble* (1944), *Black Jack* (1950), *Gog* (1954), *Five Weeks in a Balloon* (1962)

Gene Martel
Producer, director
Born: New York City, New York 1916

Milestones: Producer: *Stranger From Venus* (1954)
Millstones: Director, producer: *Diplomatic Passport* (1954), producer: *Doorway to Suspicion* (1957)

Paul Maslansky
Producer, writer, actor
Born: Rego Park, New York 1933
Milestones: Producer: *Police Academy* (1984), *Police Academy 2: Their First Assignment* (1985), *The Russia House* (1990)
Millstones: The Stinkers Bad Movie Awards: Producer: *Cop & ½* (1993)

Richard Matheson
Screenwriter, novelist
Born: Allendale, New Jersey 1926, died Calabasas, California 2013
Milestones: Novel: *I Am Legend* (1954) filmed as *The Last Man on Earth* (1964), *The Omega Man* (1971), *I Am Legend* (2007), Novel/co-screenplay: *The Incredible Shrinking Man* (1957), *House of Usher* (1960), *Pit and the Pendulum* (1961), *Night of the Eagle* (1962), *The Raven* (1963), *The Comedy of Terrors* (1963), *The Devil Rides Out* (1968), *Duel* (TVM, 1971)
Millstones: *Fanatic* (1965), co-writer: *De Sade* (1969), *Jaws 3-D* (1983)

Carole Mathews
Actress
Born: Jean Defeil Montgomery, Illinois 1920, died Murrieta, California 2014
Milestones: *Meet Me at the Fair* (953), *Port of Hell* (1954), *The Stranger Awakening* (1958)
Millstones: *Swamp Women* (1956), *13 Fighting Men* (1960)

Kerwin Matthews
Actor
Born: Seattle, Washington 1926, died San Francisco, California 2007
Milestones: *The 7th Voyage of Sinbad* (1958), *The 3 Worlds of Gulliver* (1960), *Jack the Giant Killer* (1962)
Millstones: *Octaman* (1971), *Nightmare in Blood* (1977)

Victor Mature
Actor
Born: Louisville, Kentucky 1913, died Rancho Santa Fe, California 1999
Milestones: *I Wake Up Screaming* (1942), *My Darling Clementine* (1946), *Kiss of Death* (1947), *Samson and Delilah* (1949), *After the Fox* (1966)
Millstones: *Safari* (1956), *Zarak* (1956), *The Bandit of Zhobe* (1959), *Firepower* (1979)

Arthur Mayer
Producer
Born: Demopoulos, Alabama 1886, died New York City, New York 1981
Milestones: Author (with Richard Griffith) *Merely Colossal: The Story of the Movies from the Long Chase to the Chaise Long* (1971)
Millstones: *High Hell* (1958)

Doug McClure
Actor
Born: Glendale, California 1935, died Sherman Oaks, Los Angeles, California 1995
Milestones: *The Unforgiven* (1960), *Shenandoah* (1965), *The Virginian* (TV series 1962-1971)
Millstones: *The Land that Time Forgot* (1975), *The House Where Evil Dwells* (1982)

Roddy McDowall
Actor
Born: Roderick McDowall, London, England 1928, died Studio City, Los Angeles 1998
Milestones: *How Green Was My Valley* (1941), *My Friend Flicka* (1941), *Lassie Come Home* (1943), *Cleopatra* (1963), *Planet of the Apes* (1967), *The Poseidon Adventure* (1972)
Millstones: *Killer Shark* (1950), *Big Timber* (1950), *The Cool Ones* (1967), *It!* (1967), *Angel, Angel, Down We Go* (1969), *Mean Johnny Barrows* (1976), *Cutting Class* (1989), *Going Under* (1990)

William "Biff" McGuire
Actor
Born: New Haven, Connecticut 1926
Milestones: *The Thomas Crown Affair* (1968), *The Heart is a Lonely Hunter* (1968) *Serpico* (1973)
Millstones: *Station Six-Sahara* (1963)

Burgess Meredith
Actor
Born: Cleveland, Ohio 1907, died Malibu, California 1997
Milestones: *Winterset* (1936), *Of Mice and Men* (1939), *The Story of GI Joe* (1945), *Diary of a Chambermaid* (1946), *Batman The Movie* (1966), AA nomination Best Actor in a Supporting Role: *Day of the Locust* (1975), AA nomination Best Actor in a Supporting Role: *Rocky* (1976), *Grumpy Old Men* (1993)
Millstones: *Stay Away Joe* (1968), *Skidoo* (1968), Director/screenwriter/actor: *The Ying and Yang of Mr Go* (1970), *Beware! The Blob!* (1972), *Santa Claus* (1985)

Gary Merrill
Actor
Born: Hartford, Connecticut 1915, died Falmouth, Maine 1990
Milestones: *12 O'Clock High* (1949), *All About Eve* (1950), *The Human Jungle* (1954), *A Blueprint for Murder* (1953), *Mysterious Island* (1961)
Millstones: *Navy Wife* (1956), *Destination Inner Space* (1966), *Run, Psycho, Run* (1968)

Beverly Michaels
Actress
Born: New York City, New York 1928, died Phoenix, Arizona 2007
Milestones: *Wicked Woman* (1953)
Millstones: *Women Without Men* (1956)

Cameron Mitchell
Actor
Born: Cameron McDowell Mitzell Dallastown, Pennsylvania 1918, died Pacific Palisades, California 1994
Milestones: *Death of a Salesman* (1952), *Les Miserables* (1952), *How to Marry a Millionaire* (1953), *Love Me or Leave Me* (1955), *Carousel* (1956), *Hombre* (1967)
Millstones: *Island of the Doomed* (1967), *Nightmare in Wax* (1969), *Medusa* (1973), *Ninja Assassins* (1976), *The Swarm* (1978), *Cataclysm* (1980), *Frankenstein Island* (1981), *Dixie Ray Hollywood Star* (1983), *Low Blow* (1986), *Space Mutiny* (1988)

Thomas Mitchell
Actor
Born: Elizabeth, New Jersey 1892, died Los Angeles, California 1962
Milestones: *Lost Horizon* (1937), AA nomination Best Actor in a Supporting Role: *The Hurricane* (1937), *Make Way for Tomorrow* (1937), AA Best Actor in a Supporting Role: *Stagecoach* (1939), *Our Town* (1940), *The Black Swan* (1942), *The Sullivans* (1944) (1944), *Alias Nick Beal* (1949), *Tumbleweed* (1953)
Millstones: *Too Young to Love* (1959)

Douglass Montgomery
Actor
Born: Los Angeles, California 1907, died Norwalk, Connecticut 1966
Milestones: *Waterloo Bridge* (1931), *Little Women* (1933), *The Cat and the Canary* (1939)
Millstones: *Forbidden* (1945)

Terry Moore
Actress
Born: Helen Luella Koford Los Angeles, California 1929
Milestones: *Mighty Joe Young* (1949), AA nomination Best Actress in a Supporting Role: *Come Back, Little Sheba* (1952), *Beneath the 12-Mile Reef* (1953), *Daddy Long Legs* (1955), *Portrait of Alison* (1955)

Millstones: *Platinum High School* (1960), *A Man Called Dagger* (1968), *Death Dimension* (1978), *Going Overboard* (1989), *American Southern* (1995)

Wayne Morris
Actor
Born: Bert DeWayne Morris Los Angeles, California 1914, died Oakland, California 1959
Milestones: *Kid Galahad* (1937), *Paths of Glory* (1957)
Millstones: *The Return of Dr X* (1939), *The Gelignite Gang* (1956)

Jeff Morrow
Actor
Born: Leslie Irving Morrow New York City, New York 1907, died Canoga Park, California 1993
Milestones: *The Robe* (1953), *This Island Earth* (1955), *Pardners* (1956),
Millstones: *The Giant Claw* (1957), *Fugitive Lovers* (1975)

Mary Murphy
Actress
Born: Washington DC 1931, died Beverly Hills, Los Angeles, California 2011
Milestones: *The Wild One* (1953), *The Desperate Hours* (1955), *Crime and Punishment USA* (1959), *Junior Bonner* (1972)
Millstones: *Escapement* (1957), *Two Before Zero* (1962)

Don Murray
Actor
Born: Hollywood, California 1929
Milestones: AA nomination Best Actor in a Supporting Role: *Bus Stop* (1956), *The Bachelor Party* (1957), *A Hatful of Rain* (1957), *The Hoodlum Priest* (1961),
Millstones: *The Viking Queen* (1967)

N

George Nader
Actor
Born: Pasadena, California 1921, died Los Angeles, California 2002
Milestones: *Away All Boats* (1956), *The Unguarded Moment* (1956), *Away All Boats* (1956)
Millstones: *Robot Monster* (1953), *Sins of Jezebel* (1953), *Miss Robinson Crusoe* (1954), *The Human Duplicators* (1965), *The Million Eyes of Su-Muru* (1967)

William Nassour
Producer
Born: Colorado, 1903, died Los Angeles, California 1987
Milestones: *Street of Shadows/The Shadow Man* (1953)
Millstone: *Sheena: Queen of the Jungle* (TV series 1955-1956)

Patricia Neal
Actress
Born: Packard, Kentucky 1926, died Edgartown, Massachusetts 2010
Milestones: *The Fountainhead* (1949), *The Day the Earth Stood Still* (1951), *A Face in the Crowd* (1957), AA Best Actress in a Leading Role: *Hud* (1963), AA nomination Best Actress in a Leading Role: *The Subject Was Roses* (1968)
Millstones: *Something for the Birds* (1952), *Stranger From Venus* (1954), *Flying By* (2009)

Gene Nelson
Actor, director
Born: Eugene Leander Berg Seattle, Washington 1920, died Los Angeles, California 1996
Milestones: Actor *Tea for Two* (1950), *Lullaby of Broadway* (1951), *Oklahoma!* (1955) Director: *Your Cheatin' Heart* (1964)
Millstones: *Thunder Island* (1963)

Sam Neufeld/Sam Newfield/Sherman Scott/Peter Stewart

B movie director, producer
Born: New York 1899, died Los Angeles, California 1964
Milestones: 277 credits as director
Millstones: *White Pongo* (1945), *The Flying Serpent* (1946), *Wild Weed* (1949), *Lost Continent* (1951), *The Gambler and the Lady* (1952) etc, etc

Joseph M Newman

Director
Born: Logan, Utah 1909, died Simi Valley, California 2006
Milestones: *711 Ocean Drive* (1950), *This Island Earth* (1955)
Millstones: *Lady in the Fog* (1952)

Richard Ney

Actor
Born: New York City, New York 1916, died Pasadena, California 2004
Milestones: *Mrs Miniver* (1942), *Premature Burial* (1962)
Millstones: *Babes in Baghdad* (1952)

James H Nicholson

Producer, co-founder, with Samuel Z Arkoff, American International Pictures
Born: Seattle, Washington 1916, died Los Angeles, California 1972
Milestones: *The Pit and the Pendulum* (1961), *Premature Burial* (1962), *Tales of Terror* (1962), *The Raven* (1963), *X: The Man With the X-Ray Eyes* (1963), *The Comedy of Terrors* (1963), *The Tomb of Ligeia* (1964), *Die, Monster, Die* (1965), *The Abominable Dr Phibes* (1971), *Dr Phibes Rises Again* (1972)
Millstones: *She Creature* (1956), *Voodoo Women* (1957) *The Saga of the Viking Women and their Voyage to the Waters of the Great Sea Serpent* (1957), *Earth Versus the Spider* (1958), *How to Stuff a Wild Bikini* (1965), *Blacula* (1972)

Alex Nicol
Actor, director
Born: Alexander L Nicol Jr Ossining, New York 1916, died Montecito, California 2001
Milestones: *Meet Danny Wilson* (1952), *The Man From Laramie* (1955)
Millstones: Director/actor: *The Screaming Skull* (1958), *Ape* (1976)

Leslie Nielsen
Actor
Born: Regina, Saskatchewan 1926, died Fort Lauderdale, Florida 2010
Milestones: *Forbidden Planet* (1956), *Airplane!* (1980), *Airplane II: The Sequel* (1982), *The Naked Gun: From the Files of Police Squad!* (1988), *Naked Gun 2 1/2: The Smell of Fear* (1991), *Naked Gun 33 1/3: The Final Insult* (1994), *Dracula: Dead and Loving It* (1995)
Millstones: *Night Train to Paris* (1964), *Project Kill* (1976), *The Patriot* (1986), *Dangerous Curves* (1998), *Repossessed* (1990), *Stan Helsing* (2009)

Edmund H North
Screenwriter
Born: New York City, New York 1911, died Santa Monica, California 1990
Milestones: *Young Man with a Horn* (1950), *The Day the Earth Stood Still* (1951), *Sink the Bismarck!* (1960) AA (with Francis Ford Coppola) Best Writing, Story and Screenplay Based on Factual Material or Material Not Previously Published or Produced: *Patton* (1970)
Millstones: *Meteor* (1979)

O

Hugh O'Brian
Actor
Born: Hugh Charles Krampe Rochester, New York 1925
Milestones: *There's No Business Like Show Business* (1954), *The Fiend Who Walked the West* (1958), *The Shootist* (1976)

Millstones: *Ten Little Indians* (1965), *Doin' Time on Planet Earth* (1988)

Pat O'Brien
Actor
Born: William Joseph Patrick O'Brien Milwaukee, Wisconsin 1899, died Santa Monica, California 1983
Milestones: *The Great O'Malley* (1937), *Angels With Dirty Faces* (1938), *The Fighting 69th* (1940), *The Last Hurrah* (1958), *Some Like it Hot* (1959), *Ragtime* (1981)
Millstones: *Kill Me Tomorrow* (1957)

Willis O'Brien
Special effects
Born: Oakland, California 1886, died Los Angeles, California 1962
Milestones: *The Lost World* (1924), *King Kong* (1933), AA Best Effects, Special Effects: *Mighty Joe Young* (1949)
Millstones: *The Black Scorpion* (1957)

Cathy O'Donnell
Actress
Born: Ann Steely, Siluria, Alabama 1923, died Los Angeles, California 1970
Milestones: *The Best Years of Our Lives* (1946), *They Live By Night* (1948), *Detective Story* (1951), *Ben-Hur* (1959)
Millstones: *My World Dies Screaming* (1958)

Dan O'Herlihy
Actor
Born: Wexford, Ireland 1919, died Malibu, California 2005
Milestones: *Odd Man Out* (1947), *Macbeth* (1948), AA nomination Best Actor in a Leading Role: *Robinson Crusoe* (1954), *The Cabinet of Caligari* (1962)
Millstones: *Invasion U.S.A.* (1952), *Sword of Venus* (1953), *The Big Cube* (1969)

Dennis O'Keefe
Actor
Born: Edward Vance Flanagan Ford Madison, Iowa 1908, died Santa Monica, California 1968
Milestones: *Topper Returns* (1941), *The Leopard Man* (1943), *Brewster's Millions*, (1945), actor, co-writer: *T Men* (1947) *Dragoon Wells Massacre* (1957)
Millstones: *Siren of Atlantis* (1949), *The Fake* (1953), *Las Vegas Shakedown* (1955), *Lady of Vengeance* (1957), *Naked Flame* (1964)

James Olson
Actor
Born: Evanston, Illinois 1930
Milestones: *Rachel, Rachel* (1968), *The Andromeda Strain* (1971), *Ragtime* (1981),
Millstones: *Moon Zero Two* (1969), *Crescendo* (1970), *The Mafu Cage* (1978)

Wyatt Ordung
Actor, writer
Born: Shanghai, China 1922, died California 2005
Milestones: Director/producer/writer//actor: *Walk the Dark Street* (1956)
Millstones: Writer: *Robot Monster* (1953), director/actor: *Monster From the Ocean Floor* (1953)

P

Jack Palance
Actor
Born: Vladimir Palahnuik, Lattimer Mines, Pennsylvania 1919, died Montecito, California 2006
Milestones: AA nomination Best Actor in a Supporting Role: *Sudden Fear* (1952), AA nomination Best Actor in a Supporting Role: *Shane* (1953), *I Died a Thousand Times* (1955), *The Big Knife* (1955), *Mon-*

te Walsh (1970), AA Best Actor in a Supporting Role: *City Slickers* (1991)
Millstones: *Craze* (1974), *The Shape of Things to Come* (1979), *Cocaine Cowboys* (1979), *Gor II* (1988)

Willard Parker
Actor
Born: Worster Stat Van Eps New York City, New York 1912, died Racnho Mirage, California 1996
Milestones: *Kiss Me Kate* (1953), *The Earth Dies Screaming* (1964)
Millstones: *The Devil's Saddle Legion* (1937)

Larry Parks
Actor
Born: Sam Klusman Lawrence Parks Olathe, Kansas 1914, died Studio City, California 1975
Milestones: AA Nomination Best Actor in a Leading Role: *The Jolson Story* (1946), *Jolson Sings Again* (1949)
Millstones: Blacklisted by the House Un-American Activities Committee (1951*), Tiger by the Tail* (1955)

Robert Parrish
Director, editor
Born: Columbus, Georgia 1916, died Southampton, Long Island, New York 1995
Milestones: Editor AA (with Francis D Lyon) Best Film Editing: *Body and Soul* (1947), AA nomination (with Al Clark) Best Film Editing: *All the Kings Men* (1949), Director: *Cry Danger* (1951), *The Purple Plain* (1954), *The Wonderful Country* (1959)
Millstones: *The Bobo* (1967), *A Town Called Bastard* (1971) *Doppelganger* (1969)

Christopher Plummer
Actor
Born: Toronto, Ontario, Canada 1929

Milestones: *The Fall of the Roman Empire* (1964), *The Sound of Music* (1965), *Waterloo* (1970), *The Return of the Pink Panther* (1975), *The Man Who Would be King* (1975), *Twelve Monkeys* (1995), AA nomination Best Performance by an Actor in a Supporting Role: *The Last Station* (2009), AA Best Performance by an Actor in a Supporting Role: *Beginners* (2010), *Danny Collins* (2015)

Millstones: *The Sound of Music* (1965), *Lock Up Your Daughters!* (1969), *The Pyx* (1973), *The Spiral Staircase* (1975), *Starcrash* (1978), *Highpoint* (1982), *The Boss' Wife* (1986), *I Love N.Y.* (1987), *Red Blooded American Girl* (1990), *Firehead* (1991), *Crackerjack* (1994), *Dracula 2000* (2000)

Tom Poston

Actor

Born: Columbus, Ohio 1921, died Los Angeles, California 2007

Milestones: *Cold Turkey* (1971)

Millstones: *Zotz!* (1962), *The Old Dark House* (1963), *The Happy Hooker* (1976)

Stefanie Powers

Actress

Born: Stefanie Zofya Paul Hollywood, Los Angeles, California 1942

Milestones: *Experiment in Terror* (1962), *The Girl From U.N.C.L.E.* (TV series 1966-1967), *Hart to Hart* (TV series 1979-1984)

Millstones: *Fanatic* (1965), *Crescendo* (1970), *Gone With the West* (1975), *The Astral Factor* (1978)

Robert Preston

Actor

Born: Robert Preston Meservey Newton Highland, Massachusetts 1918, died Montecito, California 1987

Milestones: *Beau Geste* (1939), *The Macomber Affair* (1947), *Tulsa* (1949), *The Dark at the Top of the Stairs* (1960), *The Music Man* (1962), *All the Way Home* (1963), AA nomination Best Actor in a Supporting Role *Victor Victoria* (1982)

Millstones: *Cloudburst* (1951), *Island of Love* (1963)

Vincent Price
Actor
Born: St Louis, Missouri 1911, died Los Angeles, California 1993
Milestones: *Tower of London* (1940), *Brigham Young* (1940), *Dragonwyck* (1946), *His Kind of Woman* (1951), *House of Wax* (1953), *The Story of Mankind* (1954), *The Ten Commandments* (1956), *The Fly* (1958), *The Tingler* (1959), *The Fall of the House of Usher* (1961), *The Pit and the Pendulum* (1961), Tales of Terror (1962), *Comedy of Terrors* (1963), *The Tomb of Ligeia* (1964), *Scream and Scream Again* (1970), *The Abominable Dr Phibes* (1971), *Theatre of Blood* (1973), *Edward Scissorhands* (1990)
Millstones: *Nefertite, regina del Nilo (1961), Beach Party (1963), Dr Goldfoot and the Girl Bombs* (1966), *The Trouble With Girls* (1969), *Percy's Progress* (1974)

Edmond Purdom
Actor
Born: Welwyn Garden City, Hertfordshire, England 1924, died Rome, Italy 2009
Milestones: *The Student Prince* (1954), *The Egyptian* (1954), *Athena* (1954), *The Comedy Man* (1964)
Millstones: *Moment of Danger* (1960), *Horror Safari* (1982), *The Rift* (1990)

Q

Robert Quarry
Actor
Born: Santa Rosa, California 1925, died Woodland Hills, California 2009
Milestones: *Count Yorga, Vampire* (1970), *The Return of Count Yorga* (1971), *Deathmaster* (1972), *Dr Phibes Rises Again* (1972), *Madhouse* (1974)
Millstones: *Agent for H.A.R.M.* (1966), *Moon in Scorpio* (1987), *Beverly Hills Vamp* (1989), *Sexbomb* (1989), *Droid Gunner* (1985)

R

Lewis J Rachmil
Producer, art director
Born: New York City, New York 1908, died Beverly Hills, California 1984
Milestones: AA nomination Best Art Direction, Black-and-White: *Our Town* (1940), Associate Producer: *Androcles and the Lion* (1952), Producer: *Footloose* (1984)
Millstones: Producer: *The 30 Foot Bride of Candy Rock* (1959), *Mosquito Squadron* (1968)

George Raft
Actor
Born: George Ranft New York City, New York 1901, died Los Angeles, California 1989
Milestones: *Scarface* (1932), *Bolero* (1934), *Each Dawn I Die* (1939), *Some Like it Hot* (1959)
Millstones: *I'll Get You For This* (1951), *Five Golden Dragons* (1967), *Skidoo* (1968), *Sextette* (1978)

Ella Raines
Actress
Born: Snoqualmie Falls, Washington 1920, died Sherman Oaks, California 1988
Milestones: *Hail the Conquering Hero* (1944), *The Suspect* (1944), *Brute Force* (1947)
Millstones: *Singing Guns* (1950)

Tony Randall
Actor
Born: Arthur Leonard Rosenberg Tulsa, Oklahoma 1920, died New York City, New York 2004
Milestones: *Will Success Spoil Rock Hunter?* (1957), *Pillow Talk* (1959), *Send Me No Flowers* (1964), *Seven Faces of Dr Lao* (1964), *The Odd*

Couple (TV series 1970-1975)
Millstones: *Our Man in Marrakesh* (1966), *The Gong Show Movie* (1980)

Ron Randell
Actor
Born: Sydney, New South Wales, Australia 1918, died Los Angeles, California 2005
Milestones: *Kiss Me Kate* (1953), *I Am a Camera* (1955),
Millstones: *The Sea Creature* (1956), *Morning Call* (1957)

Gregory Ratoff
Actor, director
Born: Samara, Russia 1897, died Solothurn, Switzerland 1960
Milestones: Director: *Rose of Washington Square* (1939), *Intermezzo* (1939), *Adam Had Four Sons* (1941), *Song of Russia* (1944), *Moss Rose* (1945) *Oscar Wilde* (1960)
Actor: *What Price Hollywood* (1932), *The Corsican Brothers* (1941), *All About Eve* (1950), *The Sun Also Rises* (1957)
Millstones: Director: *My Daughter Joy* (1950)

Dale Robertson
Actor
Born: Harrah, Oklahoma 1923, died San Diego, California 2013
Milestones: *Fighting Man of the Plains* (1949), *Call Mr Mister* (1951), *The Farmer Takes a Wife* (1953), *Devil's Canyon* (1953), *Sitting Bull* (1954), *Dakota Incident* (1956), *Iron Horse* (TV series 1966-1968)
Millstones: *Blood on the Arrow* (1964), *Coast of Skeletons* (1965)

Edward G Robinson
Actor
Born: Emmanuel Goldenberg, Bucharest, Romania 1893, died Hollywood, Los Angeles 1973
Milestones: *Little Caesar* (1930), *The Whole Town's Talking* (1934), *A Slight Case of Murder* (1934), *Dr Erlich's Magic Bullet* (1940), *The Sea Wolf* (1941), *Double Indemnity* (1944), *Key Largo* (1948), *The Ten*

Commandments (1956), *Two Weeks in Another Town* (1962), *The Cincinnati Kid* (1965)
Millstones: *My Daughter Joy* (1950)

Albert S Rogell
Director, producer
Born: Oklahoma City, Oklahoma 1901, died Los Angeles, California 1988
Milestones: *Heaven Only Knows* (1947), *Before I Wake* (1955)
Millstones: *No More Women* (1934), *Unknown Woman* (1935), *Roaming Lady* (1936), *Love, Honour and Goodbye* (1945)

Ruth Roman
Actress
Born: Lynn, Massachusetts 1922, died Laguna Beach, California 1999
Milestones: *The Window* (1949), *Champion* (1949), *Strangers on a Train* (1951), Joe *Macbeth* (1955), *The Bottom of the Bottle* (1956), *Love Has Many Faces* (1965)
Millstones: *A Knife for the Ladies* (1974), *Echoes* (1982)

Cesar Romero
Actor
Born: New York City, New York 1907, died Santa Monica, California 1994
Milestones: *The Devil is a Woman* (1935), *Wee Willie Winkie* (1937), *The Captain from Castile* (1947), *Donovan's Reef* (1961), *The Joker* (Batman TV series 1966-1968), *Batman: The Movie* (1966), *The Computer Wore Tennis Shoes* (1969)
Millstones: *Seven Women from Hell* (1961), *Sergeant Dead Head* (1965) *Skidoo* (1968)

Mickey Rooney
Actor
Born: Joseph Yule Jr Brooklyn, New York 1920, died North Hollywood, Los Angeles, California 2014
Milestones: *A Midsummer Nights Dream* (1935), *Ah Wilderness* (1935), *A Family Affair* (1937), Won Juvenile Award (Special Oscar) with Dean-

na Durbin (1939), AA nominated Best Actor in a Leading Role: *Babes in Arms* (1939), nominated Best Actor in a Leading Role: *The Human Comedy* (1943), nominated Best Actor in a Supporting Role: *The Bold and the Brave* (1956), *It's a Mad, Mad, Mad, Mad World* (1963), nominated Best Actor in a Supporting Role: *The Black Stallion* (1979)

Millstones: *Everything's Ducky* (1961), *How To Stuff a Wild Bikini* (1965), *Skidoo* (1968), *The Manipulator* (1971), *Maximum Force* (1992), *Revenge of the Red Baron* (1994), *Internet Love* (2000)

Max J Rosenberg
Producer
Born: New York City, New York 1914, died Los Angeles, California 2004
Milestones: Producer: *The Curse of Frankenstein* (1957), formed Amicus Productions with Milton Subotsky (1962), *Dr Terror's House of Horrors* (1965), *The Skull* (1965), *Dr Who and the Daleks* (1965), *Torture Garden* (1967), *The Birthday Party* (1968), *Scream and Scream Again* (1970), *The House that Dripped Blood* (1971), *The Vault of Horror* (1973)
Millstones: *The Beast Must Die* (1974), *Invasion Earth: The Aliens are Here* (1988)

Cy Roth
Director, producer, screenwriter
Born: Chicago, Illinois 1912, died 1969
Milestones: Director/producer/screenwriter: *Fire Maidens from Outer Space* (1956)
Millstones: Director: *Combat Squad* (1953), director/producer/screenwriter: *Air Strike* (1955)

Mann Rubin
Screenwriter
Born: Brooklyn, New York 1927, died Los Angeles, California 2013
Milestones: *The Best of Everything* (1959), *Warning Shot* (1967)
Millstones: *The Bionic Woman* (TV series episode 1976)

S

Boris Sagal
Director
Born: Bernard Louis Sagal in Yekaterinoslav, Ukrainian SSR (now Dnipropetrovsk, Ukraine, died Portland, Oregon 1981
Milestones: *Twilight of Honor* (1963), *The Omega Man* (1971)
Millstones: *Girl Happy* (1965), *Mosquito Squadron* (1968)

Sidney Salkow
Director, screenwriter
Born: New York City, New York 1909, died Valley Village, California 2000
Milestones: Screenwriter: *Anything Goes* (1936), director: *Twice-Told Tales* (1963), *The Last Man on Earth* (1964)
Millstones: *The Murder Game* (1965)

Harry Saltzman
Producer
Born: Sherbrooke, Québec, Canada 1915, died Paris, France 1994
Milestones: *Look Back in Anger* (1959), *The Entertainer* (1960), *Saturday Night and Sunday Morning* (1960), *Dr No* (1962), *From Russia With Love* (1963), *Goldfinger* (1964), *The Ipcress File* (1965), *Thunderball* (1965), *Funeral in Berlin* (1966), *You Only Live Twice* (1967), *Battle of Britain* (1969), *Diamonds Are Forever* (1971), *Live and Let Die* (1973), *The Man With the Golden Gun* (1974)
Millstones: *On Her Majesty's Secret Service* (1969), *Toomorrow* (1970)

George Sanders
Actor
Born: St Petersburg, Russia 1906, died Castelidefeis, Barcelona, Spain 1972
Milestones: *The Saint* (five films 1930s,1940s), *The Moon and Sixpence* (1942), *The Picture of Dorian Gray* (1944), AA Best Actor in a Supporting Role: *All About Eve* (1950), *Village of the Damned* (1960)

Millstones: *Bluebeard's Ten Honeymoons* (1960), *Five Golden Dragons* (1965), *The Body Stealers* (1969), *Psychomania* (1973)

Donald S Sanford
Screenwriter
Born United States of America 1917, died Atlanta, Georgia 2011
Milestones: *Midway* (1976)
Millstones: *Submarine X-1* (1968), *Mosquito Squadron* (1969)

Telly Savalas
Actor
Born Aristotelis Savalas, Garden City, Long Island, New York 1922, died Universal City, California 1994
Milestones: AA nomination Best Actor in a Supporting Role: *Birdman of Alcatraz* (1962), *Cape Fear* (1962), *The Battle of the Bulge* (1965), *The Dirty Dozen* (1967), *The Scalphunters* (1968), *On Her Majesty's Secret Service* (1969), *Kelly's Heroes* (1970), *Kojak* (TV series 1973-1977)
Millstones: Director/screenwriter/star: *Beyond Reason* (1977), *A Town Called Bastard* (1971), *Crime Boss* (1972), *The House of Exorcism* (1975), *Beyond Reason* (1977), *The Border* (1980), *Fake-Out* (1982), *Mind Twister* (1994), *Backfire* (1995)

Charles H Schneer
Producer
Born Norfolk, Virginia 1920, died Boca Raton, Florida 2009
Milestones: *It Came From Beneath The Sea* (1955), *Earth vs. the Flying Saucers* (1957), *The Seventh Voyage of Sinbad* (1958), *The 3 Worlds of Gulliver* (1960), *Jason and the Argonauts* (1963), *The Valley of Gwangi* (1969), *The Golden Voyage of Sinbad* (1974), *Sinbad and the Eye of the Tiger* (1977) *Clash of the Titans* (1981
Millstones: *It Came from beneath the Sea* (1955) *Earth vs. the Flying Saucers* (1956)

Lizabeth Scott
Actress
Born Emma Matzo Scranton, Pennsylvania 1922, died Los Angeles, California 2015
Milestones: *Dead Reckoning* (1947), *I Walk Alone* (1948), *Pitfall* (1948), *Too Late for Tears* (1949), *Paid in Full* (1950), *Stolen Face* (1952), *Loving You* (1957)
Millstones: *Pulp* (1972)

Zachary Scott
Actor
Born Austin, Texas 1914, died Austin, Texas 1965
Milestones: *The Mask of Dimitrios* (1944), *The Southerner* (1945), *Mildred Pierce* (1945), *The Southerner* (1945), *Flamingo Road* (1949), *Born to be Bad* (1950)
Millstones: *Stallion Road* (1947), *One Last Fling* (1949)

Bert Shefter
Composer
Born Poltova, Russia 1904, died West Hollywood, California 1999
Milestones: (All with Paul Sawtell) *Voyage to the Bottom of the Sea* (1961), *Jack the Giant Killer* (1962), *The Last Man on Earth* (1964)
Millstones: (All with Paul Sawtell) *It! The Terror From Beyond Space* (1958), *The Cosmic Man* (1959)

Gary Sherman
Director, producer, screenwriter
Born Chicago, Illinois 1945
Milestones: Director/story: *Death Line* (1972),
Millstones: Director/co-writer: *Poltergeist III* (1988)

Phil Silvers
Born Philip Silver/Phillip Silversmith New York 1911, died Century City, California 1985
Milestones: *Cover Girl* (1944), *The Phil Silvers Show* (TV 1955-1959), *It's*

a Mad, Mad, Mad, Mad World (1963), *A Funny Thing Happened on the Way to The Forum* (1966)
Millstones: *Carry On ... Follow That Camel /Follow That Camel* (1967), *The Happy Hooker Goes to Hollywood* (1980)

Walter Slezak
Actor
Born Vienna, Austria 1902, died Flower Hill, New York 1983
Milestones: *Once Upon a Honeymoon* (1942), *Lifeboat* (1944), *Cornered* (1945), *The Pirate* (1948), *The Inspector General* (1949), *Call Me Madam* (1953)
Millstones: *Salome Where She Danced* (1945), *24 Hours to Kill* (1965), *The Mysterious House of Dr C* (1975)

Jerry Sohl
Screenwriter
Born Los Angeles, California 1913, died Thousand Oaks, California 2002
Milestones: *Monster of Terror/Die Monster Die* (1965)
Millstones: *Frankenstein Conquers The World/Furankenshutain tai chitei kaijû Baragon* (1965)

Harry Spalding
Screenwriter, producer
Born Victoria, British Columbia, Canada 1913, died Oakland, California (2008)
Milestones: Screenwriter: *Witchcraft* (1964), *The Earth Dies Screaming* (1964),
Millstones: Producer: *7 Women From Hell* (1961), Screenwriter: *Womanhunt* (1962), *The Day Mars Invaded The Earth* (1963), *Night Train To Paris* (1964), *Raider From Beneath the Sea* (1964), *Curse of the Fly* (1965), *Spaceflight IC-1* (1965), co-writer: *Wild on the Beach* (1965), screenwriter: *Witchery* (1988)

R G Springsteen
Director
Born Tacoma, Washington 1904, died 1989

Milestones: *Marshal of Laredo* (1945), *Fabulous Senorita* (1952) *Operation Eichmann* (1961) *Johnny Reno* (1966)
Millstones: *Secret Venture* (1955), *Battle Flame* (1959)

Betta St John
Actress
Born Betty Streigler Hawthorne, California 1929
Milestones: *The Robe* (1953), *The Student Prince* (1954), *High Tide at Noon* (1957), *Corridors of Blood* (1958), *The City of the Dead* (1960)
Millstones: *Alias John Preston* (1955), *The Snorkel* (1958)

C Ray Stahl
Screenwriter, director, producer
Born California 1920, died 1959
Milestones: Associate producer: *Tokyo File 2* (1951)
Millstones: Co-director/screenwriter: *Oriental Evil* (1951), co-director/co-writer: *The Scarlet Spear* (1954)

Craig Stevens
Actor
Born Gail Shikles Jr. Liberty, Missouri 1918, died Los Angeles, California (2000)
Milestones: *Abbott and Costello Meet Dr Jekyll and Mr Hyde* (1953), *Peter Gunn* (TV series 1958-1961), *Gunn* (1967)
Millstones: *The Deadly Mantis* (1957), *The Limbo Line* (1968)

Venetia Stevenson
Actress
Born Joanna Venetia Invicta Stevenson born London, England 1938
Milestones: *Day of the Outlaw* (1959), *Seven Ways from Sundown* (1960), *The City of the Dead* (1960)
Millstones: *Holiday* (1938), *Island of Lost Women* (1959), Executive in charge of production: *Born American* (1986)

Donald Ogden Stewart
Screenwriter
Born Columbus, Ohio 1894, died London, England 1980
Milestones: *The Prisoner of Zenda* (1937), AA Best Writing, Screenplay: *The Philadelphia Story* (1940)
Millstones: *Blacklisted* (1950), *Moment of Danger/Malaga* (1960)

Elaine Stewart
Actress
Born Elsy Steinberg, Montclair, New Jersey 1930, died Beverly Hills, California 2011
Milestones: *The Bad and the Beautiful* (1952), *Young Bess* (1953), *Take the High Ground!* (1953), *Brigadoon* (1954), *Night Passage* (1957), *The Tattered Dress* (1957)
Millstones: *High Hell* (1958)

Susan Strasberg
Actress
Born New York City, New York 1938, New York City, New York 1999
Milestones: BAFTA Film Award nomination Most Promising Newcomer to Film: *Picnic* (1955), *Kapo* (1960), *Taste of Fear* (1961), Golden Globe nomination Best Motion Picture Actress—Drama: *Hemingway's Adventures of a Young Man* (1963), *Psych-Out* (1965), *The Trip* (1967)
Millstones: *So Evil My Sister* (1974), *The Legend of Hillbilly John* (1974), *The Returning* (1983)

Elaine Stritch
Actress
Born Detroit, Michigan 1925, died Birmingham, Michigan 21014
Milestones: *A Farewell to Arms* (1957)
Millstones: *The Spiral Staircase* (1975), *September* (1987)

Milton Subotsky
Producer, screenwriter
Born New York City, New York 1921, died London, England 1991

Milestones: Producer/co-writer: *Rock! Rock! Rock!* (1956), co-writer: *Jamboree* (1957), co-producer/co-writer: *The Last Mile* (1959), executive producer/story: *The City of the Dead* (1960), Formed Amicus Productions with Max J Rosenberg (1962), *Dr Terror's House of Horrors* (1965), *The Skull* (1965), *Dr Who and the Daleks* (1965), *Torture Garden* (1967), *The Birthday Party* (1968), *Scream and Scream Again* (1970), *The House that Dripped Blood* (1971), *The Vault of Horror* (1973), *From Beyond the Grave* (1974), *The Uncanny* (1977), *The Monster Club* (1981), co-producer: *Maximum Overdrive* (1986)

Millstones: Co-producer/screenplay: *It's Trad, Dad!* (1962), co-producer/screenplay: *Just for Fun* (1963), *The Deadly Bees* (1966), *The Beast Must Die* (1974), *Invasion Earth: The Aliens are Here* (1988), *Dominique* (1979)

T

Akim Tamiroff

Actor

Born Tiflis, Georgia 1899, died Palm Springs, California 1972

Milestones: AA nomination Best Actor in a Supporting Role: *The General Died at Dawn* (1936), AA nomination Best Actor in a Supporting Role: *For Whom the Bell Tolls* (1943), *The Great Gambini* (1937), *The Way of All Flesh* (1940), *The Corsican Brothers* (1941), *Touch of Evil* (1956), *Topkapi* (1964), *Alphaville* (1965)

Millstones: *The Great Flirtation* (1934), *La Vedova X* (1955), *Invasion Europe* (1962), *Spuit Elf* (1964), *The Vulture* (1966)

Kent Taylor

Actor

Born Louis Weiss, Nashua, Iowa 1907, died Woodland Hills, Los Angeles, California 1987

Milestones: *Merrily We Go To Hell* (1932), *Death Takes a Holiday* (1934), *Tombstone: The Town Too Tough to Die* (1942)

Millstones: *Secret Venture* (1955), *The Day Mars Invaded the Earth* (1963), *The Crawling Hand* (1963), *The Mighty Gorga* (1969), *Brain of Blood* (1971), *Angels' Wild Women* (1972), *Girls For Rent* (1974)

Irving Temaner
Producer
Born Chicago, Illinois 1923, died United States 1975
Milestones: Associate producer: *How To Succeed in Business Without Really Trying* (1967)
Millstones: Executive producer: *Submarine X-1* (1968), *Attack on the Iron Coast* (1968)

Roy Thinnes
Actor
Born Chicago, Illinois 1938
Milestones: *The Hindenburg* (1975), *Falcon Crest* (TV series 1982-1983)
Millstones: *Doppelganger* (1969)

Robert Thoeren
Screenwriter, actor
Born Brno, Czech Republic 1903, died Munich, Germany 1937
Milestones: Story *The Prowler* (1951), story: *Some Like it Hot* (1959)
Millstones: Cowriter: *My Daughter Joy*/US: *Operation X* (1950)

Marshall Thompson
Actor
Born James Marshall Thompson Peoria, Illinois 1925, died Royal Oak, Michigan 1992
Milestones: *Homecoming* (1948), *Battleground* (1949), *Port of Hell* (1954), *Daktari* (TV series 1966-1969), *White Dog* (1971)
Millstones: *Cult of the Cobra* (1958), *It! The Terror From Beyond Space* (1958), *Fiend Without a Face* (1958), *Bog* (1983)

Peter M Thompson
Actor
Born Ottumwa, Ohio 1920, died Palm Springs, California 2001
Milestones: *Santa Fe* (1951)
Millstones: *A Yank in Ermine* (1955), *Monster a-Go Go* (1965)

Jacques Tourneur
Director
Born Paris, France 1906, died Bergerac, Dordogne, France 1977
Milestones: *Cat People* (1942), *I Walked With a Zombie* (1843), *The Leopard Man* (1943), *Experiment Perilous* (1944), *Out of the Past* (1947), *Night of the Demon* (1957), *The Comedy of Terrors* (1963)
Millstones: *Doctors Don't Tell* (1941), *The City Under the Sea* (1965)

Richard Travis
Actor
Born William Justice, Carlsbad, New Mexico 1913, died Pacific Palisades, California 1989
Milestones: *The Man Who Came To Dinner* (1942)
Millstones: *Mask of the Dragon* (1961), *Mesa of Lost Women* (1953), *Women Without Men*/US: *Blonde Bait* (1956), *Missile to the Moon* (1958)

Forrest Tucker
Actor
Born Plainfield, Indiana 1919, died Woodland Hills, Los Angeles, California 1986
Milestones: *Sands of Iwo Jima* (1949), *The Abominable Snowman* (1957), *Auntie Mame* (1958), *F Troop* (TV series 1965-1967)
Millstones: *The Strange World of Planet X* (1958), *The Trollenberg Terror* (1958), *The Wild McCullochs* (1975)

Irve Tunick
Screenwriter
Born New York City, New York 1912, died Carmel, New York 1987
Milestones: Co-writer: *Murder Inc.* (1960)
Millstones: *Lady of Vengeance* (1957)

Lana Turner
Actress
Born Julia Jean Mildred Frances Turner Wallace Idaho 1921, died Century City, California 1995

Milestones: *Somewhere I'll Find You* (1942), *The Postman Always Rings Twice* (1946), *The Bad and the Beautiful* (1952), AA Nomination Best Actress in a Leading Role: *Peyton Place* (1957) *Imitation of Life* (1959), *Portrait in Black* (1960), *Madame X* (1966)
Millstones: *The Big Cube* (1969), *Persecution* (1974), *Witches Brew* (1980)

U

Edgar G Ulmer
Director
Born Olmütz, Moravia, Austria-Hungary 1904, died Woodland Hills, Los Angeles, California 1972
Milestones: *People on Sunday* (1930), *The Black Cat* (1934), *Detour* (1945)
Millstones: *Babes in Baghdad* (1952) *The Amazing Transparent Man* (1960)

V

Victoria Vetri
Actress
Born Victoria Cecilia Vetri, San Francisco 1944
Milestones: *Playboy Magazine* Playmate of the Year 1968 (as Angela Dorian), AA nomination Best Effects, Special Visual Effects Jim Danforth, Roger Dicken: *When Dinosaurs Ruled the Earth* (1970)
Millstones: *Invasion of the Bee Girls* (1973), Sentenced to nine years in prison after pleading no contest to charges of attempted voluntary manslaughter for allegedly shooting her husband of 25 years (2011)

Charles F Vetter
Producer, screenwriter
Born USA
Milestones: Producer: *Fiend Without A Face* (1958), executive producer: *The Secret Man* (1958), co-producer: *Corridors of Blood* (1958), pro-

ducer/co-writer: *First Man Into Space* (1959), executive producer/story/screenplay: *Battle Beneath the Earth* (1967)

Millstones: Co-producer: *Assignment Redhead* (1956), co-producer: *The Counterfeit Plan* (1957), co-producer: *West of Suez* (1957), associate producer/co-story: *The Crooked Sky* (1957), co-producer: *Man in the Shadow* (1957), co-producer: *Escapement* (1957)

W

Robert Walker Jr

Actor

Born New York City, New York 1940

Milestones: *The Hook* (1963), *The Ceremony* (1963) *Ensign Pulver* (1964)

Millstones: *The Face of Eve* (1968), *Beware! The Blob* (1972), *Gone With the West* (1975)

Sam Wanamaker

Actor, director, producer

Born Chicago, Illinois 1919, died London, England 1993

Milestones: *The Spy Who Came in From the Cold* (1965), Director: *Sinbad and the Eye of the Tiger* (1977), Founded International Shakespeare Globe Centre, The Globe Theater, Bankside, Southwark, London (1997), *Guilty By Suspicion* (1991)

Millstones: Blacklisted by House Un-American Activities Committee 1950, *Danger Route* (1967), *The Spiral Staircase* (1975), *Billy Jack Goes to Washington* (1977)

Robert Webber

Actor

Born Santa Ana, California 1924, died Malibu, California 1989

Milestones: *12 Angry Men* (1957), *Hysteria* (1965), *Harper* (1966), *The Dirty Dozen* (1967), *Revenge of the Pink Panther* (1978), *10* (1979)

Millstones: *The Dangerous Mission* (1975), *Madame Claude* (1977), *Wild Geese II* (1985),

Robert D Weinback
Producer, screenwriter
Millstones: Producer: *Blind Man's Bluff* (1970), producer: *Hot Pants Holiday* (1971), producer/screenplay: *The Mutations* (1974), producer/screenplay:Herbert g luf *Shiver* (2012)

Paul Wendkos
Director
Born Abraham Paul Wendkos Philadelphia, Pennsylvania 1925, died Malibu, California 2009
Milestones: *The Burglar* (1955) *Face of a Fugitive* (1959), *Gidget* (1959), *Angel Baby* (1961), (1963), *Guns of the Magnificent Seven* (1969)
Millstones: *Gidget Goes to Rome* (1963)

Myles Wilder
Screenwriter
Born New York City, New York 1933, died Temecula' California 2910
Milestones: *The Dukes of Hazzard* (TV series 1981-1985)
Millstones: *Phantom from Space* (1953), *Manfish* (1956), *Fright* (1956), *Seven Guns to Mesa* (1958), *Spy in the Sky!* (1958), *Bluebeard's Ten Honeymoons* (1960)

W Lee Wilder
Director, producer
Born Sucha, Galicia, Austria-Hungary 1904, died Los Angeles, California 1982
Milestones: Nomination Golden Lion, Venice Film Festival: *Once a Thief* (1950)
Millstones: Director/producer: *Phantom from Space* (1953), *Killers from Space* (1954), *The Snow Creature* (1954), *Manfish* (1956), *Fright* (1956), *The Man Without a Body* (1957), *Spy in the Sky!* (1958), *Bluebeard's Ten Honeymoons* (1960), *Caxambu!* (1967), *The Omegans* (1968)

Bill Williams
Actor
Born Herman August Wilhelm Katt Brooklyn, New York 1915, died Burbank, California 1992
Milestones: *The Great Missouri Raid (1951), Son of Paleface* (1952), *The Adventures of Kit Carson* (TV series 1951-1955)
Millstones: *Space Master X-7* (1958), *Spaceflight IC-1* (1965), *The Giant Spider Invasion* (1975), *Night of the Zombies* (1981)

Elmo Williams
Editor, producer, director
Born James Elmo Williams Lone Wolf, Oklahoma, died Brookings, Oregon 2015
Milestones: AA Best Documentary, Features Editor: *Design for Death* (1947), AA (with Harry W Gerstad) Best Film Editing: *High Noon* (1952), AA nomination Best Film Editing: *20,000 Leagues Under the Sea* (1954), associate producer: *The Longest Day* (1962), editor: *Cleopatra* (1963), executive producer: *The Blue Max* (1966), producer: *Tora! Tora! Tora!* (1970),
Millstones: Co-editor: *Women Without Men* (1976), producer: *Soggy Bottom, U.S.A.* (1981)

Keenan Wynn
Actor
Born Francis Xavier Aloysius James Jeremiah Keenan Wynn New York City, New York 1916, died Los Angeles, California 1986
Milestones: *Annie Get Your Gun* (1950), *Kiss Me Kate* (1953), *The Absent-Minded Professor* (1953), *Son of Flubber* (1963), *Doctor Strangelove or: How I Stopped Worrying and Love the Bomb* (1964), *Once Upon a Time in the West* (1968), *The Great Race* (1965)
Millstones: *Escapement* (1957), *The Monitors* (1969), *The Manipulator* (1971), *The Devil's Rain* (1975), *The Lucifer Complex* (1978), *Hard Knocks* (1979), *The Dark* (1979), *The Clonus Horror* (1979)

Y

Philip Yordan
Screenwriter, producer
Born Chicago, Illinois 1914, died La Jolla, California 2003
Milestones: Screenwriter AA nomination Best Writing, Original Screenplay: *Dillinger* (1945), AA nomination (with Robert Wyler) Best Writing, Screenplay: *Detective Story* (1951), AA Best Writing, Motion Picture Story: *Broken Lance* (1954), *Johnny Guitar* (1954), *Joe Macbeth* (1954), *The Harder They Fall* (1956), *The Bravados* (1958), *King of Kings* (1961), *El Cid* (1961), *The Fall of the Roman Empire* (1964) Producer: *The Harder They Fall* (1956), *Battle of the Bulge* (and cowriter 1965)
Millstones: Producer/screenplay: *Bloody Wednesday* (1987), co-writer: *The Unholy* (1988)

Roland Young
Actor
Born London, England 1887, died New York City, New York 1953
Milestones: *One Hour With You* (1932), *David Copperfield* (1934), *The Man Who Could Work Miracles* (1936), AA nomination Best Actor in a Supporting Role *Topper* (1937), *King Solomon's Mines* (1937), *The Young in Heart* (1939), *The Philadelphia Story* (1940), *Bond Street* (1948)
Millstones: *That Man From Tangier* (1953)

Epilogue

Paradoxically, perhaps, while second and co-features have long been replaced by hundreds of made-for-television movies and small-screen series, Hollywood-in-Britain is far from extinct.

Many major movies have been made in Britain over the years, thanks in part to the country's excellent but considerably less-expensive-than-Hollywood studios and, of course, because many first-rate British supporting actors also tend to cost less than their Hollywood counterparts.

Conspicuously the first *Star Wars* was filmed at Britain's Shepperton and Elstree Studios in 1977, while 2015's blockbusting box-office-breaking reboot *Star Wars: The Force Awakens* was based at Britain's Pinewood Studios.

Long may Britain remain a force in filmmaking (and perhaps one day revive the B feature as well?).

About the Author

Alan Frank was Network Film Publicist for ITV (Britain's commercial television network) before becoming a film researcher for Granada Television. He is the author of some 15 books on the cinema, including several on horror and science fiction films and biographies of Frank Sinatra, Clint Eastwood and Humphrey Bogart.

He served a two-year term as a Governor of the British Film Institute.

He was film critic of the *Daily Star* (a leading popular British national newspaper) for over 30 years and now reviews films weekly for the *Morning Star* newspaper.

He has written on cinema for various magazines including *Film Review*, *Photoplay*, *TV Times* and was for many years the world's first Teletext film critic (with Oracle) and has been a regular contributor on cinema for various British radio stations.

www.ingramcontent.com/pod-product-compliance
Lightning Source LLC
Chambersburg PA
CBHW071658160426
43195CB00012B/1510